1968

JOHN DONNE

A STUDY IN DISCORD

ANNO DNI. 1591
ÆTATIS SVÆ 18

This was for youth, Strength, Mirth, and wit that Time
Most count their golden Age; but t'was not thine.
Thine was thy later yeares, so much refin'd
From youths Drosse, Mirth, & wit; as thy pure mind
Thought (like the Angels) nothing but the Praise
Of thy Creator, in those last, best Dayes.
    Witnes this Booke, (thy Embleme) which begins
    With Love; but endes, with Sighes, & Teares for sins.

Will: Marshall. sculpsit.   IZ: WA

JOHN DONNE
A STUDY IN DISCORD
by
HUGH I'ANSON FAUSSET

'PALLIATION OF A SIN IS THE HUNTED CREATURE'S
REFUGE & FINAL TEMPTATION. OUR BATTLE
IS EVER BETWEEN SPIRIT AND FLESH.
SPIRIT MUST BRAND THE FLESH,
THAT IT MAY LIVE'
G. MEREDITH

NEW YORK / RUSSELL & RUSSELL

FIRST PUBLISHED IN 1924
REISSUED, 1967, BY RUSSELL & RUSSELL
A DIVISION OF ATHENEUM HOUSE, INC.
BY ARRANGEMENT WITH THE ESTATE OF HUGH I'ANSON FAUSSET
L. C. CATALOG CARD NO: 67–28776

PRINTED IN THE UNITED STATES OF AMERICA

CONTENTS

PORTRAITS

to
MY WIFE

MANY writer on Donne must be under a deep obligation to Mr. Edmund Gosse's *The Life and Letters of John Donne*, Mr. E. K. Chambers' edition of the *Poems*, and Isaac Walton's exquisite but too devout miniature.

Upon all of these I have inevitably and gratefully drawn. My aim, however, has been to explore anew, and, if possible, more profoundly, a personality of absorbing significance, and to present it both critically and biographically on such a scale as may introduce it to many who are unable to possess themselves of Mr. Gosse's monumental work.

H. I'A. F.

PROLOGUE

RELIGIOUS systems, like other imperfect organisms, wax and wane. Wrought by man, they partake of man's daring and decline. The ecclesiastic is as powerless to preserve his dogmas against the march of human reason as the dead leaf is to stay the upward urge of the sap. Religious emotion indeed persists, a hunger for deeper and wider experience, an aching sense of the flesh's insufficiency, a longing, as of some exile turning his thoughts homewards, to be one with the heart of stars and seas and sunsets, to prostrate the self blindly before the unknown and unknowable, or to discover consciously some guiding principle for harmonious life. The essence of religion, whether we name it a desire for beauty, an intuition of immortality, or a thirst for God, survives alike the advance of thought and the paralysis of formalism, because it is no less than life itself aspiring out of insensate matter after ever completer consciousness. And this aspiration implies a battle. The physical, it would seem, is loath to divulge its secret; it resents the exploitation of its latent consciousness; it would drag the soul back into servile nescience and subject ideal life to natural death. Religious experience is therefore in all but its final phase a condition of conflict between the forces of imagination and of nature, a life-and-death struggle in very truth between spiritual creativeness and physical passivity, a struggle in which every moment of a man's life has its significance, and is, as it were, a rehearsal for the great crisis of death itself.

It is only, however, in the most vital individuals that the battle is fought with vigour and decisiveness, and the life-force may be observed gradually defining and refining itself through the human faculties, being disintegrated at first into conflicting elements of instinct and intelligence, and, if the battle is carried to a victorious issue, being resolved at last into an exquisitely modulated spiritual harmony.

Few men, it is safe to assert, have achieved that victory in all its positive completeness, nor have the majority of those who accepted the battle owed allegiance to any specific system of faith. The struggle is a burningly personal one, and those who engage in it are of necessity rebels against convention and conformity, which would cut a soul to pattern. We are more likely to find them among artists and outcasts, seers, solitaries and heretics than on a Bishop's bench, — in the wastes of Siberia than in the pews of a conventicle.

For true religion, like true art, is an immediate image of reality. It rejects all compromise and all qualification. But every institution is built upon compromise, and implies a surrender of the particular to the general. And general truths are at best half-truths. All true religion is in its development vehement and impetuous, because it is the hazardous adventure of a pioneer fighting through the dust and beating distracted hands against the walls of the world. And because its aim is the discovery of an art of life, it is, like all good art, intensely preoccupied and personal.

The timid, tired or average man finds an easy escape from his difficulties in the impersonal image and the systematized type. He gladly accepts a sanctified routine in place of an open battle, and it is for him that institutional religion exists.

Yet so long as there is a heaven above him and an earth beneath, man will continue to break down the sanctuary in which he has taken refuge, if only to build it up anew. It was fear, weakness, and poverty of imagination which compelled man first to construct a Church and a set of doctrines about a faith which he had accepted rather than originated. The creative souls in whom all religions have originated felt no such need, but like the artist gloried only in expressing themselves from day to day 'in spirit and in truth.'

But no edifice of dogma can stay the tide of life. Man is born of earth, and aspires to the heaven of intelligence, his mortality is stung by immortal longings, his blind instinct gropes towards consciousness. For a time in the stress of conflict he may barter his liberty for security. For a period, long or short according to the vitality of the age or the elasticity of the doctrine, religious emotion may be pent within the walls of orthodoxy. But little by little the soul languishes, the body pants for air, the mind grows peevish with questions. What proved at first a delicious respite from battle, a port after storm, an illusion of peace that caressed and consoled nerves harassed by uncertainty, degenerates imperceptibly into a solemn, a somnolent, a meaningless routine.

Life, with its perpetual motion, its progress, and its retrogression, has been sacrificed to comfort and rigidity. The very forms which once embodied a vital, if imperfect, sense of reality are become idols that minister to a senseless genuflexion: the dogmas, once beaten out of the rock of ignorance by men striving to escape from the animal to the human and divine, are but formulas which the tongue reiterates. The priest is grown unctuous, his congregation lethargic. In place of moral fervour and a spontaneous social enthusiasm, linking man to man in vital communion, we find casuistry, bigotry and corruption, idle ceremonial and cowardly obscurantism. The temple built to protect a spiritual fire is become the theatre of social manners. Man's religious home, so lovingly, so laboriously wrought, roofs him over – a spiritual tomb.

This picture is not too darkly drawn for the Catholic Church in the fifteenth or eighteenth centuries. Protestantism, however, has never degenerated to this extent because it has allowed so wide a latitude to dissent, avoiding thereby the extremes alike of spirituality and of corruption. Rather than a medium of revelation, it has served as a school of practical, and consequently often conventional, morals for respectable people, and in its very breadth and colourlessness has often proved a serviceable organ on which visionary souls could play their personal themes. It has been least guilty too of that vice which comes near annulling all the services that organized religion has rendered humanity in dark times – the interested enslavement of the human mind.

Nevertheless, it is scarcely an exaggeration to say that the most vitally religious souls to be found in English history for the last three centuries have been, if not for the whole of their career, for some considerable part of it, rebels against organized Protestantism. They have been inevitably more loyal to life than to labels.

The goal of all religious emotion, it may be admitted, is the Absolute. But although the Absolute may be apprehended, it cannot be permanently imprisoned in any frame of doctrine. It is an idea, a condition of consciousness which demands perpetual reconception and redefinition. To postulate finality for any idea, to wall it round with dogmas founded upon an unproven hypothesis, to withdraw it from the arena of criticism, and to impose it on men as a categorical imperative, is to reduce it very speedily to a moribund formula.

Life congeals into form, only to melt into anarchy. Her form is, like that of musical counterpoint, the condition of motion: it is both momentary and perpetual, consistent and yet eternally new. Stagnation is unknown to Nature; she images her idea from hour to hour, and season to season, afresh. The rational in man is dismayed by so profligate an activity, lavish alike in its florescence and its waste. Deep into this whirling motion he plunges, seeking for some immutable centre, some directing unity answering to the coherent idea of which his mind is the human principle. None can honestly say whether such an absolute principle underlies the interplay of elements which we know as the universe, or whether man finds it only because he needs it.

Philosophy argues about it inconclusively, science doubts, art seems to express it with the same multiple profusion as Nature. Organized religion alone claims certainty, and names its discovery God. But history belies it. For God has proved a very variable symbol. He has lacked just that permanence and incontrovertibility which his worshippers have claimed for Him. He has changed with the needs of men, with their intellectual growth and refining sensibility. He has proved, in short, a relative reflection of man rather than an absolute conception, demonstrably achieved beyond revision or conjecture.

The devout in all ages have, however, refused to admit this. They have enthroned, as an immutable Absolute, what has imaged all the imperfections of their consciousness. And their God divorced from life, life has taken its revenge. Nature detests fixity no less than a vacuum. She is content to leave the abstract to die of its own inanition. Thus have Religions died beneath, or lagged behind, the feet of progress. The soul divorced from the body, the idea from the active mind, are divorced too from the struggle and the nakedness of which life is generated and by which it is preserved.

By subjecting at an early age to a rigid formula of faith man's instinct and intellect, the two active principles in human nature to the conflict of which all development can be traced, Religions have often not only impoverished human potentialities, but have themselves lapsed into dead custom and superstition, and as such have been spurned by new and positive minds in every age.

Ideally no institution has the right to substitute its creed for the personal and provisional reading of the Infinite which every man must make for himself. It may be admitted that few individuals, even in our own age, are capable of making any such reading, and that the function of Religion in the past has necessarily been not to develop man's potentialities but to curb his primitive impulses. Such an argument is a reasonable defence, if we regard a Church as an instrument of social or political expediency. But while it explains, it does not disprove the general failure of organized Religion either as an inspirer or repository of creative truth. And indeed the free-thinker, that bane of conventional sanctity, is actually Religion's benefactor. He restores the reality of Religion by relating it to vital thought; he exchanges a spiritual twilight for a spiritual daylight; he shatters a formula to renew a faith.

Philosophy, for ever adventuring along new paths after the secrets of life, for ever assimilating the new knowledge which each generation acquires, adds its positive contribution to that accepted store of ideas which the devout are content merely to inherit and preserve, and which, without constant reinforcement, fall into inevitable decay. A Voltaire, denounced as an atheist by contemporary prelates, is yet the purifier of an age's corruption, and it is well to remember that there have been many times when Churches have had to be instructed by deists, agnostics, or atheists, not merely in the spirit of tolerance, but even in the principles of common humanity. As Samuel Butler wrote: 'I have met with many very godly people who have had a great knowledge of divinity, but no sense of the divine; and again, I have seen a radiance upon the face of those who were worshipping the divine either in art or nature – in picture or statue – in field or cloud or sea – in man, woman or child – which I have never seen kindled by any talking about the nature and attributes of God.'

Life then in her passionate creativeness is ever at war with the formulas into which faith so often congeals.

B

Man, in building a shrine about his religious emotion, is apt to build a prison. Comes a new age, a new jet of spiritual and intellectual energy, and, like the prison gates for Peter, the doors are flung wide and the more vital souls escape to build their house anew. So was it with Christ driving the money-changers forth; so was it when rude Luther pinned his propositions to the walls of Wittenberg; so was it with Abelard in the twelfth century and Bruno in the seventeenth; so was it with Voltaire, consumed by intellectual arrogance and outraged humanity as he riddled a corrupt priesthood with his sarcasms, or with Diderot mapping out a world of exact knowledge to confound the selfish prejudice of sacerdotalism, or with Renan rising triumphantly above preciosity in his attestation of the assured destiny of the human reason, or with Ruskin and Morris, opposing the values of art to a utilitarian morality. So is it, we believe, to-day, when the most creative minds no longer deny the reality of spirit in a subservience to Victorian science, but oppose the tribal conception of God, and all its accretions of error and superstition, with the demand for verification; claiming that religion shall do more than offer its converts a sentimental consolation, that it shall rather marshal all the faculties under its banner in a fearless attempt to comprehend the governing principles of life, in order that man may no longer sanctify his own brutality in the name of God, or tyrannize over his brother in the name of faith, or shelve personal responsibility in the assurance of an omnipotent and omniscient providence.

Our modern world, with the emphasis which it lays

upon the rights of individual judgment and the duties of human discretion, may be dated from the Reformation, if only because from that moment men began to resent the conception of an arbitrary God, Who had made man in His own image, and to strive, however darkly, to make God in theirs, to realize the divinity in themselves rather than fall prostrate before the divinity of Life or yield blindly to its errant passions; in short, to be rational as well as vital, and, by the union of the social and scientific ideas, of instinct and intelligence, to transcend the violence of the beast and verify the revelation of the seer.

The Reformation is the religious expression of the Renaissance: the one announces the liberation of life, of generous, abounding, and increasingly self-conscious instinct; the other the first step in the distinctive emancipation of mind.

And as with ages, so with individuals. The two are related and even analogous, but while the microcosm reflects the macrocosm, it also forestalls its processes by speedier and more concentrated development. While therefore the vital man is of his time, he is also behind it and before it. He is a 'little world made cunningly' to demonstrate in his short span of years both the depths out of which man has emerged and the heights to which he may yet attain.

Such men are rebels against the conventions of their times because they are driven to explore the realities of all times. It is not only for their greater sincerity that they are most worthy of study, but also for their wider reach. They renew the past in their lives and image the future. Exulting in the primitive impulses of nature, they doff the garment of contemporary civilization, and by ways of bitter experience re-fashion it to clothe their nakedness. And since life's verities are most luminous when its form is no longer congealed by convention and its elements are for the moment resolved, the rebel whom passion animates and who is also self-conscious enough to record and analyse the phases of his experience is a history in miniature. His errors and distractions, even his failure, are more charged with significance for posterity than all the maxims of complacent conformity.

Such a man was John Donne, a genius physically and intellectually 'possessed,' one who ranged almost every scale of experience, and upon each struck some note, harsh, cunning, arrogant or poignant, which lingers down the roof of time; a poet who was at times near a monster, full-blooded, cynical and gross, a thinker, curious, ingenious and mathematical, a seer brooding morbidly over the dark flux of things, a saint aspiring to the celestial harmony.

This catholicity of faculty and experience is rare. History shows us few men who serve the flesh with the same ardour with which they seek the ideal. The sensualist is seldom the thinker, or the poet the priest, or the Pagan the Christian. Donne was all of these; his carnality blossomed into spirituality as a flower that springs from the dung.

And not only is his personal history a parable of 'Everyman,' and, as such, applicable to any age, but he also represents, more fully than any of his contemporaries, the three aspects of life which met in confused association in the England of the seventeenth century, those of Mediævalism, the Renaissance, and the Reformation. Sensual, scientific, egotistic, he is alike Pagan, Scholar, Courtier, and Puritan, a child of the old darkness and the new dawn. He has shed the stupor of mediævalism and most of its superstition, but not its innate savagery, nor its fear of the unknown. That sudden intoxication with life, which led the men of the Renaissance to enthrone anew in a burst of artistic adoration the body in its beauty and its pride, is his also, but with him the intoxication is not æsthetic but realistic; and so, in common with the ascetic whom the Renaissance renounced, he discovers the ugliness of the body by observing with critical detachment the gross impulses by which it is mastered. His passion for life, in brief, is not ecstatic enough to subdue his mediæval fear of death or console with a renaissance sense of beauty. And lastly the Puritan in him, the awaking rationality which he shared with his own age and country, led him to associate the fact of death with the idea of sin, and the state of virtue with the hope of immortality.

Thus, to simplify the elements which his personality expressed, we see in him a Pagan, stricken with that longing for spiritual consciousness which is the Christian's eventual compensation for ceasing to enjoy uncritically a state of Nature. And his peculiar value to us, as an expression of life, lies in the fact that he never compromised.

He never confused the spiritual and the sensual either through false fear or false reverence. He is never sentimental, because he experienced and expressed the physical with complete candour, and so was never tempted to linger over it in secretive cunning, sanctifying the sensuous with fine phrases, or smudging the spiritual with vague emotions. He knew that there can be no escape from the physical to the spiritual. Each is the condition of the other, and the transmutation must be complete and unqualified like some sudden fusion of elements.

And so the physical, intellectual and spiritual elements in him preserve for most of his life a singular detachment from each other. They do not mix, but each in turn dominates his personality.

The whole purpose of his life, unconscious as it must for the most part have been, was to bring this trinity of forces into harmony, and by so doing discover a new and deeper unity in the Universe itself. To what extent he succeeded the following pages will attempt to show, but beyond the enthralling personal record, the tortured history of such a genius, successful or not, lays bare the potentialities of humanity and of civilization.

Writing to a friend in his thirty-fifth year, he said: 'For we consist of three parts, a soul, and body, and mind: which I call those thoughts, and affections, and passions, which neither soul nor body hath alone, but have been begotten by their communication, as music results out of our breath and a cornet.' With most men one faculty is developed at the expense of another, so that their experience lacks fullness and proportion, is either too anæmic or too gross. With Donne each faculty is exercised in turn, under the co-ordinating presidency of the mind. He marches forward by the regular milestones of nature, from the riotous valley

of physical indulgence, up the tortuous hill of intellectual questioning, to the summit of mature experience, from which earth and heaven may be viewed in
true perspective, and where imagination may spread
its wings.

As a lover he is in turn the sensualist and the cynic,
passion's slave and passion's critic, the Platonist and
the devoted husband.

In religion he escapes from Catholicism to agnosticism,
becomes the paid casuist and the learned theologian:
embraces at last, at the bidding of circumstance, the
ministry of the English Church, and in the anguish of
his spirit converts a professional into a spiritual vocation, which for pure intensity of expression has never
been surpassed.

Intensity is the keynote of his career. All his days he
is on fire. His experience deepens, his wisdom matures,
his body decays, but the flame of life within him does
not fail. Rather it burns brighter and more lurid, as
emaciation heralds dissolution.

For, to vary the metaphor, his life is one long battle
with death, with the death of physical grossness and
mental conceit, of worldly ambition and spiritual
complacence. And this life-and-death struggle, so long
protracted, is only comparable, as Walton suggests,
with that recorded of some of those Early Fathers,
for whom Christianity had not yet degenerated from
an ordeal into a system — that of a St. Austin, a St.
Ambrose, or a St. Augustine.

Donne never lived prudently, and so he came to know
life profoundly, piercing through the world of appear-
ances and easy illusions to cruel and ecstatic reality.

He had explored the secrets of the senses and the subtleties of the mind. And so, psychologist and sensualist as he was, he was competent in the later days of his spirituality to report adequately of the soul.

And as one who refused both Catholicism and Anglicanism and went into the wilderness to seek religion from life, he is essentially modern. He escaped the yoke of a creed for all his most impressionable years, so that when he was driven at last to conform to the doctrine of a Church, he was able to make its dogma serve as a medium for his own vital and personal experience.

In such times then as Religion tends towards an elegant cult or a social convention, such a life as his is pre-eminently bracing. For muscles grown oversoft, for spirituality sapped by indulgent sentiment, there could be no healthier astringent. With him we learn that religion is real. He, like all of us, was limited by his age: keen as his intellect was, he lacked the knowledge which renders many of the dogmas that he ultimately accepted utterly void of reality to-day. But far beyond the limits of his time, he related poetry to religion, and religion to truth. He teaches us, not how to worship God, but how to relate ourselves to God, and he shows that spiritual satisfaction, however exquisite, is unworthy of the name if it be achieved at the sacrifice of intellectual honesty; that religious experience is the prize of perpetual conflict, of that battle between life and death which is the agony and exultation of the creature in us striving after the divine.

¶ PART ONE
THE PAGAN

THE PAGAN

§ 1

JOHN DONNE was born in London in 1573. Through his mother he was related to Sir Thomas More, John Rastell, the lawyer, and John Heywood, the dramatist, and it was to his mother's family that he referred when he wrote in 1610: 'No family, which is not of far larger extent and greater branches, hath endured and suffered more in their persons and fortunes for obeying the teachers of Roman doctrine.'

Throughout his childhood, indeed, he was steeped in Catholicism, and with all the aggravated sentiment which attaches to a fugitive faith, assailed in an alien land by the insolent forces of Reform. The blood of martyrs and controversialists beat in his veins, and persecution darkened his home.

A royal commission confiscated the lands of his grandfather, John Heywood, whose epigrams had so excellently diverted Queen Mary in her dejection; one uncle was expelled from his house in Antwerp by a mob, and died of the shock; another, Father Jasper Heywood, visiting England on a mission from Rome and parading as Papal Legate with more pomp than discretion, narrowly escaped execution, languished in prison for more than a year, and shortly after receiving a sentence of lifelong banishment, died at Naples in disconsolate exile. These are but select examples of a generation which was decimated by its faith. The cruelty of Mary bore bitter fruit for her partisans, when death withdrew her favour. The tide flowed with a

kindred strength in the opposite direction: so strong
indeed was its current that it was to sweep John Donne,
the latest offspring of a loyal fraternity, into the camp of
his traditional foes.

The topic of persecution must have been a tragically
common one in his home, and if, as seems probable,
he accompanied his mother, when a boy of twelve, on
her visits to an uncle in prison, the lean pursuit of religious controversy must have at an early age assumed
for him an exaggerated importance. Moreover, the
fact that cultivated Catholics were forced into the position of aliens, exposed to insult and suspicion, suffering
for their faith with not a little conscious pride in a
hostile environment, cannot have failed to stimulate
that haughty spirit of independence and originality
which was to characterize John Donne throughout
his life.

The situation was enhanced by the early death of his
father. The evidence of a coat-of-arms favours the conjecture that John Donne, senior, was of Welsh descent,
and it is even possible that the violent sensuality manifest in the son is traceable to this source. Of the father
himself little is known, save that he engaged in trade
with the Ironmongers' Company and prospered so well
that on his death in 1576 he left his widow in comfortable circumstances, and his son John a handsome legacy
when he should come of age.

The fatherless boy's upbringing, as was natural, erred
if at all on the side of tenderness. His mother gave
strict orders that he should be spared the rod and most
cautiously corrected. The remarkable precocity of a
child who impressed his elders as one rather 'born wise

than made so bye study,' may have encouraged his in-
structors to adopt so patient and persuasive an attitude
towards him. Nevertheless, with our knowledge of his
character in later years, it is difficult to credit the picture
which the gentle Walton has drawn for us of a child
prodigy, sage as 'another Picus Mirandola,' and submissive as another Samuel, who irradiated the light
of pure intelligence, when most boys are content to
pummel each other in outer darkness.

Donne, to whom passion was the breath of life from
adolescence to middle age, can scarcely have wanted it
in childhood. His mother may indeed have found him
tractable enough, but we suspect that her agents, from
whom the right of vigorous correction was withheld,
were not ignorant of a wilful and very physical com-
bativeness; and if the description in one of his sermons
late in life of the 'tenderness of our childhood,' when
'we suffer, and yet are whipt if we cry,' has the personal
significance attaching to so much of his pulpit illustration, it seems possible that they did not too strictly
abide by their instructions.

The history of these early years, however, is dim
enough. Probably Donne was sent, as a small child, to
his grandfather, John Heywood, who lived in exile at
Malines or Louvain, after whose death in 1580 his education was entrusted for three years to a private tutor
who grounded him in Latin and French. In the autumn
of the following year, observing the practice of many
Catholics who wished their sons to profit by a university
course, without taking the oath of allegiance involved in
matriculation, he was entered with his younger brother
at Hart Hall (later merged in Magdalen Hall), Oxford.

Here he resided for two years and satisfied the author-
ities of his ability, without, for political reasons again,
taking a degree.

In a time healthily averse to forcing the faculties of
childhood, it is strange to think of Donne as a capable
classic in his thirteenth year, stranger still to learn
that during his residence at Oxford he first turned his
mind to the study of Spanish, and particularly to those
fierce, tender, and fantastical Spanish mystics in whom
transcendentalism combined so unusually with intellectual audacity and fanciful conceits. Yet, alien
as such a form of literature might seem to the taste of
boyhood, it was in fact to prove a lifelong obsession,
and to leave a pronounced mark upon the trend of his
genius. And we may even see in this precocious
attachment to mystical literature the earliest, and as
yet subconscious, effort of escape from that egotism
which was to prove his lifelong anguish and exultation.
Possibly too it was something of a homesick impulse
which led a boy, devoutly reared in the Catholic faith
and painfully conscious of its forlorn standing in a
Protestant university, to turn to such agitated and
exotic souls as St. Teresa or Luis de Granada. It is
true that Spanish thought was at the time a fashionable
subject in some Oxford circles, and Donne's interest
was doubtless first excited in this way, but the singu-
larity of taste evinced was typical of that persistent
attraction which the unconventional in literature was
to exercise over his mind, and serves to illustrate as
it emphasized that sense of detachment which his
family's misfortunes and what he called later his
'conversation with men of a suppressed and afflicted

religion, accustomed to the despite of death, and hungry of an imagined martyrdom,' had already instilled.

Thus were circumstances destined always to reinforce a native originality.

From Oxford the young Donne turned, in the language of a contemporary gossip, 'like a laborious bee, desirous to gather from more flowers than one,' to 'our other renowned nursery of learning.' He remained at Trinity College, Cambridge, until the autumn of 1589. If Oxford encouraged the pursuit of esoteric cults, we can believe that Cambridge, true to a distinction which survives even to-day, redressed the balance by strengthening in his young mind that tenacious geometric faculty, by which he was to chart with Euclidean subtlety the stark, tangled, and recondite tracts of experience with which a rapacious instinct was to supply him. Oxford ministered to his mysticism, Cambridge to his casuistry, to that faculty for close and ingenious logic, by which, like Goethe two centuries later, he was to anatomize his sensations, and in the manner of some curious apothecary reduce to their chemical elements the wayward impulses of his blood.

Here too he became acquainted with two brothers, Christopher and Samuel Brooke, who were fated to play a loyal but uneasy part in the adventure of his life most charged with grievous consequence.

On leaving Cambridge, he worked, at any rate for some months, with private tutors, who concentrated particularly on mathematics and 'other liberal sciences,' and who, in still further training the mind of the precocious pupil in exact thought, furnished him quite unintentionally with the equipment for questioning the Catholic faith which they professed, alike the pride and cross of his own family.

Every intelligent youth, on approaching manhood, is distracted by two impulses – that of sentiment, which tempts him to accept all that is familiar, picturesque, inexplicable, and sensationally coloured; and that of reason, which commands him to criticize and form his own opinions even at the cost of ruthlessly rejecting things hallowed by association.

The second of these impulses is the slower to develop, but also the sterner and more permanent. In Donne it was preternaturally early and resolute. Sentiment too was the quality with which he was least endowed. He was passionate, as he was rational, to a high degree, but between these two forces there was little of that tolerant affection, which fortunately in the majority of men softens the acerbity, while diminishing the intensity, of each. Doubtless Cambridge, less sympathetic than Oxford to the Gothic strain in any temperament, did much to make him a rationalist. While he remained at home, however, the peculiar position of his family as a forlorn outpost of Catholicism and 'the example of his dear and pious parents almost obliged him to their faith.' Not yet could there be any open rebellion.

Yet anyone acquainted with his wilful, inquiring nature would have doubted his ability to accept even the faith for which his ancestor had forfeited his head, out of any 'custom of credulity.' The very spirit of independence which his position as a Recusant had encouraged would in its turn predispose him to rebel, if he should once feel, as he wrote later, 'wounded and maimed in the Roman Church.' Nor was he one ever to be checked by any scruples concerning either domestic or public opinion from going his own determined way. It only needed the cutting of his direct family connexion to convert a subconscious ferment into considered revolt. This was not long delayed. Early in 1592 he and his friend Christopher Brooke were admitted to Lincoln's Inn, where they shared a set of chambers.

At the age of nineteen, Donne's appearance, it must be confessed, was more arresting than amiable. A brow slightly receding and narrowing at the temples, in conjunction with a pointed chin, suggested mental keenness rather than breadth; the dark eyes, large and a trifle prominent, were both shrewd and enigmatic; the full, complacent lips more than hinted at hot appetites, which the gigantic nose, coarsely flattened at the base, confirmed, while promising a determined will. But behind the rather unsavoury arrogance of the face lurked, scarce perceptible, a haunted look, as of a soul fearful of the form that housed it. On a first glance it was fulsomely pagan, it obtruded a sinister self-sufficiency, and the swollen nostrils argued grossness. But anyone looking closer, and particularly at the eyes, might have detected an uneasiness, a fastidiousness, even a premonition of self-disgust, rich in possibilities. And in truth the great battle of Donne's life, destined to pass through so many painful fluctuations, was already begun.

§ 2

Lincoln's Inn, we may conjecture, did not find in its new resident either a docile or a regular student.

Among the lesser services which the law, like the universities, has rendered to mankind is the fact that it has offered to so many talented or generous spirits a polite refuge, where, shielded from the importunities of life and of exacting parents, they might cultivate their personality undisturbed.

That Donne applied himself to the study of law we cannot doubt. For he applied himself to the study of everything, mental or physical, with an unappeasable voracity, but it was rather to relieve an exacting hunger than to equip himself professionally.

From his earliest days Donne is remarkable for the close connexion which existed between his appetites and his intelligence. A man's thought generally functions with some degree of detachment from his body, while it is as the truant or weary fugitive from thought that he turns to the consolations of the flesh. But Donne was driven to brainwork as the athlete to the gymnasium. He could only relax mental tension as he could muscular, by constant and violent activity. And so, while his thought had an almost physical constitution, his lusts were, so to say, inlaid with logic, and he pursued mathematics, law or theology with the same tenacious passion as an ephemeral liaison.

The three or four years, therefore, subsequent to his admission to Lincoln's Inn were a time of violent and varied experiment, nor is it fanciful to see in him a very exact reflection of the insatiable curiosity of his age.

As the sixteenth century draws to its close, a change is noticeable in the tone of its expression. The blend of instinctive romance and happy imitation, typical of early Elizabethan lyricism, begins to give place to

increasing sophistication and a more studied originality. The energy which had been so lavishly squandered
both in literature and in life shows signs not indeed of
exhaustion but of self-consciousness. The romanticism
of Marlowe and his immediate successors was both
brutal and sublime. It was certainly unpondered, and
achieved greatness by the generous sweep of its impulse
and the earthly richness of its resource rather than
by any fine discrimination. Similarly the Elizabethan
lyric was in substance as gracefully superficial as it
was conventional in form. The love of which it sang
was either a pure impulse of joy as spontaneous as
a bird's, or a mannered gesture borrowed with its
form and many of its images from other and older
literatures.

Such symptoms, whether in an age or an individual,
are typical of the first condition of youth, that period
in human consciousness when it is enough to range
over the external in a fine frenzy of excitement or
delicately beautify the superficial, when any closer
scrutiny of life, any subtler degree of experience is
alien to the hasty beat of the blood, to the feet that
cannot halt for swiftness, and the hands that cannot
enough clutch a miraculous world before the day is
done. Impatient, facile, omniverous, man would take
space and time themselves in his stride, sweep the
oceans of their merchandise, mix himself with the loam
of earth, and plunder the heavens for stars.

But by the end of the sixteenth century man was no
longer thus virgin in his apprehension. The physical
had had full play: in a naturalistic orgy he had ranged
the elemental scale from the bestial to the ecstatic; his

nerves, a little jaded, felt the first twinges of disillusionment; humanity, with its criticism and its conscience,
intruded upon the forces of savagery. The instinctive
was not enough: pseudo-classic graces, pastoral conventions, allegorical fantasies, amatory madrigals – all
began to cloy. They had served well as gardens of
retreat from the surge of unreined passion, but as the
storm began to subside, their decorations palled, their
pillars seemed wrought of plaster, and their flowers
false. Premonitions of satiety manifested themselves,
and man, grown slightly morbid, turned to a more
solid playground and a more calculated diet.

Between the healthy imagination of the boy and the
mature imagination of the man there is, as Keats proclaimed, a period in which 'the soul is in a ferment,
the character undecided, the way of life uncertain,
the ambition thick-sighted.' Man brings his instincts
up to judgment, he explores curiously, he tastes and
tests. No longer is he a leaf tossed on the winds of the
world, a bird buoyant with its song, a wave borne on
its tide and flung broken up its shore. He detaches
himself from the life which he experiences, he analyses
with puzzled frenzy, he mixes sensationalism and
dialectic. Of this moody, exasperated self-consciousness broadening into harmonious vision Shakespeare
has left us a large and liberal report. In the life of
Donne it is writ no less clearly, though in a minuter
script.

§ 3

From his nineteenth to his twenty-third year Donne
surrendered both body and mind to random expe-

rience. The body took its pleasure, the mind ironically criticized, and both processes for the time were entirely superficial. Dissatisfied sensationalism and cynicism invariably go hand in hand. Meanwhile in the mazes of law and theology he began to take that violent mental exercise which an irritated brain fermenting with energy demanded. Truly it was a strange reason for joining the laborious ranks of those who –

> 'toughly chew and sturdily digest
> Th' immense vast volumes of our common law.'

But it was rather to the study of theology, as it threw light upon Catholicism, of London society, continental travel, and experimental erotics, that he applied himself with the fullest zest and the richest consequences. These we may consider briefly in turn.

The young law-student, relieved of maternal or tutorial pressure and associating with companions as frankly pagan as himself, was not slow to cast off the chains of Catholic authority. Where Donne's passions were involved (and reason for him was numbered among them), no argument based on expediency or caution could prevent him from carrying his purpose, however subversive to self-interest, to its logical conclusion. The thought of scandal, injured sensibilities, misinterpretation or even penal consequences either never presented itself to his mind, or faded before his commanding resolution.

His own account, rendered nearly twenty years later, of this second stage in his religious Odyssey, no less than that of Walton, is quite clearly gilded by a post-

dated and politic sanctity. Charming as is the picture
which Walton draws of a pensive youth, approaching
with studious and reverent humility the dogmas of the
Reformed and Roman Churches, much concerned that
his soul should 'choose the most orthodox,' and, by
prayer and supplication and abandonment of every
diversion, pleading with the Holy Spirit for right
direction, we can only suppose, to adopt the bio-
grapher's own deprecatory words on a later occasion,
that 'my affection to my friend hath transported me to
an immoderate commendation.'

For the Donne of the coarse nose and the tilted, protruding lip, the Donne who was even then composing
skits at the expense of Sectarian clerics and other world-
lings, while himself tasting the grosser pleasures of the
town, can scarcely, without outraging the probable,
be fitted into so mild and meditative a scene. He may
indeed, as Walton writes, have decided that 'an indifferent affection to both parties was the safest way,'
but, if so, the indifference, we may confidently assume,
was more noticeable than the affection.

That even in this insolent and imperturbable youth
of twenty-one there already lurked a craving for
religious experience, a germ of idealism in the rude
substance of the realist, is very probable, but it expressed itself, if at all, in a tendency to gravitate
towards the study of divinity, a detached and legal
examination of dogma and an occasional tremor of
self-disgust, rather than in any fervent search for
spiritual truth. Theology may have had its charms,
but piety as yet had none, although eventually the one
was to prepare the way for the other. For in subse-

quent years the theological hunt was to wax fast and
furious, at first in the pure joy of an athletic exercise,
later as a remunerative form of dialectic, and lastly as
forming the muscle and tissue of a panic-stricken
devotion.

But for the time life was Donne's only religion, and
the ceremonial was distinctly primitive.

We may therefore safely say that Walton has ante-
dated his hero's resort to Cardinal Bellarmine, the
eminent Roman apologist, and the weighty observa-
tions on that dignified prelate's casuistry which
Donne is reported to have shown to the Dean of
Gloucester in his twentieth year. His resort was rather
to the Babylon of his day than to any heavenly Jerusalem of whose architecture he was in doubt. His
converse was not with divines of any persuasion, but
with gallants, students, gay sparks of the town, and
those favoured and fashionable circles that camped
about the Court, upon whose fringes he hovered with
watchful and predatory eye, plunging in from time to
time to plunder and enjoy, and retiring again to his
chamber to report of the matter in satirical verse. In
short, his dissatisfaction with the Catholic faith supplied him with a convenient excuse for cherishing, for
some years at least, no faith at all.

Donne's uncompromising originality, so plentifully
revealed in the style and substance of his poetry, is
also exemplified by his choice of friends. Friendship he
was later to invoke as a second religion and to honour
with monastic devotion, but his gods were no common
gods, and their residence was other than Parnassus.
The normal young man of literary leanings, coming to

London in 1593, gravitated inevitably to the company
of poets, wits and wastrels, who gathered at the Mer-
maid Tavern. But although Donne was casually
acquainted with certain members of that fraternity
whom Tom Coryat addressed as 'Right generous,
Jovial and Mercurial Sireniacks,' he can but seldom
have been of their company. The truth is that his
temperament and genius were as completely alien to
the democracy of an artistic movement or the provincial
comradeship of a coterie as to the parochialism of a
religious sect. Only in the circle of some brilliant
Court might the aristocrat in him have been sufficiently
gratified to silence the murmurs of the rebel. He was
too essentially individual, too consciously unique to
tolerate any relationship which might tend to blur the
distinctive lines of personality, too assured to crave, as
do the journeymen of the arts or those of slender
talent, the support of an informal literary republic, and
too haughtily fastidious to bring his genius into any
common market where he might barter its fruits for
profit or applause.

It is arguable that the truest genius has always felt
this need of standing alone, even at the price of disregard; of avoiding infectious contact and so preserv-
ing its integrity. It is generally, though perhaps not
always, the smaller men who flock together in Grub
Street and fan the flame of a sickly egotism with mutual
self-applause.

Donne's upbringing, as we have shown, served to
emphasize an inherent spirit of detachment from pre-
valent opinions, and this in his attitude towards the
literary fashions of his age amounted even to active

aversion. Of this the first evidence is found in both the
form and substance of his earliest poetry.

At a time when the fruits of the Renaissance in English poetry had ripened to luxuriant harvest, when
Spenser slid through summer meadows like a drowsy
stream, when men still mourned and emulated the
courtly manner of a Sidney but seven years dead,
when Lodge and Peele distilled their honey, Daniel
moulded his grave and gracious lines, Shakespeare (in
this very year) wove his extravagant youth into the
rich tapestry of 'Venus and Adonis,' and the plaintive,
pastoral tones of Greene yet lingered in the air —
Donne betook himself to satire.

The silken folds of fashion which charmed the rather
exotic taste of contemporary poets irked him as the
iron of naked fetters. Neither tradition nor reputation
cowed the self-sufficiency of one who, some years later,
was to dismiss three princes of the classical manner in
such scornful parody as this:

'Here sleep's house by famous Ariosto,
  By silver-tongued Ovid and many moe
  — Perhaps by golden-mouthed Spenser too, pardie —
  Which builded was some dozen stories high,
  I had repair'd, but that it was so rotten,
  As sleep awaked by rats from thence was gotten.'

But for the most part he was to disdain 'these wits
that say nothing' by the decisive method of denying in
his own work all their cherished values.

This morose originality is the more remarkable in a
young poet first venturing a cast upon the sea of verse.
Imitation is the school through which even genius

generally must pass on its way to self-discovery; it cannot launch itself unfriended into the unknown. And at a time when a studied manner was so universal it argues an astonishing self-reliance in one so hardy as to repel the contagion.

But always in Donne's combative nature a fashion provoked antagonism. Certainly, had he known it, he was not alone in his revolt. He synchronized with a turn in the tide of taste which was spreading over Europe, but which was not to manifest itself fully in England for another half-century. Mr. Gosse has traced its origin to the class-room at Geneva, where Casaubon first championed with brilliant and novel force the claims of Persius in particular and of the Latin satirists in general to the attention of cultivated men. The satire of the Middle Ages had been little more than humorous and mannered allegory. Acquaintance with such writers as Lucilius or Juvenal revealed its possibilities as a tart and ruthless criticism of the corruptions and complacencies of everyday life. The first approach therefore to realism on the part of men surfeited by decadent culture, by attenuated elegancies, and posturing conceits, was through satire. Unfortunately, however, this movement ran parallel with another which modelled itself on Horace: both currents were eventually to emerge in the English satire of the seventeenth century, percolating through Jonson to Dryden, and filtering through Dryden to Pope. And thus candid realism was submerged in the commonplaces of common sense and delayed until the time of Crabbe.

But 'movements' are unreal things. Men borrow

what they need at the dictates of their nature, shaped
as that is to some extent by their age and its contin-
gencies. English poets would have turned satirical
even if there had been no Latin literature to school
them in technique. Certainly the young poets, who at
the end of the sixteenth century experimented for a
few years in satire, had little if any knowledge either
of Casaubon or of each other. They represent a curious
and prophetic pocket of revolt against contemporary
standards, and if their directly satirical activity was
quenched by the hostility of times still too sentimental
to tolerate, not to say encourage them, the intellectual
and physical realism for which they stood found other
means of expression than calculated satire. In Mar-
ston, Hall and Guilpin the revolt was trivial and
derivative, and so persisted little beyond the youth
which inspired it. In Donne it represented a profound
attitude of mind and so came to a vital fruition. For
his honesty, his irony owed little to that fastidious
savouring of evil, typical of the Latin Renaissance
spirit. Donne's northern blood made him serious,
even as a sinner; and his cynicism, at least after a few
precocious experiments, was that of hurt idealism
rather than of sensuality sharpening its taste with
wit. Proud he was, but with a pride that in its
very insolence hungered for purity of idea and of
experience.

Donne's early satires are valuable as the first manifestation of his attitude towards life. The spiced or
merely dainty flavour of so much Elizabethan verse
was obnoxious to his robust taste. Like the attenuated
sweetness of some lingering perfume, it offended his

crude virility, and he launched his defiant challenge:

> 'I sing not, siren-like, to tempt, for I
> Am harsh.'

His hostility went far deeper than the senses: it was his reason too that rebelled. These poets, it seemed to him, with their chivalries and graces, their pondered affectations and swooning sentiments, were but spinning webs about the mind and the world of fact. Such gossamers might shimmer prettily enough in the morning sunlight, but they were ephemeral and delusive as the dew. The winds of the world swept them up and the thunder mocked their fragility. Most of his contemporaries were still too naïve to appreciate any such craving for intellectual honesty. They gravitated between purely instinctive violence and an almost ceremonious assumption of perfect manners. Like children, between bouts of animal extravagance, they played with beauty as with some charming and still sufficiently novel toy.

Paradoxically enough this indifference to reason and reality drove such a conscious mind as Donne's into brutality. Nothing excites the Goth in man so surely as Hellenic grace grown decadent. No one is so intolerant of the idyllic as the idealist. Revolts from cloying sentiment have always tended to extremes, and three centuries later Zola, Whitman and Nietzsche were to be the over-zealous servants of a kindred impulse.

Yet neither pure truth nor pure poetry are born of revolt. It is possible to make romanticism real or realism romantic. A poet will choose one or the other

approach to life according to the needs of his temperament and the influence of his age. Donne chose the
latter. But until the real is heightened by romantic
imagination into the ideal, it is as imperfect, even
trivial as, and considerably less pleasant than the delicate or simpering fancies against which it raises its
ruthless sword.

Donne, it seems probable, extended his dislike of
pastoral sweetness even to the persons of its practi-
tioners. Some years later he was to accept as his
patroness one who gathered about her most of the distinguished poets of the day. Many of these Donne
cannot have failed to meet on the easiest terms at her
informal court, and particularly the grave and affable
Daniel; while another, Michael Drayton, the cele-
brated sonneteer and author of *Polyolbion*, was the intimate of one of his greatest friends. Yet in all Donne's
many letters, crowded with personal reference, no mention of either appears. That a man of sincerity should
deprecate the swarm of conceited versifiers which
every new age of creative endeavour generates to swarm
about the heels of genius, is intelligible. But such poets
as these had charm and originality enough to command
any man's cordial attention, and what can only seem in
Donne a calculated taciturnity — as if even the eminent
among contemporary poets shared, in his view, the

'tasteful flat humidity
In dough-baked men . . .'

— argues an extraordinary aversion to their temper.

Ben Jonson was the only exception. There was a
rugged honesty in both these men which, while it

limited their æsthetic capacity, refused the painted masques, the insinuating melodies behind which emptiness too often lies. Each was to hail the other from the rough fastnesses of his native solitude, and of the two Jonson was to be more generous in his admiration. Donne, however, had a strength of silence in his dislikes to which Jonson could never pretend. He spurned the exquisite manner of his contemporaries, not by diatribe or execration, as Jonson was known to do, but by a calm ignoring of their very existence.

In Donne then we see the first manifestation of the Nonconformist conscience in literature. Puritanism, it may be argued, is in its earliest phases, more brutal and licentious than the cultivated manners which, by right of intrinsic truth, it is destined to replace. The pioneering moralist seems and often is superficially the most immoral of men. His only claim to morality is in fact an insistence upon mental and physical honesty, which he opposes ruthlessly to every form of unreality, however gilded or revered. He is too much in love with life to abstract love from experience and exalt it as an idea or a principle. He can only denounce its decay in convention. And while he intrudes a savage countenance upon a graceful but insipid scene, the measure of his brutality and cynicism is also that of his opponents' sentimental insincerity. Resolute to strip the veils from the face of life, to purge poetry of the parasites that overrun it, the realist, that youngest and least conscious of moralists, plunges into ugliness in his suspicion of all beauty, with the relish of a healthy man, escaped from prim devotions to the rush and sting of physical life. The coarsest fact is food to one starved by bloodless fancies; a stormy darkness in the streets is refreshing after too long a spell in the theatre stalls. And between this urgent experimentalism and calculated depravity there is a world of difference.

Such a realist was the young Donne, but his was no simple reaction to physical truth. His mind craved candour no less than his body. It was this which gave such force and superciliousness to his revolt against the latest and deteriorating echoes of a once ebullient Renaissance. Indeed, in his 'worst voluptuousness, an hydroptic immoderate desire of human learning and languages,' no less than in his eagerness to taste violently every thrill, bodily, mental and spiritual, which life could offer, he was as much renewing the spirit of the Renaissance under more sombre skies as revolting against its latter-day decadence.

In at least one aspect his nature reflected that type which in Italy had risen magnificent in range and enormity out of the night of mediævalism. Donne may have been but a poor understudy of that 'universal man,' inexhaustibly playing in the time of the Medici the courtier, warrior, poet, lover, scholar, compelling for a short hour life's opposites into unity, philosophy and poetry, mysticism and sensuality, violence and fastidiousness, love and hate; yet if circumstances prevented his realization of so gallant or so criminal a catholicity of experience, the will to realize was in his heart, and he too on his more straitened stage was to luxuriate in sin and penitence, to drive forward in insolent disdain and lapse into brooding sarcasms.

But, as we have said, his distinction was to be both more mediæval and more modern than the Renaissance.

He is the brother of Montaigne, not of Sidney. The Renaissance was the last, the ripest, the most nearly calculated flowering of Paganism, before self-consciousness definitely crept like a fever into the blood of man, and the mind was born, and weaned of its mother Nature. It stands therefore like some lovely holiday season between two toiling terms, a season in which men lost their conscience and with it their sense of sin and fear of death, in the concentrated ecstasy of life. At least one element in Donne yearned for that delivery from mind, that immoderate and yet finely poised surrender to instinct. But in him the conscience of mediævalism with all its *macabre* preoccupation with the loathsome aspects of the physical is restored, yet with a difference. It is penetrated by modern rationalism; it expresses itself not merely in an instinctive reaction from, an agonized distortion of, the sensual – in superstition and self-mutilation and a frenzied asceticism – but in a cold and conscious criticism of the naturalistic. Consequently the spontaneity of grace, which Greece and Italy inherited from the childhood of the world, is withheld from him.

The price which every man has to pay as he advances through critical self-consciousness from a physical to a spiritual harmony would seem to be a temporary loss of that instinctive beauty which for so long was humanity's highest expression, that inevitable felicity of rhythm and gesture in which the natural man reflected, to some extent unconsciously refined, but in no sense attempted to sublimate, the native impulses of his blood. That rhythm is rudely disturbed in Donne from his earliest years by intrusive thought. He can never surrender passively to rapture; he is in conflict with his sensations in the very process of indulging them. Herein lies his peculiar modernity.

For thus it was that he came to scrutinize the vicious in himself in microscopic detail, to cross-examine his impulses with cunning dialectic, to convert his passion by argument, and finally, in the maturity of his powers, to direct them into the channels of vital virtue.

§ 4

Even Donne's earliest verse then (for we pass over some mythical verse of his boyhood, said to have been of a devotional character) mirrors a pagan licence and a puritan preoccupation. His first four satires, composed mainly in 1593 and 1594, are too experimental and too topical to reflect, save superficially, his individuality. Yet they do succeed in conveying an impression both of his opinions and his way of life during these early London years, and in their abrupt and rugged versification they reveal him extending his revolt against a pampered substance to assail a polished style.

The knots and compressions in which Donne's prosody abounds, combining with the complicated casuistry of his thought and the extravagance of his imagery, must always alienate those who look for easy returns from poetry. Yet Jonson erred in imputing his rhythmical peculiarities to want of ear, adding that 'Donne, for not keeping of accent, deserved hanging.' Donne could and indeed did, when least sincere, practise an entirely conventional prosody. But style, truly realized, is dictated by its matter, and the more intellectual a poet's

D

imagination be, the less smooth and mellifluous is his language.

The natural rhythm of poetry, like the natural rhythm of life, is inevitably broken up and reconstituted by the very individual rhythm of thought. And so, as Coleridge wrote: 'In Poems where the Author *thinks*, and expects the reader to do so, the sense must be understood in order to ascertain the metre.' A regular rhythm, a soft and sinuous cadence, are the fruit of sensation, little halted by criticism. They reflect the lulling flow of a stream, the measured march of the seasons, the stately glide of the clouds, the swing of the tides, the imperceptible unfolding of a flower. They conform in short to Nature, unharassed and serene. The more conscious, inquisitive personality intrudes on passive sensibility, the more is this rhythmic current crossed and fretted by warring eddies. The rhythm of sense plays a costive counterpoint upon the fluid rhythm of sound.

With so critical a personality as Donne's this condition was likely to be exaggerated; and unless we can adapt ourselves to the gymnastics of his thought, for ever turning upon itself, halting or darting on some new or diagonal course, his prosody will baffle and annoy. For we shall judge it by standards appropriate only to poets of a different character.

The prosodical audacities, however, of his early satires are as little dictated by urgent necessity as the verse itself. They are rather conscious experiments in a new versification, calculated, like the cynical realism of his subject-matter, to affront those mechanical felicities of style which seemed to him to have degenerated into a

passionless etiquette. And although even here we find
many examples of that same virile revolt against accen-
tual monotony which spurred Shakespeare and, to a
somewhat less degree, Milton, to deliver blank verse
from its fetters and relate it to living speech, such
devices as

'He knows who hath sold his land, and now doth beg
 A licence, old iron, boots, shoes, and egg-
 Shells to transport;'

are merely the flings of an impertinent nonconformity.

   As to the matter of these satires – we see at first only
a truculent young critic, dropping his books to dip
carelessly into the book of life, returning anon to his
rooms in self-satisfied disgust, and penning malicious
comments on the motley scene. But if we look closer,
we discover a personality more complex than the brag-
gart youth lashing at a world of which he is still essentially ignorant, and consoling himself for his 'coarse
attire' and unfashionable solitude by pretending to an
austere detachment from those 'many-coloured pea-
cocks' and that frivolous society, in which at heart he
longs to play a romantic part.

   These elements are prominent enough in this youthful
satirist, but as in many of his weaker poems, whether
licentious, fantastic or ceremonial, there are what he
called in later life 'minutes of true light in a natural
death.' He was too urgent, too excessive a being to
be merely clever, and so he seldom fails to be self-
revealing.

   In these early satires we see one who indulged himself
by lampooning the London life about him as he was

shortly to lampoon the love of women. Without the power or the patience to plumb to its human depths, he was yet too allured by the glamour of the town to preserve a haughty isolation. He tasted and was repelled; he surrendered to some momentary dissipation and awoke disgusted. And so concentrating on all its gaudy, mannered show, the hypocrisies of priests and lawyers and feathered fools, he poured out his hate with sombre exultation on a London which to his jaundiced eye was little better than a painted strumpet.

Yet his victims, unlike those of later satires, were neither recognizable individuals nor yet mere puppets fashioned to receive the onslaught of a general spleen. 'Coscus,' the insolent lawyer of one of them, may in fact be identifiable with Sir John Davies; and the various sectarians of the third satire, representatives of Rome, Geneva, the Anglican Church, the Puritans and the Brownists, doubtless had their counterpart in the London of the day, and were indeed to provide Donne some years later with a sorely needed source of income; but in reality they are all offshoots of their young satirist, say rather aspects of his anti-self, disturbing refractions from the central light of his vacillating personality.

In the 'fine, silken, painted fool' of a society man, for example, who seeing his mistress in a window

'. . . like light dew exhaled, he flings from me,'

he imaged a common type. But in the bitter realism of the portrait, he images also a personal craving for the life of luxurious ease, a craving which, in a modified

form, was to persist, until Necessity haled him into the
Church. The Pagan in him

> 'with amorous smiles allures,
> And grins, smacks, shrugs and such an itch endures,
> As prentices or school-boys, which do know
> Of some gay sport abroad, yet dare not go.'

To which that other element of his dual personality,
the reproving Puritan, replies in another place:

> 'and as
> The world's all parts wither away and pass,
> So the world's self, thy other loved foe, is
> In her decrepit wane, and thou loving this,
> Dost love a wither'd and worn strumpet; last
> Flesh, itself's death, and joys which flesh can taste,
> Thou lovest; and thy fair goodly soul, which doth
> Give this flesh power to taste joy, thou dost loathe.'

The Puritan in him dictates the scorn, the Pagan its
savagery. And although such passages are but the light
and preliminary passes of a swordsman preparing for a
duel of the severity of which he is still in comparative
ignorance, yet they do already reveal the animal appetite
for life, and the half-animal, half-moral disgust of death,
which, gathering intensity with every year, were to subject Donne's personality to a continual crisis of battle.

In particular, then, as well as in general these early
satires reflect their author. Donne may ridicule a
Mirreus or a Crantz, a Phrygius or a Gracchus, for the
theological quibblers they were: but he, too, was all at
sea in religious dogma and widowed of religious faith.

He may pour scorn on a Coscus for his pride of law and his paddling in poetry; but the young law student of Lincoln's Inn, dabbling in satirical verse, bore a striking resemblance to his butt. Donne, we need hardly say, was quite unconscious of expressing himself in the victims of his wit, but often a man is even more illumined by his scorn than by his praise.

And to complete the representative character of these satires, the Puritan moralist from time to time emerges completely for a moment from his Pagan setting to preach a positive sermon, or in the rôle of intellectualist to attest that Rational ideal, in which Donne's peculiar and precocious value lies.

> 'On a huge hill,
> Cragged and steep, Truth stands, and he that will
> Reach her, about must and about must go,
> And what th' hill's suddenness resists, win so.
> Yet strive so, that before age, death's twilight,
> Thy soul rest, for none can work in that night.'

This is no tart wit at a world's expense, but the very prophecy by heart and mind of all which lay before him, of the attempt to take life by direct assault, the long years of baffled deployment and the eventual, if precarious, capture of the citadel. But youth may be sage in utterance and yet possessed by seven devils in action. The young Donne has no poise either of body or of mind. He is the prey of lusts that drive him hither and thither. His very moralizing is spasmodic. Pity chokes his spleen, and fury blinds his reason, and 'in his ravenous maw, Rankly digested' truth and falsehood mingle. 'Is not,' he cries, ·

'our mistress, fair Religion,
As worthy of all our soul's devotion,
As virtue was in the first blinded age?'

As worthy doubtless! But where to find true religion,
how to distinguish her in a world of drifting landmarks
and amid the convulsed antagonisms of his own nature,
was beyond his powers. He might set his mind to the
disentanglement of dogma, and in the heat of the quest
find some relief, but casuistry led nowhere. It left
essentials untouched and was at best but a passing
sedative to fermenting egoism.

Thirty years later the inadequacy of reasoning was to
prove an argument for faith, as when he asked scornfully from the pulpit: 'What Anatomist knows the body
of man thoroughly, or what casuist the soul?' But now
it seemed an argument for scepticism. Indeed, a sullen
agnosticism seemed the only possible attitude.

'Doubt wisely; in strange way,
To stand inquiring right, is not to stray.'

In kindred words was Milton to excuse his physical
blindness before the judgment seat of Heaven. And
although Donne in his spiritual blindness could not
preserve this dignified, speculative isolation from
popular error, but in the flux of an internal chaos struck
wildly at the world, only to wound himself – his refusal
to accept the easy road of conventional faith, despite
a craving, even in these years of physical fever, for
religious satisfaction, attests a character bold and
vigilant for truth, and one whose faith, if ever he attain
to it, will have its roots in the well-ploughed earth, and
its foundations on the rock,

§ 5

Sometime between the years 1593 and 1596 it seems
probable that Donne travelled abroad, it may be to
Spain, in which his reading had awoken an interest, to
Italy, and even, if we are to believe Walton, to the
Holy Land, although we fancy that it was less for the
pious purpose of 'viewing Jerusalem and the sepulchre
of our Saviour' than out of a passion, always a trifle
exotic, for seeing the world. Donne's thirst for experience was overpowering, and in his youth, as was
natural, it was predominantly physical.

The intriguing bypaths of foreign literatures, the
mazes of law and theology, the sinuosities of mordant
versifying, the convolutions of the social scene – all
ministered to, without appeasing, his appetite. And
since on coming of age he inherited a handsome
fortune, it is reasonable to suppose that continental
travel as well as the ladies of the town accounted for
its headlong consumption.

Our evidence for the former supposition is however
at best conjectural: for the latter it is even brutally
circumstantial. We do not need a Freud to convince
us that the religious and the erotic impulses are closely
related. Each in a different degree bespeaks a hunger
for life, and although the one does not necessarily imply
the other, their extravagance is often complementary.

In Donne the two are almost exactly analogous. He
who was to abandon the conventional ideal of religion,
and through bitter and baffled years seek to rediscover
and renew it for himself, was first to pass through
identical phases of experience as a lover.

The cynic, it is safe to say, is almost always the dis-
appointed idealist, as the sentimentalist is the satisfied
materialist. The more savage a man's disillusionment
of the physical is, the fiercer is his desire to achieve an
experience that transcends it. Those who can accept
religious faith without question are as fortunate as
those to whom love is adequately realized in the simple
satisfaction of an instinct. There are rare souls in whom
faith and instinct are so finely attuned that such an attitude to life implies no lack of spiritual intensity. They
are the saints of this world, who by some happy creative
destiny are born above the strife of good and evil, mind
and sense. But they are few. And, with the majority,
acceptance implies spiritual lethargy. Years later
Donne was to describe this state in its religious aspect
from the pulpit :
'We never put the soul home, we never bend the soul
up to her height; and the extent of the soul is this mind.
When David speaks of the people, he says They imagine
a vain thing; it goes no farther than to the fancy, to the
imagination; it never comes so near the mind as Consideration, Reflection, Examination, they only imagine,
fancy a vain thing, which is but a waking dream, for
the fancy is the seat, the scene, the theatre of dreams.'
No one could accuse Donne himself of lapping himself
round in a dream of sense and so eluding the warfare
of human life. Such an escape is not possible to the
virile and the rational. They must do battle with the
devils of the flesh and the inquisitions of the mind. It
is only through licence, conceived, if not indulged,
and through scepticism, that they can rise to assured
'spirituality,' if rise they do. For them neither faith

nor love are opiates, fugitive transcendentalisms or
conditions of nature. They are mysticisms measured
by the mind.

It was thus that Donne became 'Love's Martyr' in a
sense which no mannered Petrarch could conceive.
Elizabethan love-poetry originated, not in nature, but
in affectation. The coarse passion which so often dis-
gusts in the drama, while rising in its animal impulse to
such elemental heights, was excluded from the lyrics.
For here convention held sway, the exquisite unreality
of the later Renaissance, borrowed intact, and for long
unblended with any native realism. The lady of the
Elizabethan lyric is a choice type, a pretty, wayward
phantom. Our feelings are as little involved in her as
were the poets' own. She is the classical nymph somewhat domesticated, a miniature Grace in porcelain for
the fancy to handle delicately. Euphuism made her the
centre of an elaborate code of courtesy as charming
and artificial as herself. But if a mannered maid sufficed
the jaded appetite of the late Renaissance, she could
not long content a younger and cruder taste. She could
at best but offer a temporary diversion to men who were
labouring on from savagery to cultivation and through
realism to reality.

The same is true of the Platonic ideal. This was in its
origin something of a spiritual abstraction. As affected
by such a poet as Petrarch it was little more than a
gracious gesture, a dainty piece of etiquette, a recognized formula in the game of love. The Elizabethans
accepted the convention and for a time played agreeable
and even ingenuous variations upon it. But very soon
their plaything proved a poison. They became rational

enough to appreciate the Platonic ideal as an abstraction,
but they were too healthily realistic to succeed in reconciling it with their desires. And so behind the Platonic
manner, which they still affected, we read, only too
poignantly, a baffled hunger. Sidney might assume
the spiritual manner and indeed nobly conceive its
chaste and courtly truth, when he cried to Stella:

> 'So while thy beauty draws the heart to love,
> As fast thy virtue bends that love to good.'

But the thought brings him no relief, for

> 'Ah, Desire still cries, give me some food.'

This disturbing naturalism made it very difficult for
the romantic poets to preserve their ideal decorum. In
the modern jargon they were forced to suppress desire
in the interests of a convention. They had either to
lapse into lifeless sentimentality or to plunge fearlessly
into realism. Donne was the first to play the man by
acknowledging the beast. He cut the convention,
bursting through the tender, trivial and sophisticated
code of love, like a satyr trampling on a bed of flowers.
And in so doing he not only released the flesh, but
eventually liberated the spirit. He exchanged a Platonic
manner for that Platonic essence which is reborn in the
soul of every man who aspires from the mire of sense
to the heaven of intelligence, and he brought it into
vital and lacerating conflict with the forces of the brute.

His early years in London synchronized with the first
and most violent stages of that conflict. To credulous
youth, stepping with so generous a faith into a sophisticated world, dazzled by its movement, allured by its

colour, intoxicated by the plastic flow of its elements, woman commonly seems the apotheosis of all things desired, the image, say rather the emanation, of life's bounty and beauty and mystery.

But Donne was not a romantic youth in this fond sense. From his earliest years he was driven, but not deluded, by desire; he saw the cobweb in the gossamer. Before his impudent scrutiny the strategies which Nature adopts to achieve her purposes became painfully transparent. For only the pure Realist can continue to enjoy, even to triumph in, his destructive cleverness. Donne had his hour of realistic satisfaction, but the Idealist in him made it of short duration. The same yearning, latent in his social satires, for some constant principle, for some idea animating the senseless flux of things, pervades with ever more conscious and caustic intensity his early love poetry. 'The divine impression of stolen kisses,' as we shall see, was soon enough to prove a mockery of 'empty blisses,' and while the realist did not shrink from attesting the brutal facts, the religious soul quickly grew sick with satiety, and the outraged reason barbed its disgust with cynicism.

We do not know, nor is it of any importance to know, who served as subjects for these cold anatomizations of love. It is enough that the tortured story is writ small and large over the 'Songs and Sonnets.' For Donne penned few lyrics which do not bear the stamp of genuine experience, repellent though it be. They are never the manufactured flowers of sentiment, if occasionally the dead-sea fruit of clever but callous invention. Generally the thought, the fact and the image are so physically attached to one another, that clearly he who wrote thus wrote out of the flesh's exultation or the burning soul's disgust, careless of the 'tinsel trappings of poetic pride,' if also devoid of that exquisite play of fancy, that melodious magic, that grace of diction, which even the trivial courtiers of the ideal learn to lisp.

It may be indeed that the worst brutalities which Donne expresses do not accurately correspond with his actions. For, as psychology has long ago discovered, human nature often relieves itself in the abstract of what it would scorn to express in the concrete, and Donne's revolt against the affected Platonisms of contemporary verse may have aggravated his realistic excess. Nevertheless many of the grossest passages in his verse have an insolent impulsiveness which refutes any suggestion of merely sportive unpleasantness. In such Elegies, for example, as that beginning:

'Who ever loves, if he do not propose
　The right true end of love, he's one that goes
　To sea for nothing but to make him sick;'

or that 'On His Mistress Going to Bed,' the anatomy of the body is catalogued with a ferocity beside which Carew's 'Rapture' is a piece of dainty confectionery. Nor is it any abstract realist, but rather a kind of masculine maniac, who, defying every scruple of taste or morality, snarls:

'Makes virtue woman? Must I cool my blood
　Till I both be, and find one wise and good?
　May barren angels love so. But if we
　Make love to woman, virtue is not she,
　As beauty is not, nor wealth.'

We are driven indeed to the very logical conclusion
that Donne was as demoniacal in his early materialist
hunger for life as in his later idealistic craving for God.
Yet, if we wish to understand life, his candour is not to
be deprecated.

A hard mental arrogance is inevitable to one who has
exposed all that is divine and sensitive in man or woman
to the touch of naked fact, and known it mocked and
scandalized. Donne's physical insolence is but the
complement and forerunner of spiritual shame; his icy
tones reflect with an extremity of paradox a blazing
soul. And unless we study the stages of his early licence
we lose the significance of his later sanctity. Certainly
these realist days are neither gracious nor edifying, but
they are extremely enlightening. And it is because our
realist's vision is so limited that his experience is so
alarmingly pronounced, so real to the cheated senses,
so disturbing to complacent sentiments, sleeping their
drugged sleep of amiable abstraction, so valueless to the
serener eyes of truth.

§ 6

Donne, the realist, advances by regular and definable
stages towards reality, and each stage registers an
increase in rational consciousness. He is in turn the
trivial sensationalist and the impudent cynic, sincerely
passionate and sincerely disillusioned.

These stages we shall now proceed to trace.

His earliest lyrics were doubtless, in Walton's words,
'facetiously composed and carelessly scattered.' He
was still the light-headed pagan to whom life is vicarious
piracy, and woman the objective of an illicit and tran-

sient adventure. He exults in the prospect of desire,
clamouring for absolute freedom and promiscuity, and
scoffing at those 'poor heretics in love,'

'Which think to stablish dangerous constancy,'

crying:

'Love, let my body range, and let
Me travel, sojourn, snatch, plot, have, forget,
Resume my last year's relict; think that yet
We'd never met,'

bidding the woman of the moment

'Rob me, but bind me not, and let me go.'

He is ready, in short, with an entire complacency to love
every one, and yet love none, or to love and hate together
in a moment of savage climax. His highest conception
of purity is physical fearlessness:

'That love is weak where fear's as strong as he;
'Tis not all spirit, pure and brave,
If mixture it of fear, shame, honour have.'

In this sort of naturalism he applauds an inconstancy,
which is one with the law of life.

'The heavens rejoice in motion; why should I
Abjure my so much loved variety,
And not with many youth and love divide?
Pleasure is none, if not diversified.

.   .   .   .

'All things do willingly in change delight,
The fruitful mother of our appetite;
Rivers the clearer and more pleasing are,
Where their fair-spreading streams run wide and clear;

And a dead lake, that no strange bark doth greet,
Corrupts itself, and what doth live in it.

    .   .   .   .   .

'The last I saw in all extremes is fair,
And holds me in the sunbeams of her hair;

    .   .   .   .   .   .

'How happy were our sires in ancient time,
Who held plurality of loves no crime.

    .   .   .   .   .

'The golden laws of nature are repeal'd
Which our first fathers in such reverence held;'

So far then liberty to Donne is identical with licence,
with Nature's exuberance and cruel unconcern, nor is
there yet to be heard even a faint undertone of dissatisfaction with the faithlessness of it all. Yet as the concluding couplet of this Elegy shows, he is quite conscious of the licence, which he applauds, accepting it as
fit and proper for the season of youth, and reserving for
'firmer age' the task of

> 'Beauty with true worth securely weighing;
> Which being found assembled in some one,
> We'll leave (? love) her ever, and love her alone.'

Little indeed did he now guess what a harvest of
remorse he was to reap in the 'penitential years,' from
this wilful sowing, how then he was to return again and
again to the bitter theme

> 'Base love, the stain of youth, the scorn of age,'

how urgently he was to bid others

> 'Cross thy senses, else both they and thou
> Must perish soon, and to destruction bow,'

how grimly he was to admit that

> 'Vengeance will sit above our faults; but till
> She there do sit,
> We see her not, nor them.'

Very different is the victorious gusto with which he
sings now of woman's treason:

> 'Go and catch a falling star,
> Get with child a mandrake root,
> Tell me where all past years are,
> Or who cleft the devil's foot,
> Teach me to hear mermaid's singing,
> Or to keep off envy's stinging,
>   And find
>   What wind
> Serves to advance an honest mind.

> 'If thou be'st born to strange sights,
> Things invisible to see,
> Ride ten thousand days and nights
> Till age snow white hairs on thee,
> Thou, when thou return'st, wilt tell me
> All strange wonders that befell thee,
>   And swear
>   No where
> Lives a woman true and fair.

> 'If thou find'st one, let me know;
> Such a pilgrimage were sweet.
> Yet do not, I would not go,
> Though at next door we might meet,

E

> Though she were true when you met her,
> And last till you write your letter,
> Yet she
> Will be
> False, ere I come, to two or three.'

Triumphant as this is, we remark the first vibrations of sarcasm. But they are as yet in no sense acrid. Donne, in fact, at this point in his devastating career was literally pleased to be cynical. It added spice to an enjoyment which was beginning unawares to prove a little tedious. But it is important to distinguish such cynicism from that which was later to issue from the roused moralist. Quite certainly Donne would at this time have been pained and embarrassed if the lady whom he chid for loving him but one whole day, had expressed her willingness to love him for another. Love, as he repeats more than once, is simply an honest meal, in which a succession of courses is imperative.

> 'Changed loves are but changed sorts of meat;
> And when he hath the kernel eat,
> Who doth not fling away the shell?'

or

> 'I spring a mistress, swear, write, sigh and weep;
> And the game kill'd, or lost, go talk and sleep.'

But even with a constant change of diet this Pagan feeding began to pall; it entailed too such a snatching at, such a speedy dispatch of dishes. There was no possibility of resting on enjoyment, of relaxing from effort and serenely cultivating the digestion. For

'Love is a growing, or full constant light,
And his short minute, after noon, is night.'

Soon Donne's mind imperceptibly detaches itself
from the process. As a first sign of this he begins to
indulge in scurrilous but much relished abuse of his
fare. He gloats over Love's deformity. He denounces
love as a 'canker' with the same violent superficiality as
he had acclaimed it a 'fruit.' He expends all his virtuosity on the delighted imaging of physical ugliness and
the enunciation of all its rankest manifestations. Or in
superlative vituperation, kindred to that of the 'blood
and thunder' dramatists, he relieves his pent passions,
concluding with a sigh of content:

'Now have I cursed, let us our love revive;
In me the flame was never more alive.'

And soon the mental detachment becomes even more
pronounced. He indulges, we might say, in a certain
quibbling talk at meals. That fantastical vein in his
nature, which had drawn him to the Spanish mystics,
appears, if at first in rather foppish guise. He extemporizes upon the theme of desire in far-fetched allu-
sions and conceits. His lambent wit and learning begin
to play about the crude fact, as in the geographical and
cosmographical imagery, which was to entangle the
minds of the later metaphysical poets:

'On a round ball
A workman, that hath copies by, can lay
An Europe, Afric, and an Asia
And quickly make that, which was nothing, all.

So doth each tear
Which thee doth wear,
A globe, yea world, by that impression grow,
Till thy tears mix'd with mine do overflow
This world, by waters sent from thee, my heaven
    dissolvéd so.'

And then into this quibbling there creeps a faint strain
of pathos, almost of tenderness, affected it may be, and
yet wistful with a wisdom of heart and mind newly born.
  In brief he is beginning to weary of the trivial: the
featureless joys of the creature sadden the awakening
creator in him. At moments he is ready to bid farewell
to such love as this; for

  'What before pleased them all, takes but one sense,
    And that so lamely, that it leaves behind
    A kind of sorrowing dullness to the mind.
    Ah, cannot we,
    As well as cocks and lions, jocund be
    After such pleasures. . . ?
    I'll no more dote and run
    To pursue things which had endamaged me;
    And when I come where moving beauties be,
    As men do when the summer's sun
    Grows great,
    Though I admire their greatness, shun their heat.'

The virus of consciousness spreads and deepens into
something more than picturesque disillusionment.
Love appears no longer as a feast, but as a fever fuelled
by corruption. Pained and humbled, Donne begins to
plead with and for the passion, the summary intoxica-

tion, which reason and knowledge have begun so
insidiously to repress.

> 'Give me thy weakness, make me blind,
> Both ways, as thou and thine, in eyes and mind;
> Love, let me never know that this
> Is love, or, that love childish is;
> Let me not know that others know
> That she knows my pains, lest that so
> A tender shame make me mine own new woe.
> I may not article for grace,
> Having put Love at last to show this face.
>
> .   .   .   .
>
> 'For this Love is enraged with me,
> Yet kill not; if I must example be
> To future rebels, if th' unborn
> Must learn by my being cut up and torn,
> Kill, and dissect me, Love;'

The inconstancy of women too, which previously had
so agreeably baited his wit, can be matter now for
wretchedness.

> 'Yet send me back my heart and eyes,
> That I may know, and see thy lies,
> And may laugh and joy, when thou
>   Art in anguish
>   And dost languish
>   For some one
>   That will none,
> Or prove as false as thou art now.'

The impervious sensualist is even reduced to the senti-

mentalist's self-pitying protestation of a broken heart
and love's final decease:

> 'My rags of heart can like, wish, and adore,
> But after one such love, can love no more.'

And lastly out of the ferment and the exhaustion of the
physical there emerges a first tremulous apprehension
of Platonism. Donne begins to think of the soul as
well as of the body. The soul, he argues, must take
limbs of flesh,

> 'Love must not be, but take a body too.' . . .

Platonic gestures and abstractions, he pleads in defence
of his materialism, are lifeless nothings, and yet he admits that in determining to 'ballast love,' he has 'love's
pinnace overfraught.' So happy is he in achieving this
celestial concept that he waxes complacent at the
expense of woman. It is only man, he claims, who can
rise to the height of an idea or spread his wings upon
the air. Woman is sunk deep in the dark of nature.

> 'Just such disparity
> As is 'twixt air's and angel's purity,
> 'Twixt women's love, and men's, will ever be.'

Man is an artful casuist in his own cause. Donne had
enslaved woman to his own coarse purposes. He had
tired of the sordid business and now was grown an
angel of purity beside the mistress whom he had debased. But his apprenticeship, as a lover, to truth had
only passed through its first and most trivial course.
The Puritan in him had indeed begun to assert itself
against the slightly jaded Pagan, but the reaction was

as facile as the action which begot it. He was approaching, however, an experience which was to test to the uttermost the reality of both elements in his nature, and through which, after a parallel but profounder cycle of passion and disillusionment, he was to pass, considerably purged, to a love in which passion and Platonism were affectionately wedded. But before we trace that passage in his emotional history, we must turn for a moment to certain external events which prefaced it.

§ 7

In the summer of 1596 Donne engaged in an adventure which was destined indirectly to have a profound effect upon his life, an effect for which the lasting enrichment of his vocabulary by nautical imagery scarcely offered adequate compensation. He exchanged the quiet of Lincoln's Inn and the liaisons of London life for a period of service on the high seas. Spain's Armada had already been destroyed, but not her pretensions. These threatened England's power on the Continent, and it was determined to launch an expedition against her. The Earl of Essex was among the leaders appointed, and Donne, recommended possibly by his knowledge of Spanish, was attached to his person, and put to sea on the first of June, bound for Cadiz.

The expedition brilliantly achieved its purpose; the Spanish fleet was broken, and in the autumn the victorious invaders returned. But Donne's thirst for some rougher and more elemental contact with life than any city could offer was not yet satisfied. It is just possible, though for other reasons unlikely, that he spent some months between his return from Cadiz and a new

departure in continental travel; certainly in the summer
of the following year he attended Essex once again on
his successful raid upon the Azores. Upon that expedition, also in attendance on Essex, went the son and
stepson of Sir Thomas Egerton, the recently appointed
Lord Keeper, a circumstance which was big with issues
for Donne himself. In July a storm, of which Donne
gave his friend Christopher Brooke a rather forced
account in verse, compelled them to put back into Fal-
mouth, but late in August they set out once more, and
early in September, saw, as the twilight settled on the
sea, the sheer peak of Teneriffe:

'Rise so high like a rock, that one might think
The floating moon would shipwreck there and sink.'

At this time of what he called 'a stupid calm' – and
we can well believe that storm was more in harmony
with so chafed and turbulent a spirit, eager to drown
his thoughts in violent action – he wrote once more to
his friend a more intimate epistle. From this we gather
that three motives, beyond the general urge of adventure, had driven Donne to sea:

'a rotten state, and hope of gain,
Or to disuse me from the queasy pain
Of being loved and loving, or the thirst
Of honour or fair death.'

We have already had occasion to state that he had
squandered his fortune with remarkable promptitude,
and the growing pains of wisdom, the baffled satiety
which had begun to descend upon a pursuit of light
licence would in themselves be enough to explain the

second impulse; while some such sick indifference to
a pampered, perplexed and over-seasoned world as
drove many a young man, and for that matter middle-
aged man, in 1914 to gather war to his arms like a
bride, is sufficient explanation of the third. That
Donne on general grounds was in a mutinous distemper
with himself and the world is unmistakable:

> 'Nothing for us, we are for nothing fit;
> Chance, or ourselves, still disproportion it:
> We have no power, no will, no sense;'

But this sudden aggravation of symptoms was attributable to a particular as well as to general causes. His
passions had already centred on a single point, and
were goading him on to a distraction, in which the
deeps and not the shallows of his nature were involved.

We have seen how between his twentieth and twenty-
third years he had begun to modify the bombastic
paganism of his first approach to life. At such a moment
sensibility is particularly exposed to attack, and the
violence of youth's surrender is proportionate to the
violence of its late aggressiveness. So it was with
Donne.

Shortly before starting with Essex to Cadiz he had
met at some society function a woman who by her very
quiet artlessness had completely captivated him. He
who had been passion's jester was reduced in a moment
to passion's slave. The lady was the wife of a rich man
and a cripple; she was of no great intelligence and ill-
treated by her testy husband. She seems to have received
Donne's extravagant importunities readily enough, and
indeed only a woman of iron will in her position could

have resisted so devastating and at the same time insinuating a lover. So wholly is the erstwhile rover attached to her on the eve of his departure to Cadiz, that the adventure has lost all its glamour through entailing so intolerable a divorce:

'Till I have peace with thee, war other men,
And when I have peace, can I leave thee then?

. . . . . .

'To mew me in a ship is to enthral
Me in a prison that is like to fall;
Or in a cloister, save that there men dwell
In a calm heaven, here in a swaying hell.
Long voyages are but long consumptions,
And ships are carts for executions;
Yea, they are deaths; is't not all one to fly
Into another world, as 'tis to die?
Here let me war; in these arms let me lie:
Here let me parley, batter, bleed, and die.
Thine arms imprison me, and my arms thee;
Thy heart thy ransom is: take mine for me.'

At the same time he sent his lady 'his picture' with the parting protestation:

'Here take my picture, though I bid farewell,
Thine in my heart, where my soul dwells, shall dwell.

How different are these tones from the recent sallies of imperious, flippant promiscuity. The quality of his passion, it may be admitted, is little changed, but his heart is held. In truth destiny, to quote his own words,

'Since I loved in jest before, decreed
That I should suffer, when I loved indeed.'

On his return from Cadiz the liaison proceeded apace.
It entailed conditions humiliating enough to one at
heart so proud and candid. The lovers were

> 'ambush'd round with household spies,
> And over all thy husband's towering eyes,
> Inflamed with th' ugly sweat of jealousy.'

Their blisses were stolen, and we are given a vivid
picture of the crippled husband, who

> 'swollen and pamper'd with great fare
> Sits down and snorts, caged in his basket chair,'

or of the lovers who, seated at table, 'spoke dialogues
with our feet far from our words,' – a picture the more
repulsive because it is preceded by a conjecture of the
husband's decease, peculiarly loathsome in its *macabre*
detail. The necessity of surreptitious love-making must
have been doubly vexing to one who had but recently
justified physical passion on the grounds of freedom
and candour. It was, in short, a 'vulgar story,' and as
such repelled the aristocrat strangely present even in
the erotic free-booter. Moreover, by this time he was
increasingly conscious of Platonic yearnings, and into
these paths of finer apprehension the lady was too
commonplace to follow him. She was, it seems, dull of
faculty, to whom previously

> 'household charms, thy husband's name to teach,
> Were all the love-tricks that thy wit could reach;'

while Donne, as he was to confess, had brought to their
early intimacy little but violent devotion. He had
instructed her in the cruder alphabet of passion, and

she, who had learnt her lesson well, wished for no more subtle or transcendental sequel. But Donne was already outgrowing animalism, which he had refined from promiscuity, in binding himself to her. And so, although he continues to protest his constancy, as the months passed by, the very hyperbole of his style betrays a fading reality:

> 'I will not look upon the quickening sun
> But straight her beauty to my sense shall run'

challenges the old manner. But

> 'Rend us in sunder; thou canst not divide
> Our bodies so, but that our souls are tied,
> And we can love, by letters still and gifts,
> And thoughts and dreams: love never wanteth shifts.'

and

> 'Nay, if I wax but cold in my desire,
> Think, heaven hath motion lost, and the world fire'

approach too near that artificial style which the honest soul in Donne abhorred, to carry conviction. The flesh no longer cleaves to the bones. He protests too much and too ingeniously; he is at pains to hide, maybe from his own heart, an inner emptiness which he cannot yet bring himself to admit.

But secretly in his own chamber the truth would out. The old cynicism at woman's expense, the old assertion of inconstancy, revives, but with a difference. Inconstancy is arraigned as a lamentable principle of death, rather than acclaimed as a condition of life. Ironic wit is no longer the foil of arrogance but of despair:

nature is become a grim instead of a cheerful analogy.

'Foxes, and goats – all beasts – change when they please.
Shall women, more hot, wily, wild than these,
Be bound to one man. . . ?'

Certainly it comforted his vanity to dismiss women's
morality as one with that of foxes and goats; for thus
at least temporarily he escaped examining his own. And
subconsciously he knew that there must be some flaw
in it. Despite all his protestations of achieved loyalty,
his feelings were changing. He had been deluded;
love after all possessed no principle of permanence: he
was drifting back into the comfortless, purposeless sea
of promiscuity, from which he had thought to put
safely into port. There was after all no safety in the
world, and no refuge in himself from the ruthless
seasons of desire.

He could not bring himself to admit it. He preferred
to impute the disaster to the special circumstances that
foiled his passion and to blame his unfortunate lady
for her married infidelity. And meanwhile he played
with the conception of some chaster degree of licence
half-way between single loyalty and plural indifference.

'To live in one land is captivity,
To run all countries a wild roguery.
Waters stink soon, if in one place they bide,
And in the vast sea are more putrified;
But when they kiss one bank, and leaving this
Never look back, but the next bank do kiss,
Then are they purest; change is the nursery
Of music, joy, life and eternity.'

Yet even this precise and calculated variation of experience appealed less and less on consideration. It might satisfy a physical craving for sameness in variety, but the maturing mind in him pierced deeper into life, and now continually troubled him with its intrusive demand for something more permanent than a moment's allurement — a principle, a quality, an idea, a sense of intellectual affinity — something indeed which he could not yet properly define, but which would, in some miraculous way, impose form and significance upon haphazard and exhausting impulses. Unfortunately the lady to whom he had tied himself was temperamentally unfitted to encourage the tentative advances of a timid idealist; nor had his previous relationships with women encouraged him to think that she differed in this from the mass.

> 'A naked thinking heart, that makes no show,
>   Is to a woman but a kind of ghost,'

or

> 'That loving wretch that swears
>   'Tis not the bodies marry, but the minds,
>   Which he in her angelic finds,
> Would swear as justly, that he hears
> In that day's rude hoarse minstrelsy, the spheres.
>   Hope not for mind in women; at their best,
>   Sweetness and wit they are, but mummy, possess'd.'

We need not pursue in detail the gradual subsidence of this passion to its infuriated close in the autumn of 1597. From refusing to meet the lady in her own house, Donne descended to the basest sneers and

recriminations, imputing to her the inconstancy which
was gnawing at his own heart. Thus, as we have suggested, he

> 'thought his pain would be lesser,
> If on womankind he might his anger wreak.'

He had indulged himself with women in general and
tired of it, and now with one woman, and tired of her
also. For a little longer he tried to perpetuate his
passion by fanning the flame of a meretricious jealousy.
His mistress, he argued with exquisite but somewhat
tardy scruple, had proved false to another, in yielding
to him. The thought of this, he protested, was a worse
plague than love itself.

> 'Falsehood is worse than hate; and that must be,
> If she whom I love, should love me.'

And yet there was a thread of truth in it. Donne's
moral nature was, in fact, awakening. He was disillusioned of carnality to a degree beside which his
earlier dissatisfaction was no more than a tissue of
conceit. Sometimes he was content to brood, dignified, resigned, or sullenly indifferent, and then he
would start up and cry, with that rolling cadence which
always speaks emotional conviction in poetry:

> 'I long to talk with some old lover's ghost
> Who died before the God of love was born.'

The heart in him which in its very clamour for freedom
had bound itself in chains, the mind, which had learnt
to search the haunts of pruriency with a morbid acute-
ness, were in revolt. The question to which he was

later to give a triumphant answer had begun to haunt him:

> 'Why should our clay
> Over our spirits so much sway
> To tie us to that way?'

Might not two souls kiss like two thoughts that met each other in the air, delicately like wind and water, the sunlight and the soil? Need love be so crude, so shackled, so grovelling, above all so damaging? For sensuality, uninformed by any higher principle, any intuition of values, not only cloyed terribly but wasted like a disease. It was

> 'The Spider Love, which transubstantiates all,
> And can convert manna to gall.'

The thought of the time

> 'When my soul was in her body sheathed,'

when

> 'Thy heart seemed wax, and steel thy constancy,'

was now anguish to him, a torment too in which his whole being was involved. His body was outraged no less than his mind rebuffed, and it was physical passion which begot images like great sprawling growths out of some alluvial slime — as

> 'So careless flowers strew'd on the water's face
> The curled whirlpools suck, smack, and embrace,
> Yet drown them.'

Similarly his resort to unbridled scorn was dictated not by calculated malice, but by the despairing neces-

sity of escape from the obsession of a curdled passion.
It was the pitiless execration of an egoism blindly
infuriated with itself. For

> 'love, dull'd with pain,
> Was ne'er so wise, nor well arm'd as disdain.
> Then with new eyes I shall survey thee, and spy
> Death in thy cheeks and darkness in thine eye,
> Though hope bred faith and love; . . .
> My hate shall outgrow thine, and utterly
> I will renounce thy dalliance.'

So at last in a savage frenzy he turned upon the poor
woman, whom so short a time before he had bent to
his purpose with a militant ardour and a shameless
licence. The cold and cruel cynicism, the elemental
spite of this last farewell to one who must at least have
given as much as she received, has no parallel in our
literature. In truth no one is so ruthlessly vindictive,
so callous to every claim of sentiment and generosity,
as the moralist newly risen from the ashes of the brute:

'When by thy scorn, O murd'ress, I am dead,
And that thou think'st thee free
From all solicitation from me,
Then shall my ghost come to thy bed,
And thee, feign'd vestal, in worse arms shall see;
Then thy sick taper will begin to wink,
And he, whose thou art then, being tired before,
Will, if thou stir, or pinch to wake him, think
    Thou call'st for more,
And, in false sleep, will from thee shrink:

And then, poor aspen wretch, neglected thou
Bathed in a cold quicksilver sweat wilt lie
　　　A verier ghost than I.
What I will say, I will not tell thee now,
Lest that preserve thee; and since my love is spent,
I'd rather thou shouldst painfully repent,
Than by my threatenings rest still innocent.'

To such a sulphurous inferno as this can naked realism lead. And yet if we are tempted to wish that
Donne had learnt some of the graces of chivalry in
that artificial court of love, in which many of his contemporaries had refined their grosser manners, we
must remember that for him it was only through this
inferno that he could ascend, with infinite travail, to
the purgatory of self-recrimination and the paradise of
self-escape. It was through the agonized errors of sex
that Donne rose to the sublimities of religion.

'This,' he was to cry later from the pulpit, '*is the full
setting of the heart to do evil*, when a man fills himself
with the liberty of passing into any sin, in an indiffer-
encie; and then finds no reason why he should leave
that way, either by the love, or by the fear of God. If
he prosper by his sin, then he finds *no reason*; if he do
not prosper by it, he finds a *wrong reason*.'

Misfortune was now directing him towards a right
one.

§ 8

Gradually his hatred subsided, and, as so often after a
day of storm, there was a grandeur about the sunset.
Pity, poignant recollection, a sense of utter, irremedi-
able emptiness, succeeded the terrific malediction.

'I, by Love's limbec am the grave
Of all, that's nothing. Oft a flood
  Have we two wept, and so
Drown'd the whole world, us two; oft did we grow,
To be two chaoses, when we did show
Care to aught else; and often absences
Withdrew our souls, and made us carcasses.

'But I am by her death — which word wrongs her —
Of the first nothing the elixir grown;

  . . . .

   . . . nor will my sun renew.
You lovers, for whose sake the lesser sun
  At this time to the Goat is run
  To fetch new lust, and give it you,
   Enjoy your summer all,
Since she enjoys her long night's festival.'

Donne was not one to succumb himself to any 'long
night's festival.' Like all men of vivid sensibility, his
alternations of mood were excessive and rapid: moreover, he would always

   'be rather grown
Mad with much heart, than idiot with none,'

and fifteen years later, when time might have been
expected to have quenched somewhat his ardours, he
could write:

'I am much of one sect in the philosophy of love;
which, though it be directed upon the mind, doth in-
here in the body, and find plenty entertainment there.'

He did not therefore long remain on this occasion
'the quintessence of nothingness.' Doubtless at the

moment he was, as he confessed, neither man nor
beast, but a shadow. Conflict had reduced him to a
cypher, and listlessness was the grateful narcotic of
defeat. Nevertheless, despite his protestation to the
contrary, the spring, when it came, seems to have
'fetched new lust' for him too; for there is evidence of
his having indulged in at least two more amorous
adventures, one of which however, judging by his
interpretation of it in verse, was of a gentle and fantastical nature, a source of consolation to ragged nerves
and fit subject for 'thankful sonnets' rather than intro-
spective agitation.

New surroundings and regular employment were to
prove now the best medicine for his distraction, and
fortunately he could congratulate himself, as his passion
declined, upon having been very discreet, so that no
scandal arose to prevent his social advancement.

The acquaintanceship which he had formed, during
his attachment to Essex, with the son and stepson of
Sir Thomas Egerton served him in good stead. For it
was to this in all probability, even more than to the
fact that he was a law student of unusual ability if
irregular application, that he owed his appointment in
the winter of 1597 as the Lord Keeper's Secretary.
Thereafter he went to live at York House in the Strand,
and his own vivid personality no less than the cordiality
of his employer soon put him on easy terms with the
family.

Sir Thomas Egerton was much in favour with the
Court, a learned lawyer, cultured, influential and
popular. He had lately married for the second time,
and his household consisted not only of his own two

sons but also of the second wife's son, Francis Wooley. A frequent visitor was one Anne More, a niece of the new Lady Egerton, and one of the daughters of a rather empty-headed but ambitious country gentleman, Sir George More.

With all of these Donne quickly became a favourite. His secretarial work carried him abroad in 1598, certainly to the Low Countries and probably to Copenhagen. Here he enjoyed the prestige of a diplomatic mission, and tasted at second-hand something of the magnificence which in those days accompanied the steps of a public servant. The effect on one so sensitive to the charm of picturesque pomps and distinguished etiquette (doubtless because of the Gothic element in his nature which he had grown to fear and disdain) must have been great. We shall see, as we trace the next twenty years of Donne's life, and watch his contorted, fluctuating struggle to achieve an inward harmony of faculty, how persistently, how despairingly, he seeks to place himself in an environment where, if only conventionally, the ruder forces of life are subdued to an etiquette. In truth the internal and the external ambition are intimately related, and a recognition of this fact will help us to understand, if not altogether to condone, many acts of rather humiliating parasitism, to which later he was to stoop.

The rebel against all those forms and manners which men evolve and perpetuate as a defence against chaos and savagery, was inevitably brought face to face with himself. So near, so unnerving a view of the uncontrollable potentialities of his own nature increasingly disposed him to regard convention, in its distinguished

manifestations, with a friendly eye, until at last, after
he had by his own impulsive action become a social
outlaw, he came to hunger for it as the necessary, the
only effective barrier against that temperamental
anarchy which he could neither subdue nor indefinitely
sustain: so much so that the hope of Court preferment
was to prove one of the chief causes which kept him
for so long outside the pale of the Church, and the
final disappointment of this hope, the goad which ultimately drove him within.

His secretarial post brought him also new and influential friends; he served as the intermediary to his
master's patronage and he was the privileged witness
of high affairs of state: all of which must have tended
to encourage his innate sense of aristocracy, and blind
his eyes to the subservience of his own position. Indeed,
his appointment was singularly opportune. He was in
that state of convalescence from the fevers of youth
when a man first consciously aspires to moral and
mental stability. And his keen sense of the indignity
of dissipation must have led him to embrace the stately
gravity which pervaded York House, with corre-
sponding satisfaction. That this was so is in no way
disproved by the probability that at this time he employed his leisure in composing those 'Problems and
Paradoxes,' which many years later his son dedicated
to Lord Newport, as representing 'the primroses and
violets' of his father's spring.

For it is a quality of the social aristocrat to translate
into terms of wit what the natural man experiences as
fact and the spiritual man interprets as idea. The
experiences over which Donne had recently agonized,

and which the preacher of a later day was to convert
into sublime edification, are in the 'Paradoxes' treated
often with an infectious flippancy, a purely disinterested nimbleness of mind. Scurrilous they are at times,
and casuistical to a degree, but there is seldom a tremor
of seriousness in their argument. Donne, it is clear,
had for the moment ceased to hold that bitter personal
stake in life, which had but a year before made even
his cynicism a cry of torture. He could afford to play
facetiously with what had been fire-brands, and were
to be the torches of a later illumination; and so these
'Paradoxes' are full of mocking echoes of painful
themes, and curious prophecies of moral ones.

Thus the Collection begins with 'A Defence of
Women's Inconstancy,' in which he writes:

'For everything as it is one better than another, so is
it fuller of change; the Heavens themselves continually
turn, the stars move, the Moon changeth; fire whirleth,
air flyeth, water ebbs and flows, the face of the Earth
altereth her looks, time stays not. . . . Learning
affords no rules to know, much less knowledge to rule
the mind of a Woman.'

And then in a familiar, but quite dispassionate manner
he continues:

'Women are like flies, which feed among us at our
Table, or Fleas sucking our very blood, who leave not
our most retired places free from their familiarity.'

And while he applauds their 'sly changeableness' and
'pleasing doubleness,' he concludes with the ancient
sophistry that 'Every woman is a science,' which man

cannot learn in a lifetime. Later he extemporizes on
the theme to which his own history was to give a
significant rendering, 'That the gifts of the Body are
better than those of the Mind. . . . I say again that
the body makes the mind . . . my Body licenceth my
soul to see the world's beauties through mine eyes; to
hear pleasant things through mine ears; and affords
it apt organs for the conveyance of all perceivable
delight.' This leads him on to give a qualified assent
to the contention that 'Virginity is a Virtue.' 'But I
call that Virginity a virtue which is willing and desirous
to yield itself upon honest and lawful terms, when
just reason requireth; and until then, is kept with a
modest charity of Body and Mind' . . . for Virtue
unused can only 'putrify and corrupt.'

In these and other such 'Paradoxes' as 'That it is
possible to find some virtue in some Women,' or such
Problems as 'Why are the Fairest Falsest?' or 'Have
Women Souls?' we hear the young secretary making
riddles of the realism which he had survived. But even
more striking are those examples in which he deals
frivolously with subjects which later in his life he was
to clothe with portentous seriousness. Thus he argues
'That Women ought to Paint': for 'If her face be
painted on a Board or Wall, thou wilt love it, and the
Board and the Wall: Canst thou loath it then when it
speaks, smiles or kisses, because it is painted?' More
than twenty years later he returned to this subject in
the pulpit of St. Paul's and developed it at some
length, but with how great a difference of tone the
following brief quotation will show:

'Certainly the limits of adorning and beautifying the

body are not so narrow, so strict, as by some sour men they are sometimes conceived to be. Difference of Ranks, of Ages, of Nations, of Customs, make great differences in the enlarging, or contracting of these limits, in adorning the body; and that may come near sin at some time, and in some places, which is not so always, nor everywhere. . . . So that if they that beautify themselves mean no harm in it, therefore there should be no harm in it; for except they could as well provide, that others should take no harm, as that they should mean no harm, they may participate of the fault.'

Similarly he writes, for once with the gravity of experience: 'That Nature is our worst Guide. . . . Can she be a good guide to us, which hath corrupted not us only but herself? . . . Alas! how unable a guide is that which follows the temperature of our shiny bodies?'

With which we may compare the eventual priest's words at a christening:

'A Fountain breaks out in the wilderness, but that fountain cares not, whether any Man come to fetch water, or no; A fresh, and fit gale blows upon the sea, but it cares not whether the Mariners hoist sail or no; a Rose blows in your garden, but it calls you not to smell to it.'

How wiser, we are tempted to interpolate, was Donne in this matter of Nature than his Romantic successors!

Although the majority of these Paradoxes are no more than examples of virtuosity, certain of them reveal the philosophy which was beginning to engage Donne's mind. The reflection, for example, 'That by

Discord things increase' was a profound if unconscious interpretation of his own personality. 'All the rich benefits we can frame to ourselves in Concord, is but an Even Conservation of things; . . . Discord is never so barren that it affords no fruit. . . . For in a troubled misery Men are always more religious than in a secure peace . . . and so the Discord of Extremes begets all virtues, but of the like things there is no issue without a miracle.'

Again he writes on the subject 'That Old men are more fantastic than Young.' . . . 'To be fantastic in young men is conceiptful distemperature, and a witty madness; but in old men, whose senses are withered, it becomes natural, therefore more full and perfect.' Which is an account, such as he might have written at the end of his life, of the gradual substantiating of his own fantastic wit. Nor is the theme neglected which was to usurp the place of love as the central, the perpetual subject of menacing soliloquy – the theme of Death. The fifth of his Paradoxes is 'That all things kill themselves,' and suggests a preparatory note for the ingenious tract which he was later to write in justification of suicide. We read too of 'the last best refuge of misery, death,' but also 'that only cowards dare die' because 'Cowards suffer what cannot be avoided,' unlike a 'brave and climbing spirit,' for whom 'truly this life is a tempest and a warfare.' The self-portrait here is unmistakable, as is the following paragraph on religious cowardice:

'And lastly, of these men which die the Allegorical death of entering into Religion, how few are found fit

for any shew of valiancy? but only a soft and supple
metal, made only for cowardly solitariness.'

Flippantly then as Donne wrote at this time, he
reveals himself significantly. So absorbed an egoist
could not crack a jest, preach a sermon, write a letter
or pen a poem, without self-confession. For the
moment Donne had detached himself from life, and
his wit is the second process in his development of a
philosophy. The budding scientist is evident in such
Problems as 'Why is there more variety of green than
of other colours?' or 'Why Venus-star only doth cast a
shadow?'; the budding theologian, scornful of the
materialist prelate scheming for preferment, in 'Why
do young Lay-men so much study Divinity?' and the
budding preacher in 'Why Puritans make long sermons.' Lastly 'An Essay on Valour' which ends the
collection with the sentence 'But now I remember I
am for valour, and therefore I must be a man of few
words,' serves well as the text for the next chapter in
his imprudent career.

§ 9

Donne did not allow such secret diversions to inter-
fere with his duties. Secretarially he was all discretion.
And if through daily converse with a man of dignity,
charm and prestige, he quickly outgrew the grosser
barbarisms of his early youth, his master, we can believe, soon learnt to value highly the sharp wits and
the ingratiating manners (for this Gothic monster
could play the courtier to perfection when he wished)
of his amanuensis.

Nevertheless, neither the fear of angering so austere a master, nor any prudent regard for his own interests, now so favourably placed, were to stay the wilful motions of Donne's romantic heart. In January, 1600, Lady Egerton died, and her place as presiding hostess was taken by her favourite and indeed almost adopted niece, Anne More, a gentle and retiring girl of sixteen. This arrangement suited her father, Sir George More, well. A hot-headed and extravagant man, who had forced his way into the Queen's favour and cherished high political ambitions, he was prevented from indulging his lavish inclinations at Loseley, his home in the country, by the fact that his father, who survived to an extreme old age, preserved control over the family purse to the end. He appreciated therefore highly the privilege of being a guest at York House on the frequent occasions when he wished to escape to London, while the society which he enjoyed there was as attractive as it was influential. And while his sister's death threatened an end to this agreeable arrangement, the succession of one of his daughters to the post of honour served to prolong it at least for a time.

Donne, as an intimate of the family, must already for more than two years have been thrown into fitful but discreet contact with his master's young niece. We may conjecture, however, that the vigilant eye of her aunt had prevented a polite acquaintanceship from developing into anything warmer, although a young secretary of such pronounced talent and appearance cannot have failed to make some impression upon the susceptibilities of girlhood — nor can we fancy that any compunction would have prevented Donne, already well schooled in the strategies of clandestine love-making, from advancing his case, so far as circumstances allowed, if his feelings had been at all affected. But even in a social environment where girls quickly matured, a child of fourteen could scarcely have excited such feelings. Now, however, circumstances had conspired to make her a woman at one stride; the sentry was gone from the walls and there was no one to take her place, no one indeed in the household, save the Lord Keeper himself, of mature years.

The girl's permanent residence at York House, together with her probable incapacity at first to cope with the responsible duties so suddenly thrust upon her, duties in which a clever young secretary was so clearly competent to assist, would in themselves explain a rapid growth of intimacy. Moreover, her youth and innocency, precociously associated with the position of presiding hostess, must have appealed strongly to Donne, to his new appreciation of aristocracy and its gracious gestures, and of purity as the antithesis of his immediate past.

Indeed, what a charming picture this child must have made playing the mistress with a grave dignity which belied, while it enhanced, her tender years! Donne had degraded his own youth with women of experienced sensuality. From such muddy waters he turned to a fresh spring with the renewed thirst of a man still morally fevered, of one who desired by chaster emotions to cleanse his conscience of sin and dignify at all costs the passion of which he feared that he was yet the slave.

The manner in which he was driven to effect this was

not of the happiest, and the consequences were so painfully, so disproportionately prolonged, that we may say without exaggeration they governed the rest of his life.

For nine months Donne and Anne More pursued a secret courtship. The young lady was compliant: her own inexperience and the headstrong charm of her lover were doubtless arguments enough. Then an event occurred which brought to a head a sentimental relationship that otherwise, it is just possible, might have died of time and familiarity.

Sir Thomas Egerton announced his intention of marrying again. He did so in October, and forthwith Anne More returned to her father's house at Loseley, not however before the lovers in the distraction of parting had plighted their troth. Separation only intensified Donne's passion. He poured it out in indifferent sonnets to his friends Christopher and Samuel Brooke, in which he attested that

'Strong is this love which ties our hearts in one,
 And strong that love pursued with amorous pain,'

and lamented

'Love's hot fires, which martyr my sad mind.'

He had shed in truth the last element of that detachment from the object of his passion, which had given such precision to his earlier verse. He was too abandoned a lover to be an artist; he lived for the times when Sir George More brought his daughter to town. In his hunger for communion and sympathy he seems even to have taken the younger members of his mas-

ter's household into his confidence. He was not unduly
sensitive to the invidiousness of his position. The
same oblivious egoism which had driven him into
every kind of unpleasant liaison, now bade him cast
discretion to the winds. His only anxiety was lest
those in authority, learning of his sentiments, should
raise insuperable barriers against their gratification.
Piratical as he was, with more than youth's own haste
to win to its goal by the nearest and speediest route,
he determined to act. Anne More was not of the stuff
of resistance, even had she questioned the wisdom of
her lover's project. All her life she was eminently,
pathetically malleable. Parliament was to be dissolved
in December, and she might then be lost for ever in
the prison house of Loseley.

Donne summoned the kindly Christopher Brooke to
his assistance. He should give the bride away. His
brother Samuel had, conveniently enough, recently
taken Orders: he should perform the ceremony. Francis Wooley, always friendly and adventurous, should
requite some small services rendered to him on the
Azores expedition: he should circumvent the suspicions
of relatives, and bring the bride safe to church. A
menial should be suborned as witness. The strategy
was drafted with a general staff's precision, and it
worked according to plan. Shortly before Christmas
of 1601 Donne and Anne More were man and wife.

§ 10

The secrecy and unconventionality of the affair seems
in the exhilarating moment of achievement to have
delighted its principal perpetrator. Donne had repaid

himself in romantic coin for his losses in the realistic.
He had wiped off his past indignities with an act of
reckless devotion, such as every story-teller would
applaud, and every wiseacre deplore. He was in the
mood to boast:

> 'I have done one braver thing
> Than all the worthies did;
> And yet a braver thence doth spring,
> Which is to keep that hid.'

His exaltation, however, was to be short-lived, and, as
the immediate excitement subsided, something of the
serious indecorum of his action must have begun to
dawn upon him. It was not merely the indignation
of parent and employer which he had to face; by
marrying a minor without her father's consent he had
broken both the Canon and Common Law. To play
the part of an eloping squire was well enough, but to be
in danger of going to prison for it was, to say the least,
humiliating.

   And how to break the news to the aggressive and
dull-witted Sir George More, without which the marriage must remain no more than a piece of pretty play-
acting? The situation, he soon realized, was fraught
with perplexity. Friends were once more requisitioned.
They were asked to drop hints in Sir George More's
hearing that the Lord Keeper's secretary cherished
feelings for his daughter that exceeded respectful
admiration. The plan succeeded only too well. The
indignant gentleman determined that the intrigue, if
true, should be nipped in the bud. His daughter
should remain out of harm's way at Loseley.

Soon Donne realized that the truth must be forced by
direct assault. Yet even he flinched at the prospect of
leading the attack in person. Fortunately among his
acquaintances was one, Henry Percy, ninth Earl of
Northumberland, who shared his appreciation of law-
less passion, his intellectual and mystical audacity, and
his complete indifference to the opinions or sentiments
of others. Donne begged him to act as confessor and
mediator, and the situation appealed so strongly to
his interfering temperament that he agreed without
demur.

Early in February he journeyed to Loseley, and
doubtless, before handing to Sir George a letter from
his unacknowledged son-in-law, he prepared the
ground deftly by dwelling upon the brilliant and indis-
pensable gifts of Sir Thomas Egerton's secretary. If
Anne More was a witness of these graceful prelimin-
aries, her embarrassment must have been extreme.
The letter, when presented, proved a strange mixture
of defiance and apology, and as casuistically con-
structed as one of its author's later sermons. It concluded with the pious hope that Sir George would
deal with the matter 'as the persuasion of Nature,
Reason, Wisdom and Christianity shall inform you.'

Unfortunately in infuriated parents the first of these
persuasions is usually so paramount as to exclude all
the others. And so it was with Sir George. Doubtless
Henry Percy enjoyed the tumult as an exotic spectacle:
but for Donne it was to prove a tempest which drove
him on the rocks.

Sir George's first step was to procure his son-in-law's
discharge from the Lord Keeper – a futile, vindictive,

and, had he stopped to consider, even self-injurious
act. He did not succeed at once. Sir Thomas Egerton
was a tolerant man and had learnt to value his secretary
highly. He could scarcely corroborate too Sir George's
high estimate of his family's social importance and the
consequent severity of its disgrace. The adventure was
reprehensible, but not criminal, and he had hopes that
if the parties were reasonable a public scandal might
be avoided. But Sir George had no intention of being
reasonable. He was determined to provoke and pro-
pagate the very scandal which he accused Donne of
devolving upon his name. And the public scandal in
its turn embarrassed, and forced the hand of the Lord
Keeper.

On the first disclosure of his marriage, Donne had
been exiled from York House, and the change to a
modest lodging after the affluence to which he had
grown accustomed must have served to warn him how
costly romance can prove in a practical-minded world.
But his dismissal, which Sir George's aggravated pleas
at last procured, set a seal of catastrophe on the escap-
ade, depriving him both of a master, to whom he had
become really attached, and of the brightest prospects
of professional advancement.

How was he in his impecuniosity, without any conventional qualifications despite his extraordinary powers, to support a wife, even if he succeeded in gaining
possession of her person? In his distraction he wrote a
letter to his mother (now remarried and so a somewhat
detached spectator of these convulsed events) and
signed it with a motto eloquent indeed of despair, but
also of the fact that in even so dark an hour the

native zest of his wit did not altogether desert him:

'John Donne – Ann Donne – Undone.'

But worse was to follow. Sir George More's pride needed some stronger purge. Within a week Donne and his two rash but friendly confederates were thrown into prison for an offence against the Common and the Canon Law.

It speaks well for the character of Christopher Brooke, and the spell which Donne cast over his friends, that although he (Brooke) was confined in prison considerably longer than the chief culprit whom he had served – and that at great inconvenience to himself as a barrister due to start on an important circuit – he never uttered one word of reproach, but even went so far as to plead with the Lord Keeper on Donne's behalf, when both discretion and natural annoyance would have invited him to concentrate on his own case.

But it was too late for pleading, and Donne was reduced to supplicate his father-in-law in terms now of abject humility, but scantily veiled by an unctuous religious strain, which must have proved very exasperating to its recipient. Sir George told him curtly enough to write no more, whereon he appealed to his former master, and with more success. He was given permission to leave the prison and be confined in his lodgings. Once again, and with as barren a consequence, he addressed himself to his father-in-law, invoking God to guide his counsels, and going so far as to beg for an interview, and even for leave to communicate with the unfortunate Anne, whose probable distress had begun to weigh upon his mind.

Within a week, however, his spirits had begun to
rally. Nothing indeed but prolonged sickness was
ever to suppress the mercurial strain in his temperament, his abnormal resilience, the sudden dart up-
wards that invariably followed the plunge into the
depths. In prison he might be the prey of melancholy
and incoherent alarm: in his lodgings in the Strand,
with the sunlight filtering through the casements, and
the stir of the world in his ears, events did not present
so tragic an aspect. It was true that his fortunes were
squandered – his patrimony in the dissipation of
youth, his prospects in the improvidence of marriage –
but the spring was at hand, and life beckoned. He felt
a stir in his blood, knew the brilliance of his powers,
dreamed that Anne was restored to him beyond dispute, and dared Sir George to do his worst.

Light-heartedly as so many another gifted youth,
ignorant of the self-defensive rings, the jealousies and
interested intrigues of a professional world, he scanned
the horizon for employment. Mr. Robert Cotton,
who, though but three years Donne's senior, already
held an influential position, and whose acquaintance
he had made, inspired him with hope. He knew him
to be engaged in legal inquiries, and his own acquire-
ments fitted him to be of real assistance. He signed
himself as 'wholly yours' to command, and although
three days later no reply had been received, his spirits
were in no way damped. For by then he had completely regained his liberty, and could scribble to a
friend the latest gossip of the town, confident that the
Commissioners, who were to try the case, would uphold
the validity of his marriage, and that Anne, after

softening the heart of her malignant parent by her
gentle ways, would be surrendered to the arms of her
none too penitent husband.

But Sir George More was not so easily appeased. He
brought all his cunning and influence to bear on the
Commissioners, who were to report on the marriage.
Donne lapsed once more into melancholy and alarm.
To turn for assistance to the Lord Keeper was now out
of the question. So long as the marriage had remained
a private *mésalliance*, he had viewed it tolerantly. But
Sir George had cried it up into a public scandal, and
by so doing brought discredit upon York House, for
which its master was bitterly chagrined.

Yet the tide, had Donne known it, was even now
turning. Sir George, like all impulsive, choleric men,
could not stay the course of hate for very long. Imperceptibly the transports of his anger began to abate. It
was tiresome to have a daughter in constant tears,
the Commissioners as the days passed seemed less and
less disposed towards nullification, and perhaps too it
suddenly dawned upon him that in publishing the
affair abroad he appeared in a rather ridiculous light.

And there was another reason. The latent violence in
Donne, served as it was by a ready wit and a profligate
fancy, hinting too at an intriguing licence, exercised
over all women a powerful attraction. Women are
very tolerant of unscrupulousness, where their instinct,
eager for enslavement, detects a character capable of
dangerous living, a personality undaunted and unfore-
seeable, rich in sudden menace. Moreover, where his
interests and not his passions were concerned, none
knew better than this rabid realist how to play the

tactful courtier or twine the silken phrase. 'His winning behaviour,' as Walton notes, was of the sort 'which, when it would entice, had a strange kind of elegant irresistible art.' It was true of the lover, it was to be a marked quality of the preacher, and we shall see that under the stress of misfortune this insinuating suavity could descend almost to the level of egregious flunkeyism.

But on the present occasion it served his purpose well. Woman's susceptibility to his charm had worked his downfall; it was now to help rescue him from the ruins.

Sir Thomas Egerton's third wife was the Countess of Derby, who had three daughters by her previous marriage, all destined to brilliant matches. During the short time in which Donne had enjoyed their society at York House, he had not failed to impress himself favourably upon these ladies. And since they held no personal stake in his runaway marriage, it must have appeared to them as a highly intriguing episode, nor could they, we can be sure, withhold sympathy from so resolute and flamboyant a lover. It seems indeed that they espoused Donne's cause, and the fact coming to the ears of Sir George More, who was rather cravenly anxious to be on easy terms with the exalted inmates of York House, inclined him to regard Donne with more complacence.

Moreover, he had by this time been prevailed upon to visit his son-in-law, and personal contact, which Donne knew well how to exploit, had considerably modified his asperity. It only required a letter couched in more dutiful terms and purged of religious exhortation to persuade the volatile Sir George to reverse his

appeal of a month before, and petition the Lord Keeper
to take back his secretary. It was, however, too late.
Sir Thomas Egerton's dignity did not allow him 'to
discharge and readmit servants at the request of
passionate petitioners.'

Late in April the Commissioners confirmed the marriage; some time elapsed before the adventurers were
allowed to reunite, but Sir George could not indefinitely
delay an event which the law approved.

Donne was now almost thirty years of age, and
although his lack of either means or employment
boded ill for the comforts of married life, he was only
the more impatient to embark upon it for the hazards
and obstacles which had so long tortured his endurance.

The poetry which was at the heart of this, his last
passion, could not contain itself. His enforced separation from the object of his love compelled him to
embrace and champion that Platonism which in the
recent past had fought a losing battle with instinct.
Frustrated, discomfited, anticipating, he turned to it
as something more than a gesture or a consolation.
Bride and bridegroom were, he cried, in spirit indis-
solubly one, though their bodies lay apart. Soul had
commerce with soul, and neither time nor space, brick
nor mortar, could forbid that communion. But to the
agents of bodily disunion he poured out with a magnificent petulance this intercession:

'For God's sake hold your tongue, and let me love;
　Or chide my palsy, or my gout;
　My five grey hairs, or ruin'd fortune flout;
With wealth your state, your mind with arts improve;

Take you a course, get you a place,
Observe his Honour, or his Grace;
Or the king's real, or his stamp'd face
Contemplate; what you will, approve,
So you will let me love.

'Alas! alas! who's injured by my love?
What merchant's ships have my sighs drown'd?
Who says my tears have overflow'd his ground?
When did my colds a forward spring remove?
When did the heats which my veins fill
Add one more to the plaguy bill?
Soldiers find wars, and lawyers find out still
Litigious men, which quarrels move,
Though she and I do love.'

He was but a short time longer kept in suspense. Sir
George's extravagance made grievous inroads into his
private fortune. He grew more and more kindly disposed towards the thought that he should be relieved
of the expenses of at least one daughter. At last, having
successfully deprived his son-in-law of a promising
career, he brought himself to dispatch his prisoner to
her husband with no more generous endowment than a
paternal blessing.

¶ PART TWO
# THE PENITENT

THE PENITENT

§ 1

THE girl-bride, who was thus at last free to honour her marriage-vow, was in disposition as timid and submissive as her husband was violent and aggressive. Her father, in the first flush of a fiery indignation, had doubtless spared no effort in blackening the character of her exigent lover, and Donne for his part was only too conscious that he came to her somewhat battered in the lists of love. More than once he expressed in verse a tender regret for past infidelities, not unmixed with anxiety lest she should make these an excuse for looking with more than sisterly regard on other men

'Which have their stocks entire, and can in tears,
    In sighs, in oaths and letters, outbid me.'

But he need not have feared. Anne Donne had all the milder feminine virtues. She was without initiative, rebellion or caprice. She surrendered the easy circumstances in which she had been reared without a murmur, and with them all that complicated ritual of sociability which is the tissue of so many women's lives.

Dependent, uncomplaining, single-hearted, she was one of those fated to suffer and be dumb. Such a nature would appreciate the positive force in Donne, which it could not resist, and having once accepted its destiny, would be unquestioningly loyal. And equally her purity and gentleness were calculated to sift the gold from the alloy in her turbulent husband, to tame his arrogance and purge his passion, and upon one issue at least, in the still inconclusive conflict of his dual personality, set the seal of domestic peace.

The further stages by which Donne, as a lover, emancipated himself from the physical are clearly set out in the poems which he addressed to her, and since his ascent in the scale of love is the prelude to his parallel ascent in the scale of religion, it will be well briefly to trace its features here.

Just as fifteen years later the current of circumstance played at least as large a part as spiritual inclination in steering him into the Church, so the impulse which drove him headlong into marriage was not that pure and unpondered passion, mystical, reverential, and with all the springtide in its breath, which possesses a young heart as yet untainted by the world. That inspired innocence, whose speech is half devotion, half raillery, and whose lyric pertness Shakespeare was even then about to interpret for all time in a Rosalind or a Beatrice, could never have been Donne's, even had he walked warily in his youth. Naturalistic though he was, his roots were too deep in earth for him to dance with the fountain or wanton delicately with the wind. He was one, from his earliest youth, physically perplexed, his elements caught into some tangled flux, churned by conflicting waves, and, like the sea, straining onwards at the bidding of some demon force, towards the verge of a shadowy shore.

Upon this man, newly tormented with a consciousness of base physical enslavement, there fell the vision, soon to materialize into closest intimacy, of a girl cool and chaste, shy-souled too, as a hushed dawn after a vexatious night. Her very placidity was Paradisal to one

staggered by gross warfare. His first approach to her
then was of the nature of a reaction, but the respite
from defeat thus given to his higher nature and prolonged by the special circumstances that attended his
marriage, culminated in a positive and final conversion.
Anne More served as the bridge by which Donne, at
least as the lover, climbed from the abyss to the cheerful daylight and even to a homely eminence. It was
her modesty and mildness that defeated 'the ravenous
Vandals and Goths,' whose invasions had become to
him a source of shame.

Donne was distinct, not so much from his age as from
the poetical convention of his time, in the candour with
which he stressed the physical. That he should do so in
the private dissection of passion, of which we have
already taken notice, is nothing remarkable. But in his
public *Epithalamia*, one at least of which was written
during his residence at Lincoln's Inn, the same discon-
certing frankness appears. This candour, however,
unlike the calculated sensuality of the next generation,
is entirely free from prurience. It is innocent alike of
that exotic licence which we detect in the kindred effu-
sions of such a poet as Carew, and of that exotic affectation with which Spenser indulges and delights us.
Donne's *Epithalamia* are rather a chant to the earth-
spirit, to the enkindling flame of the sun, the cool rush
of the wind, the clean violence of life going forth in the
morning of time to its work of kindly generation; and
as he wrote them, we fancy him escaping from the
morbid introspection of his chamber into the fresh air
of the world, where 'the sunbeams in the east are
spread.'

But events did not allow of such spontaneity in his own experience. His own past history cast its shadow, and an artificial divorce halted him on the very threshold of marriage. Those weeks of doubt and prohibition proved, we can believe, a fortunate breathing-space after a whirlwind audacity, a time of probation, which his active intellect turned to good use. He began to examine his devotion for his distant wife, as he had examined his passion for his mistresses. And as the fruit of the one had been disgusted cynicism, so that of the other was ecstatic Platonism.

At first he was frankly baffled. What was this new passion, which seemed to lack all the positive traits, good and bad, that he associated with his earlier experiences? He pleaded, rather inaccurately, that in the past he had never been wholly loyal either to the physical or the moral principle:

> 'I never stoop'd so low, as they
>   Which on an eye, cheek, lip, can prey;
>   Seldom to them which soar no higher
>   Than virtue, or the mind to admire.
> For sense and understanding may
>   Know what gives fuel to their fire;
> My love, though silly, is more brave;
> For may I miss, whene'er I crave,
> If I know yet what I would have.'

But if he had learnt to be loyal to some vital impulse, which transcended either predatory instinct or intellectual abstractions, it was still as inexplicable as it was provocative. A hush had indeed fallen on the battlefield, where but recently sense and understanding had

striven so violently together. But if the combatants had
drawn apart in exhaustion, they had not come together
in reconcilement. The issue was still puzzlingly inconclusive, and neither sense nor understanding could
define and so be sure of mastering the fire which fed
them both. Yet although Donne was still, in his own
words, 'silly,' he was more brave, more loyal to life,
than to seek refuge from his dilemma or hide his
ignorance in moral formulas. He did not pretend that
he had yet solved the riddle of the flesh, but only that
for the moment the two elements of his nature, his
reason and his instinct, seemed to have reduced each
other to neutrality.

> 'If that be simply perfectest,
> Which can by no way be express'd
> But negatives, my love is so.
> To all, which all love, I say no.'

or

> 'So, to one neutral thing both sexes fit.
> We die and rise the same, and prove
> Mysterious by this love.'

After the positive crudity of his earlier experiences,
his love for Anne could not but seem at first strangely
evanescent. But so positive a spirit as Donne's could
not long rest upon negatives. If true love were a dis-
concerting emanation of 'th' eagle and the dove,' then
he would find its wings. He paused, only to advance
more buoyantly, plunging through the external, which
had shocked and wearied him, to the principle of
life that quickened nature from within. He was in

search at last of that beauty which harmonizes fact.

> 'But he who loveliness within
> Has found, all outward loathes,
> For he who colour loves, and skin,
> Loves but their oldest clothes.'

The mystic in him had superseded but not supplanted the realist. He had been deluded by gaudy draperies long enough. Henceforth we find the erstwhile lampoonist of woman, him who had crushed her brittle worth into so many a cynical epigram, or to adopt his own edifying description, as a St. Paul's congregation heard it on an Easter Day one year before his death, who had 'out of a petulancy and wantonness of wit, and out of the extravagancy of Paradoxes, and such singularities, called the faculties, and abilities of women in question, even in the root thereof, in the reasonable and immortal soul' — we find this arrogant male iconoclast bidding men defy the vulgar hostilities of sex and

> 'Virtue in woman see
> And dare love that, and say so too,
> And forget the He and She.'

He saw woman at last as a benevolent force as well as an alluring image, and he even contemplated her as an abstract symbol of beauty and intelligence.

Yet ideal as this might seem in the abstract, and possible as it was while Anne remained a picturesque prisoner beneath her father's roof, actual marriage scarcely allowed of so lofty a disregard of natural differences. The spiritual, as Donne's whole life was to advertise, could no more be achieved behind the back of the

sexual than the sexual in contempt of the spiritual. And
so the Platonism, which had been for some three or
four years growing upon Donne as a purely mental
concept in opposition to overmastering physical impulses, was gradually brought into relation with his
new experience, until the two fused in an apprehension
of love, beside which the immaculate Platonism of so
many of his contemporaries, no less than the realism
of his own youth, seemed but languid or frenzied
shadows, void of substance and significance.

In that passion not only was his soul in all its serenity,
but his body in all its impulses, with its 'rafters of bone
. . . the muscle, sinew, and vein which roof this house,'
'emparadised' in her

> 'in whom alone
> I understand and grow and see.'

This love, in short, had brought all his faculties into at
least partial harmony; the idealist and the realist, the
mystic, thinker and hedonist, were no longer at daggers
drawn; no longer did he share in

> 'Dull sublunary lovers' love
> . . . Whose soul is sense.'

For soul and sense were mixed in an exquisite consciousness of union, and the very 'eyes, lips and hands' of the
beloved, being in Donne's stilted phrase, 'inter-assuréd
of the mind,' were rescued from earthly conditions and
filled with the form and radiance, the feeling and intelligence, which the artist, whether he work in the medium
of life or of words or of pigment, brings to his meanest

H

material. Their ephemeral fact was wrought into eternal symbol. This was no 'abstract spiritual love,' such as Donne imputed to those of 'Love's divines' (his fellow poets), whose 'souls exhaled with what they do not see.' Beauty and truth, the thought and the image, desire and morality, were at last absolutely wedded. Realism had passed into reality. ·

'For, though mind be the heaven, where love doth sit,
  Beauty a convenient type may be to figure it.'

In the phrase 'a convenient type' we hear the detached sophist, from whom Donne was not yet entirely free. Perhaps Beauty never came to him spontaneously on the wings of nature to be refined instantaneously in the moment of acceptance. In turn his body and his mind disputed her coming; and yet the fact enabled him to dissect, if not to enjoy or express, this divine rapture, as no English poet had before.

In one poem, 'The Ecstasy,' the whole argument between instinct and intelligence, and incidentally the whole history of his passion, is set down step by step, until their differences are at last composed.

Hand in hand the lovers sit, and their souls go out to meet each other, negotiating, as it seems to him, in the air between them. They taste an ecstasy which does not perplex, they merge like two elements safe from the friction of sex. The two souls thus 'interanimated' lose their distinct identity in a fresh unity: mingling they form a 'new soul,' which 'no change can invade.' So far the argument has advanced along traditional Platonic lines. But now the body intervenes.

'But, O alas! so long, so far,
Our bodies why do we forbear?
They are ours, though not we; we are
Th' intelligences, they the spheres.

We owe them thanks, because they thus
Did us, to us, at first convey,
Yielded their senses' force to us,
Nor are dross to us, but allay.'

The body, in short, is no necessary enemy of the soul,
nor need it cast any stain upon it. Soul may flow into
soul, 'though it to body first repair.'

'So must pure lovers' souls descend
To affections, and to faculties,
Which sense may reach and apprehend,
Else a great prince in prison lies.

'To our bodies turn we then, that so
Weak men on love reveal'd may look;
Love's mysteries in souls do grow
But yet the body is the book.'

Donne had learnt that the body is only dishonoured if
it excludes the soul of which it should be the image
and agent, while the soul is but a phantom, if it do not
speak through the mind and the flesh. Some ten years
later he enunciated in a typical passage the general
philosophy which he had now wrested from the particular experience of love and was to repeat in the wider
sphere of religion:
'Our nature is meteoric, we respect (because we partake

so) both earth and heaven; for as our bodies glorified shall be capable of spiritual joy, so our souls demerged into those bodies are allowed to take earthly pleasure. Our soul is not sent hither, only to go back again: we have some errand to do here; nor is it sent into prison because it comes innocent, and He which sent it is just.'

The Platonism then by which gentler spirits had sought to escape from savagery into some transcendental region of pure idea, was restored at last by this reckless adventurer to its proper function as a harmonious principle shaping and animating a carnality, else chaotic. In the realization of that unity Donne was made one with the whole creation, and could cry consciously of that which transcends human consciousness:

> 'All measure, and all language I should pass,
>   Should I tell what a miracle she was.'

From this ideal, so far as 'passion' went, Donne never again seriously lapsed. No longer did the flesh rebel nor despair contend with ecstasy; instead the struggle was transferred to the plane of religious and worldly rivalries.

Inevitably married life mellowed his passion with affection. The familiar intimacies of daily life, the sufferings of many years, sanctified and tranquillized it, mixing the milder air of unpretentious sympathy with the chill breezes of the heights. But in one short year the agitations of love's fever are gone for ever. There is the same royal note in his address to his wife on the anniversary of their marriage as was to sound from the pulpit in homage to his God:

'All kings, and all their favourites,
All glory of honours, beauties, wits,
The sun itself, which makes time, as they pass,
Is elder by a year now than it was
When thou and I first one another saw.
All other things to their destruction draw,
Only our love hath no decay;
This no to-morrow has, nor yesterday;
Running it never runs from us away,
But truly keeps his first, last, everlasting day.'

Thus it was with 'souls where nothing dwells but love,' and in words which the Apollo of a later day was destined to repeat in the hearing of a convulsed world, Donne cried:

'Who is so safe as we? where none can do
Treason to us, except one of us two.'

The mariner who had read treason everywhere, in Woman, in himself, in the very elements, was come safe home to port — but not to stagnate there. The vexed path by which Donne had come to marriage, the want and difficulty which continued to embarrass it, only served to certify his fidelity. It is in the tones of some devout litany that, four years later, seeking to dissuade his wife from a picturesque but rash adventure (she wished to accompany him abroad, disguised as a page!) he recalls the phases of their passion:

'By our first strange and fatal interview,
By all desires which thereof did ensue,
By our long starving hopes, by that remorse
Which my words' masculine persuasive force

Begot in thee, and by the memory
Of hurts, which spies and rivals threatened me,
I calmly beg. But by thy father's wrath,
By all pains, which want and divorcement hath,
I conjure thee and all the oaths which I
And thou have sworn to seal joint constancy. . . .'

As the years passed, the sincerity of his devotion pervades his verse with an even greater simplicity. Imagination, stooping to serve the uses of the world, only
heightens her sovereignty. Domestic love is perhaps
less decked in mystical metaphor, perhaps

'not so pure and abstract as they use
To say, which have no mistress but their Muse;

'And yet no greater, but more eminent,
        Love by the spring is grown;
        As in the firmament
Stars by the sun are not enlarged, but shown,
Gentle love deeds, as blossoms on a bough,
From love's awakened root do bud out now.
If, as in water stirr'd more circles be
Produced by one, love such additions take,
Those like so many spheres but one heaven make,
For they are all concentric unto thee;
And though each spring do add to love new heat,
As princes do in times of action get
New taxes, and remit them not in peace,
No winter shall abate this spring's increase.'

Much love poetry (for example, Byron's) has ceased
to appeal to many modern minds because it concen-

trates too exclusively on sexual passion, because it uses
the vocabulary of appetite to catalogue only physical
charms, and to excite, as it indulged, only a superficial
sense of pleasure. A mistress has been addressed so
often, not as a note of human life which has its own
significance and with which the poet is in exquisite
sympathy, but as the provocation merely of a series of
luxurious images or sentimental metaphors. Kindred
to such Paganism, too self-engrossed for insight, has
been the poetry of Abstract Ideals – that in which the
poet has imposed the creative conceptions of his own
mind upon his mistress with the same self-absorption
as the sensualist. Seldom have these slaves of the
Concrete and the Abstract discovered liberty by coming
together, achieving intense pleasure without blind self-
gratification, sympathetic insight and idealism without
physical impoverishment.

It is by its capacity to express that perfect accord
between two beings, that delicate and yet assured sense
of welfare shared together, and modulated through all
the faculties, that blend of wonder and affection, faith
and desire, at once wayward and devout, reverential
and laughable, radiant and rational – that love poetry
rises to the heights of truth and universality. It may
be that the great lovers of the world have seldom
expressed themselves worthily, if at all, because their
experience defies or avoids definition. A superficial
passion, we are tempted to say, provokes poetry – racy,
vivid, highly-sensed. The great lovers are too near to
the silence in which everything is spoken: they are
too penetrated and possessed by each other to stand
aside and appraise in the manner of one pleasurably

anticipating or remembering. They go softly, as it were with finger to lip, lest the spell of unity should be broken or the linked souls unclasped. Theirs is the greatest work of art, but it is writ in the book of life.

Donne left little report of his love after he had learnt to live it. His *Songs and Sonnets* are, with few exceptions, the tale of his probation; and perhaps his most intimate appreciation of domestic harmony is to be found in a sermon preached at Whitehall twenty years later, in celebration of 'the peace of a royal and religious Wisdom.'

'Let thine own family be a Cabinet in this Gallery, and find in all the boxes thereof, in the several duties of Wife, and Children, and Servants, the peace of virtue, and of the father and mother of all virtues, active discretion, passive obedience; and then, lastly, let thine own bosom be the secret box, and reserve in this Cabinet, and then the best Jewel in the best Cabinet, and that in the best Gallery of the best house that can be had, peace with the Creature, peace in the Church, peace in the State, peace in thy house, peace in thy heart, is a fair Model and a lovely design even of the Heavenly Jerusalem which is *visio pacis*, where there is no object but peace.' By a very similar path to Donne's did many of the great Romantics of a later century pass, subduing animalism to imagination, and informing imagination with affection. It is the Pilgrim's Progress, and none can truly reach the goal, whom false shame inhibits at the start.

It is not necessary to act shamelessly as Donne, the distracted pioneer, was driven to do. But it is necessary to prefer truth to modesty, and danger to security.

Civilization is synonymous with repression in its rudi-
ments, and repression only begets reaction. That much
we have learnt in the last hundred years. But in Donne
we see the creature rising by harrowing steps to the
creator, undeterred by any scruples. And because
man learns most, not by textbook philosophy or
morals, but by those immediate shocks, those crises
which nature inflicts on all who abuse her, Donne's
eroticism, despite its unsavoury features, is singularly
revealing.

We see in turn the darkness of insensibility troubled
by the first rays of thought; a writhing of light with
darkness terrible to witness; the gradual triumph of
light dispersing the fractured gloom after reducing
it to a neutral grey: at last the radiant mingling of
the two hostile elements, of the substance and the
spirit, and out of chaos blossoms form. The marriage
of Heaven and Hell, as Blake was later to image it, is
consummated.

Man, as Donne once wrote to Lord Herbert of
Cherbury,

> 'is a lump, where all beasts kneaded be;
> Wisdom makes him an ark, where all agree.
> The fool, in whom these beasts do live at jar,
> Is sport to others, and a theatre.
> Nor 'scapes he so, but is himself their prey;
> All which was man in him, is eat away;
> And now his beasts on one another feed,
> Yet couple in anger, and new monsters breed.
> How happy's he, which hath due place assign'd
> To his beasts, and disafforested his mind.'

Or in another verse-letter:

> 'He just profanes whom valiant hearts do move
> To style his wandering range of passion, Love.
> Love that imparts in everything delight
> Is fancied in the soul, not in the sight.'

The essence of love indeed can only be distilled out of experience by some process that transcends without refuting the bounds of reason, by some inspired divination, which it is as impossible to achieve by calculation as to explain. Seldom if ever did Donne as a poet succeed in capturing that high imaginative moment. Paradoxically enough his mind was too insistently alert to communicate a consciousness of life, which entails a complete self-forgetfulness. He could only plead that it might not be 'express'd, 'cause infinite.'

By some such steps as these did Donne explore the tangled path of passion; and in the story of his love we read that longing for permanence in the rout of time, for mind in the flux of motion, for Beauty in the waste of death, and for peace in the storm of night, which is the impulse of all true poetry and true religion.

§ 2

The years, however, during which this metamorphosis occurred were exceedingly straitened. Donne had bought his conversion dear, and if he could offer his wife a real devotion, it was eventually at the cost of all the comforts, not to name the luxuries, to which she had been accustomed. For the moment the extremity of his situation was relieved by Sir Francis Wooley's generous offer of a home at Pyrford in Surrey, the estate which he had recently inherited. Here for more than two years the Donnes lived in complete retirement and tolerable content, and here in 1603 and 1604 the first two of the many children that Anne Donne was destined to mother were born.

Yet though the material problem was temporarily solved, the effect of this retirement on Donne himself can scarcely have been happy. He was one to whom solitude was demoralizing, as a cage would be to an eagle or prison to some sea-rover. Indeed his appearance at thirty was curiously suggestive of one of those swash-bucklers of the four seas, whose ranting oaths and uproarious manners he had reflected in one of his early Satires.

There was a strange conflict in his features of the brigand and the seer. The large eyes were quizzical and haunting, the brow already seemed broader than in early youth, and suffering sensibility had begun to draw its tell-tale lines from the nostrils to the lips. But the swarthy beard that half disclosed an insolent yet tormented mouth, the formidable nose, the thick, squat neck, the resolute shoulders, all announced power in no uncertain terms. He had the look of a baffled centaur. Such a one was not intended for a monastic life. The aggressive qualities that would have found their natural outlet in the stress of the world were without any salutary objective in the wilderness.

A neutral atmosphere worked like a slow poison on so vivid and vehement a personality, which could only spend itself in futile revolt when not engaged in active intellectual endeavour, soothed by books, those 'companions in whom there is no falsehood or frowardness,' or distracted by society. Excess of sedentary study, both early in the morning and late at night, produced some of those '1,490 authors, abridged and analysed with his own hand,' to which Walton refers – and also a disorganized digestion. The physical and the mental revolve in a vicious circle, and thus enforced solitude begot, as an inevitable consequence, that brooding melancholy which was to echo down his days, telling of volcanic fires unhealthily banked, of energies fated to smoulder, where they should have found an active vent.

His friend Christopher Brooke was alive to the danger. On various visits to Pyrford he must have noticed how indolence was inviting depression. He urged his friend to bestir himself, to come to town more frequently, to press his interests at the Court. 'It was good you did prevent the loss of any more time. . . . The King's hand is neither so full nor so open as it hath been.'

Too late was Donne to appreciate the wisdom of this advice, when through lean years he long courted in vain the favour of this pedantic monarch, but although he was probably presented to James I, when Sir George More entertained him at Loseley in 1603, he took no immediate steps to push his fortunes. Meanwhile he had abundant leisure to pursue those studies which the distractions of London life had interrupted. He applied himself once again to jurisprudence, to esoteric learning of a speculative and mystical character, and to the theological casuists whom the Reformation had multiplied. And in so doing he developed also a general philosophy of his own.

The young Dionysus, who had broken from the

restraints of Rome, seeking his way back to some primal ecstasy, which conventions seemed at best to adulterate, was now attempting to translate his ecstasy into ideas. He had turned at first to those tortured saints of the Dark Ages in whom sensuality and science melted into mysticism, and then to the pure but tenuous conceptions of Plato. But not for him were those enchanted bridals of the soul with God, of the mind with Beauty, in which the body passed away in flame or in smoke. There was too much of the satyr in his seership, and of the casuist in his mysticism. His branches might strain up heavenward, but they never forgot their native earth. His only hope was to subdue his lawlessness to logic, until the two, blended together in a rational whole, achieved such an equilibrium between mind and body as he had already discovered for his passions.

We have already remarked that in him, as in some English Abelard or Leonardo, the intellectual sceptic of the Renaissance joined with the aspiring pagan of the Middle Ages. He turned therefore to the casuistry of the one and the eccentric lore of the other, because he knew himself to be compact as they of sensuality and sublime longings, fury and fastidiousness, morbidity and rapture, the gracious and the grotesque. But as he approached his thirtieth year Science began to assert her mastery. He was impelled to conduct researches not only in the art of living, but also in the art of Faith, in the chemistry of religion as well as in that of the senses, while the new astronomy of Copernicus and Tycho Brahé supplied a semi-rational confirmation of that transcendental belief in God which organized religion seemed to reflect with such pitiful inadequacy.

Two years before, during his residence at York House, sympathy with the Pythagorean doctrine of 'Metempsychosis' had led him to undertake a metaphysical poem, later entitled 'The Progress of the Soul.' It was never completed, but, fanciful and in some ways frivolous as this fragment is, it is of real value, not only for the pregnant power of many of its lines and images, but also as an autobiographical document, and as embodying a remarkable prevision of the basic hypothesis of modern science. The poem sets out to be the history of a soul in its ascent from the vegetable to the animal, and thence to the human plane. Donne's intention was, after pursuing the idea of life from the protoplasmic cell through the hierarchy of plants, animals and men, to conduct it finally to the body of Calvin; but yielding for once to the fashion of the time, he substituted the person of Queen Elizabeth as its eventual haven.

We need not here consider in detail this fantastic fragment, but crude as his handling is (for he figured the soul's progress only through its moments of violent transit from one material prison-house to another), his conduct of the soul from the apple and mandrake to the fish, culminating in the whale and thence to the mouse and the ape, as a prelude to its impersonation in the basest of humankind and its ascent to the conscious Calvin, tallies strikingly with modern evolutionary theory. And as evidence of Donne's state of mind, it is really significant, revealing in his speculative activities an outlook exactly parallel to that which we have traced in his erotic. The Soul of the poem comes, we are to suppose, from Paradise in all its native inno-

cence and integrity, is plunged from one natural process into another. It has no control over the experiences,
often obscene, which are thrust upon it, but the mysterious force of life which it obeys is gradually driving
it upward to the higher plane of humanity. So it was
with Donne's own soul at this time, and possibly one
of the chief reasons why the poem was broken off before
conscious intelligence begins in it to function, was that
Donne did not feel himself sufficiently learned in that
state to represent it truly. There is one passage frankly
autobiographical, in which the natural man protests
against the toil involved in intellectual effort, and
though he hungers for high creative experience, cries
rebelliously:

'O let me not launch out, but let me save
   Th' expense of brain and spirit, that my grave,
   His right and due, a whole unwasted man may have.'

Just as the Pagan long resisted the Puritan in Donne's
experience of passion, preferring an easy indulgence to
the high and difficult way of the ideal, so in his thought
it strove petulantly against the pains of philosophy.
But at Pyrford the natural man had found peace, and
there was no 'distracting business' to absorb his surplus
energies. And so the philosophy which had so far
arrived at the conception that 'nature hath no goal,
though she hath law,' and the curious half-mystical
agnosticism which succeeded his abandonment of an
organized faith, proving also the condition of his eventual return to it, had time to deepen and develop, until
circumstances drove him into the narrow but concrete
channel of casuistical theology.

§ 3

In 1605 Donne left Pyrford to find a home nearer
London. Doubtless with an increasing family he was
anxious to advance his fortunes. He took lodgings for
a short time at Camberwell before moving into a small
house at Mitcham. It was not only small, but un-
hygienic, damp and draughty, as was also the lodging
in the Strand to which he resorted at first for several
days in the week. The one he named his 'Prison,' the
other his 'Hospital,' and both his 'Grave.'

His residence in this cheerless lodge in the wilderness
was to have a profound effect on his character. It is a
common experience that the solitude whether of moun-
tain-tops or of great plains can aggravate self-consciousness to a point where the individual doubts his own
identity. Eternities seem to press about him and sub-
merge the boundaries of reason. By such experiences
are we made mystics. The solitude imposed by poverty,
sickness, or distress of mind, has similar, if tardier, consequences. It separates a man from the stream of life
and the bustle of humanity; it can make him inhuman
or divine, according as selfishness or selflessness predominates in his nature, and necessarily its effect varies
with the degree of his sensibility. 'I cannot endure,'
wrote Shelley, 'the horror, the evil, which comes to self
in solitude.' But if that enveloping sense of loneliness,
which wrests man from the comfortable contact of life
to isolate him in what seems an everlasting vacuum, can
bring horror and paralysis, it can also bring exaltation.
In a verse-letter to his friend Mr. Rowland Woodward
Donne emphasized, as Carlyle was to do also in many a

letter to his friend Sterling, the value to the creative powers of 'a chaste fallowness,' and he testified also to its purifying influence upon personality, particularly 'if our souls have stain'd their first white.'

> 'So works retiredness in us. To roam
> Giddily and be everywhere but at home,
> Such freedom doth a banishment become.
>
> .   .   .   .
>
> Manure thyself then, to thyself be improved;
> And with vain outward things be no more moved.'

Yet excessive solitude can so affect a character like Donne's that only a restoration of 'vain outward things' can save it from myopia or even madness.

'Ordinary poverty,' he was later to affirm as a preacher, '(that is a difficulty, with all their labours and industry to sustain their family, and the necessary duties of their place) is a shrewd, and a slippery tentation.' In his own career it certainly encouraged morbidity, because it undermined his health, but through painful introspection came finally an addition of light. Truly that obsession by the wormy circumstances of death which was to haunt him to the end of his days seems to date from this time.

The realist who had catalogued with such relish the details of woman's anatomy, now began to visualize the features of corruption, and the situation of his study gave him every excuse.

'I have occasion,' he wrote, 'to sit late some nights in my study . . . and now I find that that room hath a wholesome emblematic use; for having under it a vault, I make that promise me that I shall die reading, since

I

my book and a grave are so near. But it hath another unwholesomeness, that by raw vapours rising from thence . . . I have contracted a sickness which I cannot name nor describe.' From henceforth, with ever sharpened intensity, death was to him, in Shelley's words, 'that contemplation of inexhaustible melancholy, whose shadow eclipses the brightness of the world.' And as the shadow deepened, like the clouds across some burning sunset, the light which radiated through it became more splendid and awesome, more sombrely and fiercely defined.

It is an interesting speculation, too, how much that fashion of ghoulish symbolism with which Donne's successors, aping his example, were to decorate death, as in the *macabre* woodcuts that headed Quarles' *Emblems*, is traceable to the unhealthy atmosphere in which he was fated to live for the next few years. There can be no doubt that the feverish and gastric conditions, to which he finally succumbed, now first appear, and with them the melancholy which became the agonizing converse of his will to live.

Temporarily, however, the removal to Mitcham must have proved beneficial. Donne was once again in touch with friends, and soon succeeded in obtaining some professional work, which, if precarious, was well suited to his powers. His knowledge of casuistical writings and of the Civil and Canon Law became known through the good offices of the Countess of Huntingdon (one of those ladies at York House into whose favour Donne had insinuated himself) to Thomas Morton. This was an urbane and dexterous cleric, who had been employed by the King to oppose with

arguments such Romish Recusants as in those years
were so vocal in their criticism of the Reformed Church.
As in all times of religious revolt, the orthodox party
were of as many shades of opinion as the heretics, and
it needed considerable knowledge and adroitness, not
to say dialectical vigour, to deal convincingly with the
many pamphleteering theologians engaged in this
solemn game of doctrinal chess, and championing their
own particular brand of faith or apostasy. After the
Gunpowder Plot in 1605 the battle of argument waxed
even more furious, as political panic primed the guns,
and Thomas Morton was only too glad to enrol Donne
as deviller and co-partner in his controversial activities.

For two years at least Donne was so engaged, travel-
ling for some time, it seems possible, on the Continent
on a secret mission of inquiry, and himself writing
many of the pamphlets issued under Morton's name.
Such work had for him something more than a purely
professional interest. It is entertaining as a sidelight
on party methods to think of this discreet agnostic,
who, if not a Romish Recusant, was certainly far from
Anglican conformity, waging war with detached mental
efficiency on fanatical theologians of every persuasion.
Nevertheless his own mind, which had rejected Catholicism in no merely frivolous spirit but at the urging of
a fundamental honesty, had now passed from a negative
to a positive phase.

He wished amid the flux of prejudiced dogma to find
at least a bare foundation that his mind could accept
and his mysticism rest upon. And doubtless it was at
this time rather than in his nineteenth year, as Walton
supposed, that he 'began seriously to survey and

consider the body of divinity,' over which the opposed
parties were so cunningly and emptily disputing. The
concentration on theology which Morton's work necessi-
tated considerably advanced the attempt, already fitfully
undertaken, to relate, if not to reconcile, a somewhat
indefinite philosophy with the specific dogmas of religion. That Donne, to whom freedom of mind was
essential, should eventually range himself on the Protestant side was inevitable, although association and
that love of ceremonial to which we have referred,
drew him powerfully towards all that was aristocratic
in the Catholic faith. Nevertheless his peculiar position
as for long owing loyalty to neither side enabled him
to see quite clearly the faults of both, and having himself a mind above small partisanship, the very strife of
tongues in which he was now briefed must have convinced him that a Church advertises its relative conception of truth by its militant exclusiveness. To that doctrinal feud he gave his mind for hire, and by so doing
learnt a certain contempt both for his employers and
his opponents, the contempt of a man too strong and
too true for compromise, which only necessity should
prevail upon him to forget.

In the summer of 1607 Thomas Morton, being
appointed Dean of Gloucester, ceased to have need of
Donne's services. Rumour of this preferment had been
rife for some time, and Donne had already without
success been seeking other employment. Morton was
anxious for him to take Orders, and sought to induce
him to do so by the offer of a benefice which was in his
gift. According to Walton, Donne refused on the
ground of his youthful irregularities, which he had not

yet had time to live down. It is possible indeed that
he made use of his wild oats to relieve him from an
embarrassing solicitation: for it was scarcely in his
interest to shock Morton's orthodoxy by confessing
himself a freethinker. Nevertheless we cannot doubt
that this was the true motive of his refusal. Donne was
not the man to fear, as Walton supposes, running the
gauntlet of public censure; his sins in all their realistic
variations were in fact to prove the rich and staple
substance of his preaching, but he was consistently
averse to practising a spiritual fraud. He knew that he
was still far from that serenity of faith in God and himself, or that rational assurance which alone justifies the
religious vocation. And on such a point, with all his
impetuosity, he had a delicate conscience. His loyalty
to truth was as absolute in things of the mind as to
fact in things of the body. Conscious of his powers,
the patronage he might expect, and his otherwise
dismal prospects, it was both foolish and courageous
of him to reject at the age of thirty-four such an
offer.

But the straitened independence which Donne, with
all his qualifications for success in any profession, had
to endure for so many years was due, far more than to
the malice of circumstance, to the almost vicious
honesty, the determined integrity of genius. For compromise is the price of professionalism, paid without
thought by most men, reluctantly by the absolute-
minded few. Donne resisted until dire necessity was
at his throat, and then he turned necessity, as only
genius can, to glorious gain. For long, however, he
refused to be bound by either Romish or Anglican

fetters, and he paid the bitter price which an orthodox world invariably exacts from the rebel.

But if Morton's suggestion had no immediate issue, it is not perhaps too fanciful to see in it the first summons from afar to the fold. In the lean years which followed, in which self-confidence began to quake, sapped by sickness and melancholy, and religion of some kind became more and more needful, Donne must often have pondered the wisdom of his refusal, and by degrees habituated himself to the idea of acceptance. Indeed so early as 1607 he is found speaking of the English Church as 'ours.'

§4

His work now for Morton decreased to a minimum and nothing appeared to take its place, so that from 1607 he was constantly on the verge of abject poverty, with its contingent evils of illness and extreme domestic discomfort. As Keats wrote: 'Until we are sick, we understand not,' and Donne himself in many passages of his later sermons paid his tribute to the desolating, chastening, cleansing and illuminating power of sickness.

'Put all the miseries that man is subject to together, sickness is more than all. It is the immediate sword of God. Phalaris could invent a Bull, and others have invented Wheels and Racks; but no persecutor could ever invent a sickness or a way to inflict a sickness upon a condemned man. To a galley he can send him, and to the gallows, and command execution that hour; but to a quartane fever, or to a gout, he cannot condemn him. In poverty I lack but other things; in banishment I lack but other men; but in sickness I lack myself. And, as the greatest misery of war is when our own Country is made the seat of the war, so is it of an affliction, when mine own Body is made the subject thereof. How shall I put a just value upon God's great blessings of Wine and Oil, and Milk and Honey, when my taste is gone, or of Liberty, when the gout fetters my feet?'

Later, as we shall see, he was to map out his conversion in all its fluctuations, by milestones of physical collapse and recovery, and we may be sure that illness was a principal, if not the deciding factor in persuading him to take a less absolute view of what liberty of mind implied.

Circumstances now suddenly intensified the growing seriousness of disposition natural to his age. We see it both in the tenour of the verse and prose which he wrote during these years, and in the letters which he dedicated to 'that short roll of friends writ in my heart.' These letters, despite their intimacy, tend increasingly towards moral and metaphysical discourses, into which Donne plainly slips unconsciously, and for which, like another but very differently sententious correspondent, Lord Chesterfield, he is found constantly apologizing, as when he writes, 'But I must not give you a homily for a letter,' or, 'I mean to write a letter and I am fallen into a discourse.'

In truth to this vehement soul, marooned in a backwater of moral introspection, often dyspeptic, or reduced to that state of listlessness in which the mind feeds on its own dejection, correspondence with sympathetic friends was a burningly necessary means of self-expression and self-release. How highly he valued it, how much it was to him in the nature of an art, an act of vital communication, may be judged from his own words:

'I make account that the writing of letters, when it is with any seriousness, is a kind of ecstasy, and a departure and secession and suspension of the soul, which doth then communicate itself to two bodies.'

Or again on a later occasion, after citing, only to dismiss, the secondary motives of letter-writing, he acclaims it as the very breath and finer spirit of friendship:

'I send not my letters as tribute, nor interest, nor recompense, nor for commerce, nor as testimonials of my love, nor provokers of yours, nor to justify my custom of writing, nor for a vent and utterance of my meditations, for my letters are either above or under all such offices; yet I write very affectionately, and I chide and accuse myself of diminishing that affection which sends them, when I ask myself why; only I am sure that I desire that you might have in your hands letters of mine of all kinds, as conveyances and deliverers of me to you, whether you accept me as a friend, or as a patient, or as a penitent, or as a beadsman, for I decline no jurisdiction, or refuse any tenure.'

In such passages we hear the first vibrations of those preludes and fugues which were to sound with infinitely richer harmonies and more involved counterpoint from the pulpit of St. Paul's. But it must be confessed that Donne was neither a graceful nor a witty correspondent. The very virtues which shone so resplendently in a place of public assembly, the involved dialectic, the

close-knit, labouring argumentation, learnt in the school
of Quintilian and scholastic rhetoric, militated against
that wilful spontaneity, that direct intimacy of style,
which makes the born letter-writer both so elusive and
so companionable. There is a solidity and seriousness
in Donne's letters, and even, when he is stirred, a
stately eloquence. But there is no charm. His personality, we feel, cannot break free from the creaking
machinery of syllogisms, of lumbering logic and
involved speculation, from the clogging formality, in
short, which, when the breath of inspiration blew,
became indeed a trumpet for the lips of Milton or an
organ for the hands of Hooker, but which for informal
occasions could only prove a vast and inappropriate
scaffolding.

Doubtless, too, Donne often turned to address his
friends straight from a prolonged study of some wordy
dialectician, or from the composition of some casuistical
tract, and his own style reflected his cramped employment, while to influential acquaintances he was driven
to adopt, and with increasing exaggeration as he became
a distraught mendicant, that tone of elaborate compli-
ment and august flattery which was the convention of a
time of patronage. He himself was certainly conscious
of the congestion of his style, but he imputes it typically enough rather to subjective than objective causes,
complaining that 'words which are our subtlest and
delicatest outward creatures, being composed of
thoughts and breath, are so muddy, so thick, that our
thoughts themselves are so, because . . . they are even
leavened with passions and affections.'

Our only regret is that the passions and affections of

the letter-writer, unlike those of the preacher, were not
lively enough to leaven the lump. All that is rich, regal
and sonorous in the sermons is laboured and heavy in
the correspondence.

Chief among all the friends to whom Donne opened
his mind, if not very expressively his heart, was Sir
Henry Goodyer. This estimable man, who came of a
merchant stock, had entered Parliament some years
earlier, and had but recently been knighted by the
King. New to the glitter of Court life and generous-
hearted to a fault, his extravagances ultimately reduced
him to poverty. But although unable to help Donne
during the worst crises of his affairs, it seems probable
that he did assist him financially, and certain that he
was of great use to him socially.

Upon the weekly letters which passed between them
our chief knowledge of Donne's circumstances and
state of mind during these years is based, and strewn
as they are with irrelevant social chatter, we can trace
in considerable detail the chastening process through
which Donne's character was passing, and his first
tentative approximation towards Anglican orthodoxy.

It is certainly amusing to find one whose life had so
far been scarcely an example of prudence and sobriety
exhorting his friend in the character of some sage
mentor to

> 'ask your garners if you have not been
> In harvest too indulgent to your sports.'

To suggest, however, that this anxiety upon his
friend's moral and material account was dictated by the
knowledge that the depletion of the good knight's

fortune would react unfavourably upon himself, would
be altogether to misread Donne's character. Truly
none knew better than he how easily and disastrously
life's capital might be squandered. He was now only
too painfully 'advantaged with discretion and experience,' and, conscious that his own past career, not to
say its fruits in the present, was hardly the best testi-
monial for a teacher to offer, he advanced it with bitter
sincerity as a warning:

'You, sir, are far enough from these descents, your
virtue keeps you secure, and your natural disposition
to mirth will preserve you; but lose none of those holds,
a slip is often as dangerous as a bruise, and though you
cannot fall to my lowness, yet in a much less distraction
you may meet my sadness; . . . make therefore to yourself some mark, and go towards it alegrement. Though
I be in such a planetary and erratic fortune that I can do
nothing constantly, yet you may find some constancy
in my advising you to it.'

We may admit that the constancy proves at times a
little tedious, and that we pay for the excitement of
Donne's twenties by the sententiousness of his thirties.
Nevertheless, these are plainly the tones of a man who,
having gone with the tide himself and been shipwrecked
on the shoals of pain, penury and perplexity, is intensely
anxious to put his experience at the service of a friend.
Again, in his mention of a sudden death he discloses
his own new sense of life as a disciplinary disease,
and his yearning for the days when the blood ran
pure:

'Perchance his life needed a longer sickness, but a man
may go faster and safer when he enjoys that daylight

of a clear and sound understanding than in the night or twilight of an ague or other disease.'

From these letters it is clear that a complete change had come over Donne, or rather the rational development which we have seen reflected in his Platonism had suddenly received a violent forward impulse. The cause, we believe, was physical. Four successive tides of sickness and solitude, by which we mean a sense, at times terrified, of isolation, were to attack the sturdy breakwaters of Donne's body and mind during the next twenty years.

The first was already well upon its way, and its effect is manifest in the high moral tone which he adopts from this time, and which, if at first surprising to the careless onlooker, is yet the quite logical issue of that Puritanism which had so troubled the Pagan's enjoyment.

Under the stress of circumstances indeed Puritanism, from being a cantankerous critic, had become a creative force. Passage after passage in these letters attests not only that experience had convinced Donne of the value of moral prudence, but that also he hungered now increasingly for higher values than those embodied in moral conduct, for communion with the creative principle of life at its purest, with some God, in fact, more real than either philosophic abstractions or conventional dogmas, a God in whom his whole nature, intellectual, sensuous and spiritual, could conclusively believe. How little either sectarians or casuists satisfied him may be gathered from the following passage:

'I begin to think that as litigious men tired with suits admit any arbitrament, and princes travailed with long

and wasteful war descend to such conditions of peace
as they are soon after ashamed to have enhanced, so
philosophers, and so all sects of Christians, after long
disputations and controversies, have allowed many
things for positive and dogmatical truths which are not
worthy of that dignity; and so many doctrines have
grown to be the ordinary diet and food of our spirits,
and have place in the pap of catechisms, which were
admitted but as physic in that present distemper, or
accepted in a lazy weariness, when men, so they might
have something to rely upon, and to excuse themselves
from more fanciful inquisition, never examined what
that was. To which indisposition of ours the casuists
are so indulgent as that they allow a conscience to
adhere to any probable opinion against a more probable. . . .'

Evidently Donne was not to prove an easy convert to
any faith. In those days he shared Coleridge's later
opinion of the religion, if not of the politics, of his
time, that it represented 'a world of power and talent
wasted on the support of half-truths.' To him, intellectually honest as he was physically fearless, no faith
prescribed for spiritual hypochondriacs, or merely
serviceable to professional divines, was of any avail.
Even in his casuistical writing he did not rest content
with the virtuosity of most of his fellows and opponents.
He spun few webs of logic in the air, but by exact
argument tried to give concentrated definition to vague
hypotheses, to advance step by step from the improb-
able to the probable, and thence to that plane of purer
probability where faith begins to be justified. He had
learnt how dangerous is the blind acceptance of passion,

and so he wished not only to love God, but to prove and know Him.

And as he revolted against spiritual lethargy, masking itself in dogma and ceremonial, so he championed positive virtue, even as earlier he had championed positive vice against the prudences of a cowardly and self-interested morality. Virtue, he claimed, could not be compromised by relative considerations. It is the mystic transcending the realist who writes that 'virtue is even, and continual and the same, and can therefore break nowhere, nor admit ends nor beginnings; it is not only not broken, but not tied together.' Or again:

'He is not virtuous, out of whose actions you can pick an excellent one. Vice and her fruits may be seen, because they are thick bodies, but not virtue, which is all light; and vices have swellings and fits and noise, because, being extremes, they dwell far asunder, and they maintain both a foreign war against virtue and a civil against one another, and affect sovereignty, as virtue doth society. . . . But men who have preferred money before all, think they deal honourably with virtue if they compare her with money, and think that as money is not called base till the alloy exceed the pure, so they are virtuous enough if they have enough to make their actions current . . . as though our religion were but an act of thrift, to make a little virtue go far.'

Donne indeed was as uncompromising, as candid, as exploring in his search for God as he had been in his pursuit of his mistress. He had not ceased to be loyal to life in the process of refining his natural values.

But how crude, how callow, those natural values had been, particularly in their contemptuous assessment of

womanhood, must have come vividly home to him in
the summer of 1607, when he became acquainted with
Magdalen, widow of Richard Herbert, and mother of
three daughters and seven sons, of whom George the
poet, now in his fourteenth year, was the fifth. She
had at this time moved from Montgomery Castle, the
family seat of the Herberts, to watch (somewhat in the
manner of Mrs. Ruskin) over the completion of her
eldest son's education at Oxford. It was probably
through some mutual friend extolling Donne's learning
that she asked him to correspond with her on religious
and educational themes. Donne in his lonely situation,
and with his unused energies, might have welcomed
correspondence with any cultured person, but with a
woman of Mrs. Herbert's distinction, so placed as she
was with a large family to rear, it must have appeared at
first a privilege rich in practical as well as spiritual and
intellectual promise. He made no delay in writing and
he wrote, we are to believe, voluminously. Acquaintance
quickly followed, and thus was begun a colloquy between two souls, which seems like some cool thread
running down the fevered fabric of Donne's days.

To her from time to time he was to resort, as to some
idyllic retreat of sanity and piety and sympathy in a
sultry world. She was, as perhaps only a good woman
can be, both innocent and experienced, practical and
devout. Prudent, almost austere, she had yet a wonderful
sweetness of disposition, that inspired as much affection
as reverence. With the 'excellent endowments of
mind, the great and harmless wit and cheerful gravity,'
which made her the intellectual equal of gifted men, she
combined the tender discretion and quiet competence

which made her the devoted mother of a gracious family, and which in later years at a time of sickness called forth from her poet son, whose nature she had so finely tempered, a tribute as near some prayer of thanksgiving and psalm of adoration as ever mediæval saint offered up to the Mother of Christ.

To Donne – once brutal derider of women and but newly read in the finer mysteries of love – Magdalen Herbert must have seemed like some accusing angel, were it not that her nature was too pure for accusation, and her spirituality too unassuming for angelic detachment.

'Yet when her warm redeeming hand – which is
A miracle, and made such to work more –
Doth touch thee, sapless leaf, thou grow'st by this
Her creature, glorified more than before.'

Through the rest of Donne's life we shall trace her influence, impalpable as some breath of virtue, soothing him in moments of perplexity, inviting to harmony and self-surrender, and girding him onward through successive hours of physical and mental crisis to the haven of a pastoral vocation. To her, in the autumn of her days, as we shall see, he addressed the lines most near perhaps to Platonic grace, Italian courtliness, and human tenderness, most irrefutably budded from the heart, of all that he ever wrote – the lines which begin:

'No Spring, nor Summer Beauty hath such grace,
As I have seen in one Autumnal face,'

and in her memory twenty years later – exclaiming with typical extravagance that he wished 'all his body were

turn'd into tongues, that he might declare her just
praises to posterity ' – he preached in the parish church
of Chelsea a sermon that is a lament, a panegyric and a
portrait.

But if intercourse with Mrs. Herbert intensified that
high seriousness expressed in the *Holy Hymns and Sonnets* to which his converted Muse was now to devote
itself, he owed her in many grave moments practical
as well as spiritual support. And not only in these early
days did she prove a bountiful benefactor, but later,
when more exalted patronesses failed him, he never
turned to her in vain. Well therefore might he confess
to her even in 1607 that by her influence and example
he had 'attained to such a step of goodness, as to be
thankful, were both to accuse your power and judgment of impotency and infirmity'; and on another
occasion: 'Your favours to me are everywhere; I use
them and have them. I enjoy them at London, and
leave them there, and yet find them at Mitcham.'

And he had increasing need of such favours; for his
affairs were rapidly going from bad to worse. His only
means of self-escape was to plunge violently into
society. Like all neurotics he was peculiarly sensitive
to his environment, and few of the company amid
which he 'kindled squibs about him and flew into
sportfulness' could have guessed the weight of depression accumulating above the husband only too conscious of the 'incumbencies of a family,' which yet
persisted in its yearly increase. His very excess of
animation, his transports of jollity in congenial society,
were significant of the disease of melancholy settling
upon his mind, a 'soul sickness' which had its roots in

K

penury and solitude. For soon he was compelled to relinquish even his unhealthy lodging in the Strand and to stay stifled at Mitcham with noisy children and an ailing wife, subject himself to periodic attacks of ague, and brooding over shining attainments left to rust, and rich connections complacently prepared to let him starve.

In such a den of domestic confusion, in which we hear of a valuable book, lent by a friend, being torn in pieces by mischievous children, amid illnesses which dragged on from one child to another through summer and autumn, a man of intellect and highly nervous temperament could not but languish. And the pagan in him was impatient of suffering; as he wrote:

> 'The honesties of love with ease I do,
> But am no porter for a tedious woe.'

At first indeed he seems to have been ironically resigned. He begins a verse-letter to his friend Mr. Rowland Woodward with the whimsical couplet:

> 'If, as mine is, thy life a slumber be,
> Seem, when thou read'st these lines, to dream of me.'

But the slumber quickly passed through bad dreams into a nightmare; and if the moralistic tone waxes for a time, poetry wanes:

> 'My Muse – for I had one – because I'm cold,
> Divorced herself, the cause being in me.'

As the dumb days dragged on, he sank through despondency into despair, morbidly arraigning his past errors or entangling himself in metaphysical mazes.

The spring of 1608, the thirty-sixth year of his life,
drew on, but it woke no response. He could only write:
'The pleasantness of the season displeases me. Everything refreshes, and I wither, and I grow older and not
better, my strength diminishes and my load grows, and
being to pass more and more storms, I find that I have
not only cast out all my ballast which nature and time
gives, reason and discretion, and so am as empty and
light as vanity can make me; but I have overfraught
myself with vice, and so am riddingly subject to two
contrary racks, sinking and oversetting, and under
the iniquity of such a disease as enforces the patient
when he is almost starved, not only to fast, but to purge.
For I have much to take in, and much to cast out.'

To experience conversion, Donne had discovered, was
one thing: to enlarge it into a satisfactory life policy in
a darkly hostile world and one perfectly callous towards
its unfortunate creditors, was another. At times he felt
an utter impotence, and laying aside the notes he was
making for what was to prove perhaps his finest tract,
the *Pseudo-Martyr*, he turned his casuistical gifts to the
defence of a more personal theme, that of suicide. It
was said later of *Biathanatos* that 'certainly there was a
false thread in it, but it was not easily found,' and possibly this ingenious piece of very superficial and special
pleading owed its persuasive subtlety to the fact that
Donne had seriously pondered the question as an intimate possibility, and composed his tract as an apology
for a conjectural event.

Just as in love he had been so often tempted to
abandon the struggle of conscience and surrender
blindly to the fact, so he may well at times have longed

to escape the conflict, which life to his eyes more and more appeared, to lose himself and his frustrations and hypochondrias in the cool embrace of death, to have done with the wear of mental argument and physical debasement, to accept the defeat of the flesh in this its last great adventure with the same ecstatic surrender as of old. It may have been so: certainly his vitality was often at a low ebb during these months, and he had not yet discovered a compensating faith. Still conventional religion, for which he had at least respect enough to study its 'peremptory judgment,' condemned suicide in no uncertain terms.

At the very time therefore when imperceptibly he was progressing towards what religion could give, he turned to examine the justification of what she denied. Did a 'Brave scorn' or a 'faint cowardliness' beget such an inclination? Could reason plead at least a good case? Is not a considered self-homicide kindred to martyrdom, a contempt for life the first principle of Christianity, and indeed typical of every heroic character who has preferred death to shame and honour to gross survival? Thus by many a specious argument, and a clever avoidance of the specific dogmas involved in the problem, he built up a defence of that act to which he fancied himself succumbing. It is unlikely that it convinced himself, but it certainly eased his mind, while in arguing the deed he lost some of his desire to perform it. The desire, we cannot believe, was ever urgent.

Donne was too violent a lover of life to be death's paramour: he could and did repeatedly henceforth threaten his mistress with infidelity whenever she withdrew her favour from him; but life was not unduly frightened. She knew that she had but to turn her face towards him and the old loyalty, the old fervour returned. Donne's despair, in fact, was an effervescence of the nerves. It was not that worst malady of a later day, a philosophic pessimism. He was too true a son of his age for that, and his power of recovery was so remarkable because the disease did not strike deep. His body was too buoyant, his mind too detached to succumb absolutely to despair. He might question the dogmas of religion as a curious scholar, but he never really descended to deny the value of life.

Even the worst melancholy too has its moments when the clouds tend to break, and the stout heart and mind of Donne are constantly visible breasting the gloom which pervaded him. Nevertheless, in August of 1608 he seems almost to have touched bottom.

'There is no one person but myself' (he wrote) 'well of my family; I have already lost half a child, and with that mischance of hers, my wife is fallen into such a discomposure as would affect her too extremely but that the sickness of all her other children stupefies her: of one of which, in good faith, I have not much hope; and these meet with a fortune so ill provided for physic and such relief, that if God should ease us with burials, I know not how to perform even that; but I flatter myself with this hope that I am dying too; for I cannot waste faster than by such griefs. As for —
From my Hospital at Mitcham,

JOHN DONNE.'

Death, however, he was to find as deaf to his flattery as king's favourites, and it was with prophetic insight that he wrote: 'I shall have many things to make me weary, and yet not get leave to be gone.'

But it was the lack of all power of decisive action, good or ill, that weighed upon him most. Ashamed of his failure to support his family, and yet impotent, he wrote:

'Every Tuesday I make account that I turn a great hour-glass, and consider that a week's life is run out since I writ. But if I ask myself what I have done in the last watch, or would do in the next, I can say nothing; if I say that I have passed it without hurting any, so may the spider in my window. The primitive monks were excusable in their retirings and enclosures of themselves; for even of them every one cultivated his own garden and orchard, that is, his soul and body, by meditation and manufactures; and they owed the world no more since they consumed none of her sweetness, nor begot others to burden her. But for me, if I were able to husband all my time so thriftily, as not only not to wound my soul in any minute by actual sin, but not to rob and cozen her by giving any part to pleasure or business, but bestow it all upon her in meditation, yet even in that I should wound her more and contract another guiltiness. As the eagle were very unnatural if because she is able to do it, she should perch a whole day upon a tree, staring in contemplation of the majesty and glory of the sun, and let her young eaglets starve in the nest.'

More and more he seemed to himself to lie rotting in a pool of corruption, his vivid faculties atrophied, the world a dust-heap, upon which, like another Job, he had been cast away. His buccaneering spirit revolted against the physical degradation:

'When I must shipwreck, I would do it in a sea where mine impotency might have some excuse: not in a sullen weedy lake, where I could not have so much as exercise for my swimming.'

He was once again reduced to that 'nothingness' which he had known in the satiety of physical passion. He was become 'rather a sickness or a disease of the world, than any part of it,' and the old desire for escape at any cost from the humiliation of life that he had known, 'when I went with the tide, and enjoyed fairer hopes than I now do,' returned doubly strong now the tide ran against him.

Early next year, however, sickness ceased to be metaphorical and became a fact. The 'continual cramp and tetane and gout,' the twistings and wrestings of which he gives so vivid an account cut violently through the morbid tangle of introspection which might well otherwise have led to insanity. When 'pain hath drawn my head so much awry . . . that mine eye cannot follow mine hand,' the head ceased to conduct its interminable moral arguments. His body reasserted in agony its rights.

§ 5

Bed was to prove more than once for Donne a happy place of composition. On this occasion he wrote a 'Litany' and dedicated it to the 'lesser chapels, which are my friends.' It is a strange mixture of dialectic and devotion. We hear in it both the tones of the agnostic wandering rather disconsolately through metaphysical labyrinths and those of the preacher of a later day, reduced to a 'gallant humbleness of faith,' Donne's religious, like his erotic verse, images the gradual absorption of the casuist in the convert, and his 'Litany' is the first poetical expression of that self-abasement already manifest in his letters – a contrition which pain has now informed with passion.

The inspired egoist, who can only be truly happy when he is making his life into an expressive act, to whom introspection or remorse is therefore a species of 'self-murder,' is conscious that he has been feeding mentally on his dejection as before he had fed physically on life. 'Who will deliver me from the burden of this death?' is the essence of his appeal and his lament, and by death he implied mental and moral obsessions. The mind in its turn has become his gaoler and his foe, and he sets out to discover a religion which transcends without denying the mind, as earlier he had discovered a love which transcended without denying the body. His effort in this his first attempt is very spasmodic. Throughout the poem the cry of his distressed soul breaks forth, and then lapses again, with a strange abruptness, one stanza being little more than an ingenious pattern, another a burning prayer; one the subtle weaving of a man who is

> 'moved to seem religious
> Only to vent wit';

another, instinct with the deep diapason note of a heart convinced that

> 'A sinner is more music, when he prays,
> Than spheres' or angels' praises be,
> In panegyric alleluias.'

He beseeches each Person of the Trinity to recreate his body 'now grown ruinous,' his 'mud walls, and condensed dust . . . half-wasted with youth's fires of pride and lust.' And then he turns reprovingly upon his mind:

> 'Let not my mind be blinder by more light,
> Nor faith by reason added lose her sight,'

or later prays

> 'That learning Thine ambassador,
> From thine allegiance we never tempt;
> That beauty, paradise's flower,
> For physic made, from poison be exempt;
> That wit — born apt high good to do —
> By dwelling lazily
> On nature's nothing be not nothing too.'

He begs forgiveness for his excess 'In seeking secrets, or poeticness,' only to indulge the vice in the next stanza, solicits the martyrs for their 'discreet patience of death, or of worse life,' and in his intercession to be delivered

> 'From being anxious, or secure,
> Dead clods of sadness, or light squibs of mirth,
> From thinking that great courts immure
> All, or no happiness . . .'

reveals the pining heart of the cultivated outcast.

Further proof of his reaction against a barren intellectualism is contained in another poem, written about this time and entitled 'The Cross.' Here also the

Christian symbol is woven, with more ingenuity than accuracy, into all the show of nature.

'Swim, and at every stroke thou art thy cross;
The mast and yard make one, where seas do toss;
Look down, thou spiest out crosses in small things;
Look up, thou seest birds raised on crossed wings;
All the globe's frame, and spheres, is nothing else
But the meridians crossing parallels.'

Although Donne's efforts to escape from self-consciousness (that 'self-despising' which 'gets self-love') are as yet too considered to be effective, the desire to heal the disease of proud thought by restoring the humble health of nature, or, to express it more grandiloquently, to relate the rhythm of life to the definitions of reason in a kind of religious ecstasy, is evident. Applying the terminology of the cross to the forces that sway personality, he urged that man should on the physical plane

'Cross thy sense, else both they and thou
Must perish soon and to destruction bow,'

and on the mental:

'So when thy brain works, ere thou utter it,
Cross and correct concupiscence of wit.'

Henceforth this latter admonition is the chief factor in Donne's development. As health returned, as his fortunes improved, and he could once more dispense with a religion, the reconciliation of life and thought seemed less pressing a problem. But sickness had only to return for him to attack it once more, and with

increased urgency, until the time when he, the once
learned casuist, might flatter his faith in public with the
words:

'How imperfect is all our knowledge? What one thing
do we know perfectly? . . . Young men mend not
their sight by using old men's spectacles; and yet we
look upon Nature but with Aristotles spectacles, and
upon the body of man but with Galens, and upon the
frame of the world but with Ptolomies spectacles.
Almost all knowledge is rather like a child that is
embalmed to make Mummy, than that is nursed to
make a Man; rather conserved in the stature of the
first age, than grown to be greater.'

This sin of intellectual lust, against which Donne had
begun to rebel ('a thirst, an appetite which had no ease')
was destined to preoccupy and distinguish the modern
mind from his day to our own. To the old world's
surrender to lust has been added the new world's
enslavement by logic. The men of the early Renaissance bridge the two eras.

They had succeeded in reconciling a newly awakened
intellectual curiosity with the primeval joy of the
senses; they fused the Pagan and the Christian impulses
in a zest for life which embraced alike depravity and
mystical exaltation. The gulf between the depths and
the heights did not trouble them; they were content
to range buoyantly up and down the scale of experience
from sin to saintliness, from bestiality to beatitudes.
Of those three Kingdoms of Consciousness which
Joachim of Flora divined, naming them those of the
Father, the Son, and the Holy Spirit, they knew but the
first two. As citizens of the one they rejoiced in the

primitive; as citizens of the other they refined sensations into an art. The distinction of the modern era is to have discovered the third kingdom, that plane where the intensity of experience, of which art is the expression, is also informed by those ideal and human values to which conventional morality is a progressive approximation.

Between this plane and the first there seems for long to be a great gulf fixed.

Modern man discovered the mind as a detached faculty. He became consciously critical, but his criticism, either through directly opposing or serving his primitive cravings, was primarily destructive. As a purely natural being he indulged his body, and all the time he longed to achieve that equilibrium between the two whereby the gulf might be closed, and the spiritual be born out of the strife of the Rational and the Natural.

Donne is a precocious example of this now so familiar complex, and in these last days at Mitchem he came appreciably nearer solving the problem of his contrarieties. Pain compelled him to arraign his pride of mind, as earlier his pride of body. Before this he had been able to satisfy his religious impulses by casuistry, because his reason had never been put to the test of anguish and exhaustion, of those moments in life when the daylight even of the mind is darkened, and logic is a straw upon the flood. The generation which succeeded him thought to bank the fires of nature beneath the formulas of wit and deism, and they suffered, despite all their outward platitude, in sickness of heart and mind. Early in the nineteenth century the smoul-

dering flames broke out once more, only however for a
Victorian generation, far less honest than Donne, to
suppress them once again under the formulas of faith
and science. To-day we name these antagonisms
rationality and mysticism, and while modern rationality
is grown less self-assured, modern mysticism is more
defined and more ready to submit to verification.
There are many signs indeed that we are beginning to
merge the two in that discriminating intuition which,
as it is the artist's purest form of perception, is also the
ultimate interpretation of Christianity's ideal — love.

But Donne's significance is to have waged this battle
of human consciousness, which is the basic metaphysic
of such a novelist as Dostoevsky, two hundred years
in advance of his time, and to have issued from it, if
not the complete victor (for assured harmony perhaps
was never his, even when 'the fire was dying in the
hearth'), at least without compromising his honour.

§ 6

Donne's worst sufferings were now to be relieved: he
was no longer to want for food and clothes, London
was to open its gates to him once more, and he was
secure at last from the sickly promptings of suicide.
In the autumn of 1608, when his affairs were at their
darkest, he had made desperate but unavailing efforts
to obtain a secretaryship in Ireland. Lord Hay, to
whose ample munificence Donne was later to owe
much, pressed his claims upon the King's attention,
but unfortunately that monarch, if weak in will, was
strong in memory, and had not forgotten 'the disorderly

proceedings, seven years since, in Donne's nonage.'
Thus Donne's amorous audacity not only nipped his
career in its first bud, but withered it indefinitely.

Donne begged Lord Hay not to be discouraged,
assuring him that all those involved had long ago for-
given his youthful indiscretion, and ended with a per-
jured protestation that 'to live in your memory is
advancement enough.' But all was in vain. Nevertheless, his eloquent appeals advertised in other quar-
ters the extremity of his situation. Each of the great
ladies whom Donne had charmed at York House
was in a position to relieve unmerited poverty; but it
was once again to the generous-hearted Sir Francis
Wooley that Donne owed immediate and solid assistance – the last service indeed this loyal friend was
destined to render.

Bold as ever in support of his friend, he approached
Sir George More, and with a frank discretion compelled him to take notice of his son-in-law's condition.
The Donnes' necessity was in embarrassing contrast
to the gilded magnificence which Sir George himself
had been most improvidently affecting. He had indeed
for some time been soothing his conscience by vague
promises of financial assistance, but Donne was too
proud to sue, and Anne too docile, and it needed a
friend's direct assault to bring him to a sense of his
obligations. And now self-interest swelled the argument; for penury is the sire of sickness, and doubtless
Sir Francis reported the health both of Donne and his
wife as being seriously affected. Sir George had no
desire to be left the guardian of a bevy of orphans,
so that an allowance was an insurance investment as

well as a benefaction. Such considerations, and, it
may be, some tardy paternal scruples, persuaded him
to offer his son-in-law a regular yearly allowance
of £80.

From this time therefore Donne was safe from in-
digence, and, what was perhaps equally important,
through its power 'to lift the smothering weight from
off his breast,' in a position to frequent again London
society. The altered tone in all he now wrote is evidence enough how much his despair was circumstantial, and we shall find that, as his strongest inclinations towards religion coincide with periods of physical
and financial dissatisfaction, so in the intervals when
the sky is comparatively clear, the wind fresh and the
sun in his eyes, he is content with the intriguing commerce of the world and the varied adventures of an
exploring but secular mind.

For the future his fortunes were to be bound up with
influential people. First among these was Lady Russell, Countess of Bedford, who, during a visit to one of
his wife's relatives at Mitcham, had discovered and
assisted Donne, when his affairs were at their lowest
ebb, while Sir Henry Goodyer, who was in her service,
had probably acquainted her with his history. When
he was once more able to frequent London, he attached
himself to the informal court which she held at Twickenham Park, and, if we are to believe his words, 'a new
world rose from her light.' 'Favourite of the Muses,'
as she was named, she seems to have revived Donne's
interest, if not his sincere activity in poetry.

Between 1609 and 1611 we mark a recrudescence of
literary energy, more reasonably attributable to the

general lift of the clouds than merely to his new patroness' personal 'radiation.' But he confined himself
mainly to prose, as we should expect of one who in his
thirties was lying in the trough between two waves of
passion, the erotic and the devotional. This was
Donne's period of critical incubation and divided aim.
Only gradually was the new tide to rise and carry his
logic on its crest.

The Countess was herself a versifier, and, in a time
when rank and culture were more generally synonymous than they are to-day, delighted to gather about
her many of the distinguished contemporary poets,
with whom she exchanged both wit and verses. Donne
himself was speedily enrolled as a private laureate, and
required to decorate the nuptials or obsequies of his
patroness' less interesting relations with complimentary
verses. That he did not find this an intolerable task
was due to his natural aptitude for spinning allegorical
imagery about a theme, and his latent appreciation
of ceremony. Moreover, just as in his pamphlets
for Morton the paid casuist would not altogether
suppress the sincere thinker, so in the excitement of
versification the poet could suddenly supplant the
laureate.

Particularly was this so in Elegies, when the theme of
death, even in relation to some lady for whom he had
neither interest nor affection, could recall him from the
multiplication of compliments to such an image as:

'But as the tide doth wash the slimy beach,
    And leaves embroider'd works upon the sand,
    So is her flesh refined by death's cold hand.'

For the great lady whom he served, and named with
a sweeping superlative

'The first good angel, since the world's frame stood,
That ever did in woman's shape appear,'

he cherished a sincere devotion. The Countess of Bedford stood to him for the rest of his life in the position
of a secular Mrs. Herbert. Each is the figurehead of
one of the two ambitions which were to dispute his
allegiance – the world's charm and the Church's peace.
Mrs. Herbert excited his mysticism, the Countess
that wit, of which he wrote:

'nor must wit
Be colleague to religion, but be it,'

and the verses which he addressed to each emphasize
the distinction. For despite the fact that in his first
enthusiasm he could address 'the good Countess' as
'that best Lady . . . who only hath power to cast the
fetters of verse upon my free meditations,' it was Magdalen Herbert who inspired poetry, while her rival in
his devotions received only lyrical flattery. In such
flattery Donne was, when he chose, a master. He
knew exactly how far to extend an hyperbole without
rousing vanity's suspicions, and his inventive powers
were prodigal. But his attachment to Lucy Russell
was inspired by something more than self-interest or
gratitude. It was no posturing courtier who confided
to Sir Henry Goodyer: 'I would write apace to her,
whilst it is possible to express that which I yet know
of her, for by this growth I see now soon she will be
ineffable,' or protested to her:

L

'You have refined me, and to worthiest things –
Virtue, art, beauty, fortune. Now I see
Rareness or use, not nature, value brings.'

She showed him how everyday life might be made
into an art, that virtue's temple need not necessarily
be the dull and doleful little chapel which his youthful
impatience had pictured it; that it might rather be
choicely adorned and served by magnificent ritual.

'What walls of tender crystal her enfold,
What eyes, hands, bosom, her pure altars be!'

he cried, and the ritual was real. It was no frozen
service, but simple, lively, intimate, a play of nature
modulated into art. And thus it awoke his latent
gallantry. Strolling about the gracious Twickenham
lawns with this 'happiest lady,' emblem of all that was
most cultivated in her time, discoursing on poetry in
elegant terms, confiding to her compositions of his own
and having the confidence returned, Donne was ready
to announce, if scarcely to believe that

'The story of beauty, in Twickenham is, and you.
Who hath seen one, would both; as, who had been
In Paradise, would seek the Cherubim.'

The tiger was indeed tamed in Twickenham Park!
   The strain of aristocracy in Donne, to which we have
already referred, led him paradoxically enough to
delight in humbling himself with a kind of affectionate
awe before his social superiors. Even as a preacher the
same debasement before notabilities existed together
with the most pronounced self-assertion that ever

menaced from a pulpit, and with perfect complacence
he would compare the King and his Court to God and
the Communion of the Saints.

There are times when this prostration before rank
becomes somewhat degrading, but it was never so in
his relations with the Countess of Bedford, because
she herself was so entirely free from pride or affectation,
so sincerely in every act and gesture the great lady.
And the devotion which Donne attested in many verses
and letters was the tribute of one who, beaten himself
about a stormy world and exposed to its humiliating
exactions, read in her an ideal of serenity, grace and
quiescence, of security from indiscreet disaster, such as
he himself was never completely to realize, even when
he had wrapped himself in the dignified ceremonial of
the Church.

For Sir George More's bounty, welcome as it was,
did not touch the root of the problem. Donne's great
gifts were still wasting themselves in featureless activities, his family was growing with monotonous regularity, his wife's energies were overtaxed, and his own
philosophy of life uncertain.

It was not that he desired the 'fluid slipperiness and
transitory migrations' of fashionable society. To one
at heart so serious, a 'giddy and feathery' life made
little appeal, and he was generally glad to be 'removed
from the scorchings and dazzlings and exhalings of the
world's glory.' But just because of his dynamic seriousness, the conditions under which he lived still
remained highly unsatisfactory. Donne was never
glacial enough to disregard his environment; rather
his inordinately fiery temperament fed angrily upon it.

Even during these first months when he was again enjoying London's diversions, he could only write: 'I live in the country without stupefying, am not in darkness, but in shadow, which is not no light, but a pallid, waterish and diluted one,' and that 'all retirings into a shadowy life are alike from all causes, and alike subject to the barbarousness and insipid dullness of the country: only the employments and that upon which you cast and bestow your pleasure, business, or books, gives it the tincture and beauty.'

Donne was too positive a force of nature himself to accept the wild nature about him in a 'wise passiveness.' The country merely irritated his egoism by its quiet; and although the mystic might write: 'If we can but tell ourselves truly what and where we would be, we may make any state and place such,' the realist soon mocked the platitude, and the 'salad and onions of Mitcham,' as he named his happiest hours, were very intermittent.

The fireside of his little parlour seemed very cramped after the spaciousness of Twickenham, the noise of 'gamesome children' fretted one fresh from sallies of wit and learning, while as he watched his wife, pale, and, like Martha, troubled with many things, he was made miserable by the thought that he had ' transplanted her into a wretched fortune.'

It is not surprising therefore that the note of religious yearning and resignation returns, even more insistently disputing in all he wrote with the social gossip which was his other preoccupation. If London society could relieve his spirits temporarily, Mitcham still remained, cold, inhospitable and chaotic, to urge a rebellious

Thomas towards the comfort of a faith. Indeed had not
fortune, before many months were past, made another
turn of her wheel, he might well have surrendered;
and although such a step would have been premature,
having regard to his convictions, it would have saved
him and his a world of trouble. Meanwhile the years
1609 and 1610 are chiefly of interest for the stages
which we can trace in his advance towards that goal,
deferred though his arrival was to be. In all his writings – and he was much engaged during this irresolute
vacation on theological study and exposition – we watch
him preparing his mind, half-consciously, for the
Anglican ministry. And the poet, as always, takes a
hand in the process, and the scientist too.

§ 7

It will be well to quote at the head of this chapter in
his life the summary and defence which he himself
wrote, in his *Pseudo-Martyr*, of his religious progress
up to this time.
'They who have descended so low, as to take knowledge of me and to admit me into their consideration,
know well that I used no inordinate haste nor precipi-
tation in binding my conscience to any local religion.
I had a longer work to do than many other men, for I
was first to blot out certain impressions of the Roman
religion, and to wrestle both against the examples and
against the reasons by which some hold was taken
and some anticipations early laid upon my conscience,
both by persons who by nature had a power and superiority over my will, and others who by their learning
and good life seemed to me justly to claim an interest

for the guiding and rectifying of mine understanding
in these matters. And although I apprehended well
enough that this irresolution not only retarded my
fortune but also bred some scandal, and endangered
my spiritual reputation by laying me open to many
misinterpretations, yet all these respects did not transport me to any violent and sudden determination till I
had, to the measure of my poor wit and judgment, sur-
veyed and digested the whole body of Divinity contro-
verted between ours and the Roman Church. In which
search and disquisition, that God which awakened
me then, and hath never forsaken me in that industry, as He is the author of that purpose, so is He
a witness of this protestation, that I behaved myself,
and proceeded therein with humility and diffidence in
myself, and by that which by His grace I took to be
the ordinary means, which is frequent prayer, and
equal and indifferent affections.'

It would be easy for the cynical-minded to quote the
less reputable incidents in Donne's early life in refutation of his assertion that he had 'behaved himself
with humility and diffidence,' but to do so would be to
confuse his life with his religion. The two were things
apart, slowly gravitating towards each other. And
even at this time he was still the curious critic of religious dogma, troubled by moments of real religious
conviction. The fault was not entirely his own, nor
indeed ever is with sincere souls. So much religion
always is mere conformity; so much theology only a
web of words. Every organized faith reveals this alloy.
Consequently candid souls and daring minds are for
long alienated; they reject the truth with the falsehood.

In disgust with the dead matter of convention, they embrace a religion of life and indulge the bright play of personality, loyal rather to the Nature of whom they claim sonship, than to the God whom withered authority would have them revere.

So it had been with Donne. Rome suffocated him, and Protestantism seemed a pallid, political compromise. Meanwhile life allured, and it was only when physically and mentally disillusioned that he began to grope tentatively towards a Church which was at least a clouded mirror of spiritual values.

Of this wary approach the account just quoted is, we may believe, an accurate summary. What is chiefly noticeable is his studious caution. No risk of misunderstanding at the hands of such orthodox divines as Morton, no financial considerations, could at this time affect his determination to be mentally honest. He might invoke Divine grace, he might, as in his 'Litany,' decry intellectual pretensions, but he would accept no irrational consolation.

Certainly he began to have moments when he seemed possessed by some supra-rational power, which it was convenient to call God, moments of heightened insight, which grew more frequent as he bore the buffets of the world. Such experiences were apt to set up a painful conflict, his keen sense of the finite disputing with this new appreciation of the infinite, the one inviting a debasement of soul by sense, the other an exaltation of character; for

'man, to get
Towards Him that's infinite, must first be great.'

But normally he was still the detached observer, clutching at any straws which might point towards conviction. It was as such that he served Morton, and his approach to Anglican conformity may be traced along two lines – that by which he convinced his mind that Protestant dogmas did not to any vital degree conflict with logical and philosophical consistency, and that by which he felt an ever more imperative need of the sustenance of religious faith in his inner life, and of the stability of the clerical profession in his outer.

His letters to Goodyer testify to both processes. The God whom he had invoked with more unction than sincerity in his agitated correspondence with Sir George More is now become not only the confidential deity to whom he speaks of commending his friend in his prayers, but also the central point about which all his curious reading in science and theology and metaphysics revolves. For Donne was original in the pioneering interest which he showed in contemporary science, little then remarked either by poets or theologians absorbed in their respective crafts, no less than in his backward sallies into the works of eccentric mystics.

We may admit that despite his keen excitement over the Copernican discovery, he did not realize its implications. His mind conceived with a dizzy rapture the immensities of space and the infinity of time, but he was also too earthbound to allow such a conception to dwarf the world he trod. The Copernican and the Ptolemaic theories corresponded indeed to the mystical and material elements in his personality, and he accepted them both without realizing the contradiction.

Thus it was that in one of his great pæans on the
Creation the future preacher could combine modern
astronomy with mediæval fancifulness. He is speaking
of 'God's company':

'Was that Heptarchie, the seven kingdoms of the
seven Planets, conversation enough for him? Let every
Star in the firmament, be (so some take them to be) a
several world, was all this enough? We see, God drew
persons nearer to him, than Sun or Moon or Stars, or
any thing, which is visible and discernible to us, he
created Angels; How many, how great? Arithmetic
lacks numbers to express them, proportion lacks
Dimension to figure them; so far was God from being
alone.'

Science then merely increased the sphere of his wonder: it gave his imagination a thousand new worlds to
range, without lessening his sense of the unique importance of the one which he still allowed God to have
created in six days. His ingenious mind, far from being
materially depressed, turned the new discovery to the
uses of the spiritual.

'Methinks,' he wrote, 'the new astronomy is thus
applicable well, that we which are a little earth should
rather move towards God, than that He which is ful-
filling, and can come no whither, should move towards
us.'

So early as 1611 he was enraptured by news of Galileo's invention of a telescope, hailing him as one 'who
of late hath summoned the other worlds, the stars, to
come nearer to him, and to give him an account of
themselves.' The materialist cleric denounced such
discoveries as infringements upon the prerogatives of

the Deity. To Donne the faculties of man were rather the criterion of divinity, and certainly to study man's creative triumphs in science was considerably more edifying than to observe his destructive cunning in theology.

Meanwhile his letters become both more sacramental and more worldly – a strange mixture of social inquiry, theological argument, and expressive piety. Plainly a possible Court appointment, diplomatic or administrative, drew him in one direction, while the Church beckoned austerely in another. He himself, we cannot doubt, favoured the former, and, until the King himself finally vetoed the matter, clung despairingly to the hope of its realization; while in the attempts which he made to flatter, cajole, bribe or weary influential men into finding him a post, he appears in a rather obsequious light. In 1610 we find him once again applying for a secretaryship, this time in Virginia, and with equal ill-success. Shortly before, he had suffered a real loss in the death of Sir Francis Wooley, and although he was soon to make new friends and profit by their influential patronage, they could scarcely fill the place of this magnanimous friend, who, without assuming the tones of a patron, had helped him to his own personal cost in three of the most serious crises of his life.

It was at such times, when some resource was withdrawn from him, or his secular efforts rebuffed, that, hopeless of worldly preferment, he turned once more to theological investigations. But Walton altogether misread the situation when he wrote that 'to that place (Mitcham) and such studies he could willingly have

wedded himself during his life,' nor was it any such
sense of unworthiness as he inferred, whether in 'strict-
ness of life or competence of learning,' which deterred
Donne from 'putting his hand to that holy plough.'
Donne was no 'meek Moses ' to question: 'Lord, who
am I?' nor was he ever, as Walton suggests, blind to
worldly considerations. Rather he was in the abstract
discontented with clerical values, and in the concrete
anxious to better his circumstances, and when every
other possibility of affecting the latter at last seemed
closed to him, he found no great difficulty in conquer-
ing the former.

The Church figured as a potential career as well as a
still suspect sanctuary for a distracted spirit. In his
happier moments he was glad to preserve his freedom
of mind, in his melancholy he really desired to find
peace by reconciling his values with those of a Church.

What particularly baulked him in this attempt was
the materialism of the ordinary prelate. He complained 'that the divines of these times are become
mere advocates, as though religion were a temporal
inheritance; they plead for it with all sophistications,
and illusions, and forgeries: and herein are they likest
advocates, that though they be fed by the way with
dignities and other recompenses, yet that for which
they plead is none of theirs. They write for religion
without it.' Or in a verse passage:

'Court, city, church, are all shops of small wares;
   All having blown to sparks their noble fire,
   And drawn their sound gold ingot into wire.'

Doubtless, as Walton wrote: 'In the first and most

blessed times of Christianity . . . the clergy were
looked upon with reverence, and deserved it,' but
degeneracy from that high ideal had long set in, and
Donne saw only men, who, without his brilliant powers
of advocacy, wanted the very religious conviction
which he wished to discover in some faith outside
himself, men who cared more for the material rewards
of a profession than the spiritual excitement of a vocation. Only an idealist could have looked for anything
else. The gross ecclesiastical materialism, which Eras-
mus had sketched with bitter irony in his *Colloquies*,
and which had brought the Reformed Church into
being, still existed to a less degree in the new foundation, because it was a cardinal quality in human nature.
Luther was material in other ways than the commer-
cialization of relics, just as a fashionable Victorian
cleric, pandering to social or national prejudice, was
material in other ways than Luther. St. Paul is material
by the side of Christ; and although it would be a libel
on many a noble, many a simple and serviceable soul to
say with Donne that the prelate has 'neither the body of
Religion, which is moral honesty and sociable faith-
fulness, nor the soul, Christianity,' yet it is safe to say
that a St. Francis is seldom found within a Church,
because absolute spirituality does not of its nature
submit to organization.

But Donne saw the materialism of contemporary
ecclesiastics with such a desolating intimacy, because
in the theological word-spinning, in which they were
engaged, he was himself a master technician, and so
knew its utter irrelevancy, unless it served a vital conviction. He needed vision, some crowning concept

which would relate casuistry to life and truth, and for this he looked in vain either in the Reformed or the Roman Church. He saw them rather as two wordy disputants, absorbed in that semi-political controversy wherein he had been a hired special-pleader. Neither side took its stand on the simple ground of a purer and more positive spirituality, but 'the wounds which they inflict . . . are all *se defendendo*.' In the panic of party hostilities they could neither preach nor practise the unaggressive faith that they were supposed to represent.

In that struggle Donne preserved himself a very open mind. He seldom lowered himself to the cheap invective of the time, although he was shortly to compose a somewhat fuliginous skit at the expense of the Jesuits. But at heart he admitted that 'both sides may be in justice and innocence,' and was sufficiently disinterested to realize that the technical details over which they fought would not have troubled the truly religious at all. This attitude he was eventually to carry into the pulpit, complaining that: 'amongst ourselves, for matters not Doctrinall, or if Doctrinall, yet not *Fundamental*, only because we are subdivided in divers *Names*, there should be such Exasperations, such Exacerbations, such Vociferations, such Ejaculations, such Defamations of one another, as if all *Foundations* were destroyed ' – and on another occasion boldly asserting: 'Beloved, there are some things in which all Religions agree; The worship of God, The holiness of life; And therefore, if . . . any man will say, this is Papisticall, Papists do this, it is a blessed Protestation, and no man is the less a Protestant, nor the worse a Protestant for making it. Men and brethren, I am a Papist, that is, I will fast and pray as much as any Papist. . . . Men and brethren, I am a Puritan, that is, I will endeavour to be pure, as my Father in heaven is pure, as far as any Puritan.'

Donne neither divorced the values of religion from those of life, nor confused them. It was on these grounds that he argued in his *Pseudo-Martyr* that a political Oath of Allegiance did not affect a man's relation to God. But interesting as was the controversy to one of a legal turn of mind, it was God whom he wished to discover, and not faction which he desired to please. 'You know,' he wrote, 'I have never fettered nor imprisoned the word Religion, not straightening it friarly . . . nor immuring it in a Rome, or a Wittenburg, or a Geneva; they are all virtual beams of one sun, and wheresoever they find clay hearts, they harden them and moulder them into dust.' Such a view he had presented satirically as a young man; he held it now with a forlorn fervency. For what Donne desired above all (in this again kindred to much religious opinion in our own day) was a speedy reconciliation of the combatants. His heart hungered for a reunited Church, delivered from partisanship, and so ripe to voice those high mysteries which his soul as yet darkly conceived. Such to him was no narrow, national unity, but that essential agreement of spirit which can afford to tolerate differences of interpretation.

'I know,' he ends a letter to his friend, 'I speak to you who cannot be scandalized, and that neither measure religion (as it is now called) by unity, nor suspect unity, for these interruptions.

'Sir, not only a mathematic point, which is the most

indivisible and unique thing which art can present, flows into every line which is derived from the centre, but our soul which is but one, hath swallowed up a negative and feeling soul, which was in the body before it came, and exercises those faculties yet: and God Himself, who only is One, seems to have been eternally delighted with a disunion of persons. They whose active function it is, must endeavour this unity in religion.'

It is strange that one who could thus comprehend the fine distinctions between πνεῦμα and ψυχή, or as we should name them to-day, intuition and sense-perception, should yet want religious conviction. But it is possible to understand the metaphysics of religion without experiencing its inspiration, and, for so concrete a mind as Donne's, religion in the void, or an impalpable essence of faith, was not enough. He needed a Church to embody and localize the abstract idea, to carry a step further 'that advantage of nearer familiarity with God, which the act of incarnation gave us'; he needed it also as a sufficiently commendable profession. But to a mind liberated by philosophic knowledge and heated by scientific (for he wrote of Galileo as seeing 'the Moon in so near a distance that he gave himself satisfaction of all and the least parts of her'), the grovelling strife of sectarians must have proved an uninviting spectacle.

Thus the worldliness of prelates combined with his own secular ambitions to discourage the latent mysticism to which he was soon to give poetical expression, but which under different circumstances might have already impelled him to accept the orders of a Church.

And indeed during 1610 it is clear that Donne renewed his efforts to obtain some secular appointment. Those begging letters, which were henceforth to flow from his pen in an even more futile, fulsome and agitated stream, begin to figure largely in his correspondence.

It is hard to distinguish between the empty language of obsequiousness and the reality, between a matter of fashion and a flaw of character. Doubtless both dictated the tone of such solicitations, and, offensive as it often sounds in the ear of a generation which has generally ceased either to patronize or to be patronized, Donne's age must be held more responsible for it than himself.

But Fortune is a wayward jade. She rejects the industrious suitor and rewards the impudent. Donne's affairs were to be startlingly bettered by more subtle and even more casual means than official wire-pulling, and through the agency of poetry instead of prose, although the Muse may at first have looked somewhat askance upon the policy she was made to serve.

¶ PART THREE
THE PENSIONER

Viri seraphici Ioannis Donne Qua=
dragenarij Effigies vera, Qui post
eam ætatem Sacris initiatus Ec=
clesiæ Sti Pauli Decanus obijt.
Ano { Dom 1631°
{ Ætatis suæ 59°

Lombart. sculp. London

THE PENSIONER

§ 1

EARLY in 1610 Sir Robert Drury of Hawsted, in Suffolk, a man of ample fortune, lost his only surviving daughter Elizabeth, a girl in her fifteenth year, daintily proportioned if we are to believe her portrait, upon whom he had lavished all his affections and centred all his ambitions. Her death made some stir in the world; for her father's pretensions on her behalf had been as exorbitant as was his despair. It was even rumoured that he had destined her for a royal consort; and that the extravagance of his grief was attributable to the fact that she had died of a box on the ear which he himself had administered.

The facts and fictions of this 'sad history' reached Donne's ears, and he composed a short funeral elegy in the girl's honour and dispatched it to her father. The act is surprising because, so far as is known, he was unacquainted with Sir Robert Drury, had never seen the subject of his verse, and must have owed the personal details which he wove into its fabric to the careful reporting of friends. Certainly, as professional Elegist for the Countess of Bedford, he was well exercised for the task, and the pathos of the story was such as appealed to the tenderer side of his nature. The thought of innocence smirched by all the squalid associations which death called up in his mind, of the bud trodden down in the mire, was exactly the kind of strong physical contrast which held him fascinated between awe and disgust. There is sincerity for example in such descriptive lines as

'One, whose clear body was so pure and thin,
Because it need disguise no thought within;
'Twas but a through-light scarf her mind to enroll,
Or exhalation breathed out from her soul.'

Nevertheless, so uncalled-for an act of homage and
the obvious artificiality of much of its expression cannot but provoke the suspicion that Donne, who was
now intent at all costs on bettering his position, conceived the plan of attracting to himself in this way the
notice of one of the wealthiest men of the time.

If so, he succeeded beyond all expectation.

Sir Robert was so delighted by the attention, that
after making Donne's acquaintance he 'assigned him
and his wife a useful apartment in his own large house
in Drury Lane, and not only rent-free, but was also a
cherisher of his studies, and such a friend as sym-
pathized with him and his in all their joy and sorrows.'

Thus Donne, much as Jeremy Taylor was to do later
in Lord Carbery's Golden Grove, found an asylum in
which he could shelter from the dust and danger of the
world: and if he scarcely turned it to such saintly uses
as that sweet-tongued prophet, whom 'a tender providence shrouded under her wings,' the breathing space
which it offered in his perplexed career was of the
highest significance. Many as were the abuses of the
patronage system, these two examples and their issue
speak weightily in its favour.

For three years Donne was relieved of his dilemma,
and although only a professional career could definitely
secure his position, he was sufficiently lulled by the
semblance of such service as he had once rendered to

the Lord Keeper to dismiss the religious problem from his mind and drift into the social tide – a tide which eventually took him to the Continent, and replaced theological by legal problems.

The 'hospital' at Mitcham, where he had loved and thought and suffered for more than six years, was thankfully abandoned, and he and his accumulating family settled in the wing of a palatial establishment, standing in its own grounds not far from Temple Bar. For such privilege he had certainly to pay, and at first in rather a debased coinage. Moreover, to be indebted to the charity of a rich man, however perfect his tact, must soon secretly have chagrined so independent a spirit. The disproportionate gratitude, too, which Sir Robert had shown for the original tribute to his daughter, and his manifest eagerness for more in the same kind, seemed to demand on each sad anniversary a repetition of the act of homage. To compose one elegy on a character for whom he had no direct attachment and therefore can at best but have felt a passing wave of sympathy, clearly taxed Donne's ingenuity to the full. To continue the meretricious service indefinitely was a doleful prospect.

Yet on the first anniversary he bravely met the bill and promised to be regular in his payments.

> 'Accept this tribute, and his first year's rent;
>   Who till his dark short taper's end be spent,
>   As oft as thy feast sees this widow'd earth,
>   Will yearly celebrate thy second birth.'

Fortunately after one more effort, in which once again he asserted that his Muse's matronly ambition was 'yearly to bring forth such a child as this,' he wisely went into default, and posterity was spared the perpetuation of what, beginning in artificiality, might have degenerated into farce.

Possibly Sir Robert's insistence on publication explains the withdrawal. Donne had always been averse to printing his poetry, while allowing it to circulate in manuscript among a select circle, and it was truly unfortunate for his reputation as a poet that these elegies should be the first to dare the full daylight. The story of their origin and the hyperbole in which they indulged could only excite derision, and reflect unfavourably upon the one quality which Donne consistently cherished – his honesty. Ben Jonson's opinion that 'the Anniversarie was profane and full of blasphemies . . . that if it had been written of the Virgin Marie it had been something,' was but a blunt version of the chatter of the coteries and the jealous insinuations of great ladies, who rather unreasonably wished their laureate to preserve his powers for the celebration of their own obsequies.

Yet although Donne may deserve censure for commercializing to some extent both his Muse and a tragic occasion, a study of these three poems (the 'Funeral Elegy,' and 'The First' and 'Second Anniversaries,' incorporated under the title 'An Anatomy of the World') can only convince us of the justice, not to say the shrewdness, of his self-defence:

'Of my Anniversaries (he wrote) the fault that I acknowledge in myself, is to have descended to print anything in verse, which though it have excuse even in our times, by men who profess and practise much

gravity; yet I confess I wonder how I declined to it,
and do not pardon myself. But for the other part of
the imputation of having said too much, my defence
is, that my purpose was to say as well as I could; for,
since I never saw the gentlewoman, I cannot be understood to have bound myself to have spoken just truths;
but I would not be thought to have gone about to
praise her or any other in rhyme, except I took such a
person as might be capable of all that I could say. If
any of those ladies think that Mistress Drewry was
not so, let that lady make herself fit for all those praises
in the book, and they shall be hers.'

In brief, although Donne could scarcely lay such a
claim to immediate inspiration as Shelley in his 'Adon-
ais,' or to personal emotion as Tennyson in his *In
Memoriam*, he, as they and Milton, Matthew Arnold,
Bion and Moschus, was paying his tribute to the idea,
not the fact, of death, and was engaged in self-expression rather than piece-work. He himself later wrote,
with considerable truth, of his elegiac efforts: 'I did
best when I had least truth for my subject.'

In the process of stringing verses and the pursuit of
images and analogies, his excitement rose. The pathetic figure of Elizabeth Drury assumed a more than
mortal significance. It was 'the Idea of a Woman,' as
he told Jonson, 'and not as she was,' which now
haunted his imagination, and in the Idea of a woman
he embodied his Idea of God, both as a perfect moral
principle and as the unity underlying all diversity. His
mysticism, freed for the time from casuistry, poured
itself into passages of these elegies, and therein lies
their usually neglected grandeur. Critics have erred

in assuming indifferently their artificiality. They have complained that when Donne compares Elizabeth Drury's death to a great earthquake in which the world is gulfed, he is forgetting self-respect and descending to preposterous absurdity. There is truth in the plea in respect of certain parts of the poems; yet even against the most venal passages it is well to weigh Donne's indebtedness to Sir Robert's 'noble estate and more liberal mind,' and the fact, as Walton expressed it, that he was 'so generous as to think he had sold his liberty when he received so many charitable kindnesses.' Moreover, the original Elegy and 'The First Anniversary,' against which the charge of artificiality can most justly be sustained, were written without any idea of publication, as a private offering to a distracted father. And, unnoticed by many critics, the leaven of artificiality rapidly diminishes on each occasion. Donne may not indeed be celebrating Elizabeth Drury any more sincerely, but he rises from versification to poetry because he is passionately expressing himself.

It is a mistake then to suppose that these three Elegies are mere catalogues of servile superlatives, or at best technical *tours de force*. There can be no real beauty of style without sincerity of substance, and we need only submit ourselves to the 'Second Anniversary,' not as derisive spectators of an act of craven professionalism, but in readiness for a great prelude embodying a gush of spiritual insight suddenly released, to discover its worth.

Each of the 'Anniversaries' is, in fact, a step upward in rapturous exploration through death of the divine. For this Elizabeth Drury is but the excuse, the pro-

vocation soon translated into burning symbol, as the
Virgin was to the Florentine artist; and in parts of the
'Second Anniversary,' entitled 'Of the Progress of the
Soul,' Donne rises to a height of metaphysical ecstasy,
which may be compared without injustice to that of
Shelley himself.

§ 2

'An Anatomy of the World' may be fitly considered
the third of Donne's attempts to image his spiritual
conception of life, of which the earlier 'Metempsychosis' and the 'Litany' already cited are the fore-
runners, and the later 'Divine Sonnets' the successors.
He had never approached the mystery of life or the
enigma of God from the purely religious standpoint.
Science and philosophy had both served as foils for his
imagination, and his advance is clearly from a fantastic
and frivolous playing with ideas to their co-ordination
in a disciplined conception, and a unified consciousness
of truth. This advance is particularly noticeable between the first and second 'Anniversaries,' and by
1612, the date of this last achievement, Donne has
clearly reached imaginative conviction.

Death as a fact and a concept was never far from his
thoughts during his last twenty years. It enriched his
negative moments with the same sensuous experience
as life gave to his positive moments. Its horror as
exquisitely tortured his nerves as its mystery exalted
his spirit. So curiously blended of the carnal and the
spiritual as he was, he found in it the crux and climax
of religious experience. Like sin, it was a denial of life,
but through the pleasure and pain of sin he had grown

to truth, so that he took comfort in the analogy; and
as the realist of the early love-poems would mock the
idealist in his own heart by listing the indecencies of
the flesh, so the seer of a later day would turn from
some rapturous vision of the hereafter to brood with
concentrated disgust upon the facts of corruption –
'death's worst,' as Gerard Hopkins words it, 'winding
sheets, tombs and worms and tumbling to decay.'

Thus 'woman' and 'death' were the two objectives
upon which the material and ideal impulses in his
nature centred and fought out the battle. Admittedly
we find in his celebration of death, as in his expression
of love, no such radiance and serenity, fresh and sweet
as the air of an early autumn morning, as we know for
example in Jeremy Taylor's *Holy Dying*. The realist
was never completely transmuted in Donne, and while
this served to give to his ideas a richly physical definition, it also touched his highest flights of imagination
with something of the damp and dolour of the tomb.
They come to us like Gregorian chants from a cathedral choir, as heard by some melancholy wanderer in
the crypt beneath.

A pure girl, untimely dead, attracted him therefore
as an ideal symbol of physical enslavement and spiritual
release. The two emblems through which he had
imaged and would image his own personal conflict
were here united, and little Elizabeth Drury, as the
poems mount from a complimentary exercise to an act
of creative expression, is sublimated into a pure idea,
comparable to the 'holy light' which Milton invoked,
Blake's 'Los,' Keats' 'Moneta,' or Shelley's 'Witch of
Atlas.'

The original Elegy then is but the material foundation upon which temples of metaphysical thought and
of mystical rapture were successively raised. It contains fine lines, such as genius will often achieve, almost
unconsciously, under the stimulus of versification, but
the rest is factory-work. Its artificial excess is, as it
were, the parody of that heightening of actuality by
imagination which occurs in its sequels. The one in-
spires ridicule, the other reverence. When Donne, for
example, announces that Elizabeth Drury

'Being spent, the world must needs decrepit be,'

and commands a tottering universe to sing her dirge
we find the extravagance tiresome and absurd. Our
feelings, it must be admitted, are very similar during
the first sixty lines of 'The First Anniversary,' the first
thirty of 'The Second,' and the concluding passages of
both.

For on each occasion Donne bent to his task laboriously, only too conscious, we may suppose, of the
weight of professional duty, and not until he has been
composing for some time does the theme begin to
possess him. He takes fire, forgets Sir Robert Drury
and his daughter, and passionately invokes all that is
hidden in the dark of death, the mysterious idea that
transcends time and space, growth and decay, the
serene perfection clouded and warped by the clotted
senses, but surely realized in its immaculate purity
when the body is brought to dust. Like Shelley, he
climbs dizzily the steeps of speculation; and then
suddenly the impulse fails, the thought of practical business intrudes, the paid Elegist returns and a laboured

conclusion crowns a dithyrambic chant to the life-spirit.
'The First Anniversary' is imaginatively as inferior
to 'The Second' as it is superior to the 'Funeral Elegy.'
Even in its highest moments we are conscious of the
dialectician. It is, in fact, a strange medley of the
thought and reading on which Donne had been engaged during the previous two years. He had filled his
mind with scientific, theological and metaphysical
ideas, and he felt strongly the need of building these
up into some symmetrical conception. Elizabeth
Drury was the incongruous personality about whom he
gathered them, at first in an effort of conscious co-
ordination, but later fusing them in the passionate
unity of a creative act.

The predominant motive of 'The First Anniversary'
is that of negative disillusionment, which Donne
emphasizes from various aspects, contrasting the
world's stained and shadowed state, as he sees it, with
the purity of her whom he celebrates – the corrupt
fact with the immaculate idea.

Thus he ponders the transiency of man:

> 'Mankind decays so soon,
> We're scarce our fathers' shadows cast at noon';

laments the ardour, the wide-ranging thought, which
are lost to him:

> 'We're not retired, but damp'd;
> And as our bodies, so our minds are cramp'd,'

and broods over the fatality of original sin:

> 'For before God had made up all the rest,
> Corruption enter'd and depraved the best.'

He records the doubts which philosophy and science
are beginning to cast upon man's primitive conception
of the universe:

> 'And new philosophy calls all in doubt;
> The element of fire is quite put out;
> The sun is lost, and th' earth, and no man's wit
> Can well direct him where to look for it.
> And freely men confess that this world's spent,
> When in the planets and the firmament
> They seek so many new,'

or in another passage announces more exactly and with
remarkable premonition the disintegrating effect of
science upon simple sense:

'For the world's beauty is decayed and gone;
— Beauty; that's colour and proportion.
We think the heavens enjoy their spherical,
Their round proportion, embracing all;
— But yet their various and perplexed course,
— Observed in divers ages, doth enforce
Men to find out so many eccentric parts,
Such diverse downright lines, such overthwarts
As disproportion that fair form; it tears
The firmament in eight-and-forty shares,
And in these constellations then arise
New stars, and old do vanish from our eyes
As though heaven suffered earthquakes, peace or war
When new towers rise, and old demolished are.

Man hath weaved out a net, and this net thrown
Upon the heavens, and now they are his own.'

With this disorder, this universe splintered by the new
spirit of criticism, this earth dwarfed amid the swarm-
ing worlds of heaven, he contrasts the girl who is
Elizabeth Drury in fact, but, in his idea of her, the
immortal and harmonious spirit of beauty,

> 'after whom what form soe'er we see
> Is discord and rude incongruity.'

In the light of such beauty as this, he exclaims:
'Thou know'st how wan a ghost this our world is,'
how small a loss it is therefore that death inflicts, and
how great a gain it promises in the realization of that
radiance, which the world sullies, that form, which
the world fumbles or distorts.

Such a hunger for ideal synthesis is raised from the
level of rather conscious argument to that of impassioned poetry in 'The Second Anniversary,' written
in the following year.

The 'Immortal Maid' whom Donne here invokes is
emancipated from the last shadow of Elizabeth Drury.
She is become the pure spirit of imaginative desire.
Drunk, as Blake, with spiritual vision, aspiring after
some ecstatic intuition of God, Donne empties his scorn
alike on the 'fragmentary rubbish of the world,' the
'carcass of the flesh,' the petty arrogance of the mind,
and that bastard learning, for which he cherished once
'so hydroptic' a thirst.

> 'Thirst for that time, O my insatiate soul,
>   And serve thy thirst with God's safe-sealing bowl;
>   Be thirsty still, and drink still till thou go
>   To th' only health; to be hydroptic so

Forget this rotten world; and unto thee
Let thine own times as an old story be.
Be not concern'd; study not why nor when;
Do not so much as not believe a man,
For though to err, be worst, to try truths forth
Is far more business than this world is worth.

     .   .   .   .

Forget this world, and scarce think of it so,
As of old clothes cast off a year ago.
To be thus stupid is alacrity;
Men thus lethargic have best memory.
Look upward.'

And then once again, only with a more dreadful concentration, an imaginative accuracy, which blends
every fearsome detail of the last hour of human life
and of the body's subsequent corruption, with a vision
of spiritual release, he turns to acclaim death as the
fulfilment of being, the crisis of achieved consciousness.

'Think then, my soul, that death is but a groom,
Which brings a taper to the outward room,
Whence thou spiest first a little glimmering light,
And after brings it nearer to thy sight;

     .   .   .   .

Think thyself labouring now with broken breath,
And think those broken and soft notes to be
Division and thy happiest harmony.

     .   .   .   .

Think thyself parch'd with fever's violence;

     .   .   .   .

Think that thou hear'st thy knell, and think no more,
But that, as bells call'd thee to church before,
So this to the triumphant church calls thee.
Think Satan's sergeants round about thee be,
And think that but for legacies they thrust;
Give one thy pride, to another give thy lust;
Give them those sins which they gave thee before,
And trust th' immaculate blood to wash thy score.
Think thy friends weeping round, and think that they
Weep but because they go not yet thy way.
Think that they close thine eyes, and think in this,
That they confess much in the world amiss,
Who dare not trust a dead man's eye with that
Which they from God and angels cover not.
Think that they shroud thee up, and think from thence
They reinvest thee in white innocence.
Think that thy body rots, and — if so low,
Thy soul exalted so, thy thoughts can go —
Think thee a prince, who of themselves create
Worms, which insensibly devour their state.
Think that they bury thee, and think that rite
Lays thee to sleep but a Saint Lucy's night.'

After this magnificent passage Donne ᵒ   ᵖ in sinks
to the level of metaphysical argument. There recurs
the very same geometrical analogy which we have
already shown him using in a letter as illustrative of
the unity existing behind all diversity:

'though all do know, that quantities
Are made of lines, and lines from points arise,
None can these lines or quantities unjoint
And say, this is a line, or this a point.'

Once again too he proceeds to versify the evolutionary
theory of the soul's progress from a life of sense to one
of motion, and thence to one of reason, which had been
the theme of the 'Metempsychosis.' But having conducted the soul through the corrupt phases of the
body to its full degree of consciousness, he once more
breaks out into splendid poetry, in which the metaphors tumble over each other in lavish profusion. He
is speaking of the body:

'Think, when 'twas grown to most, 'twas a poor inn,
A province pack'd up in two yards of skin;
And that usurp'd, or threaten'd with a rage
Of sicknesses, or their true mother, age.
But think that death hath now enfranchised thee;
Thou hast thy expansion now, and liberty.
Think that a rusty piece, discharged, is flown
In pieces, and the bullet is his own,
And freely flies; this to thy soul allow.
Think thy shell broke, think thy soul hatch'd but now.
And think this slow-paced soul which late did cleave
To a body, and went but by the body's leave,
Twenty perchance, or thirty mile a day,
Dispatches in a minute all the way
'Twixt heaven and earth; she stays not in the air,
To look what meteors there themselves prepare;
She carries no desire to know, nor sense,
Whether th' air's middle region be intense;
For th' element of fire, she doth not know,
Whether she pass'd by such a place or no;
She baits not at the moon, nor cares to try
Whether in that new world men live, and die.'

N

This is the extravagance not of fancy but of imagination. Few poets have achieved so concrete a definition of that communion with the elements, for which the pent soul of man hungers in its intensest moments.

From this point, however, the poem descends to a more material level, and we become conscious both of logic and diffuseness. We have still, it is true, those pregnant lines in which the soul and body of womanhood, her warm beauty and her impalpable essence, are miraculously incorporated:

> 'her pure and eloquent blood
> Spoke in her cheeks, and so distinctly wrought
> That one might almost say, her body thought;'

which, in its likeness and yet immeasurable superiority to a decorative passage in 'The First Anniversary,' well illustrates the difference of degree between the two poems:

> 'she, in whom all white, and red, and blue
> (Beauty's ingredients) voluntary grew,
> As in an unvex'd paradise; from whom
> Did all things' verdure, and their lustre come;
> Whose composition was miraculous,
> Being all colour, all diaphanous,
> For air and fire but thick gross bodies were,
> And liveliest stones but drowsy and pale to her.'

The rest of the poem is mainly of biographical interest. It embodies Donne's discontent with scholasticism, ecclesiasticism and the corruptions of Court life. He emphasizes man's ignorance of the truths of life and death and sin —

'Poor soul, in this thy flesh what dost thou know?
Thou know'st thyself so little, as thou know'st not
How thou didst die, nor how thou wast begot.
Thou neither know'st how thou at first camest in,
Nor how thou took'st the poison of man's sin;
Nor dost thou – though thou know'st that thou art so –
By what way thou art made immortal, know.'

Yet ignorance is not advanced as a plea for scepticism,
but rather for the enthronement of intuition, or, as
Religion names it, faith, above logic's pedantries. We
see, he writes (and no one had more assiduously cultivated the vision than he),

       'in authors, too stiff to recant,
A hundred controversies of an ant;
And yet one watches, starves, freezes and sweats,
To know but catechisms and alphabets
Of unconcerning things, matters of fact. . . .'

From these he bids men turn and

       'up unto the watch-tower get,
And see all things despoil'd of fallacies;
Thou shalt not peep through lattices of eyes,
Nor hear through labyrinths of ears, nor learn
By circuit or collections to discern.
In heaven thou straight know'st all concerning it,
And what concerns it not shalt straight forget.'

To such a mystical vision how gross do 'spongy, slack
divines' appear, who

'Drink and suck in the instructions of great men,
  And for the word of God vent them again;'

how worthless to set by the side of those

> 'apostles, who did bravely run
> All the sun's course, with more light than the sun.'

The thought spurs him anew:

'Up, up,' (he cries), 'my drowsy soul, where thy new ear
Shall in the angels' song no discord hear;'

and among the angels is she whom he celebrates, as
surely a beatific vision as was Dante's Beatrice, in whom

> 'reason still
> Did not o'erthrow, but rectify her will;
> And she made peace, for no peace is like this,
> That beauty and chastity together kiss.'

To such a height has the puzzled sensualist attained,
and we have quoted at such length because not only
the greatness of this poem, but its biographical significance has been so generally overlooked, as a result of
its rather discreditable origin and the blatant artificiality of certain of its parts. But a poet is not judged by
his motive, but by its expressive consequence. Elizabeth Drury served Donne as the site on which not
only might his fancy rear a rococo chapel, but his
imagination the spires of a Gothic cathedral.

In the act of composing a flowery elegy, he consorted
with death; it was the key which unlocked his heart,
the idea about which his thoughts had been grouping
themselves for seven baffled years. The dissatisfactions
which we have traced in his letters, his search for a
religious metaphysic which would transcend without
transgressing reason, and save him from the horror of

the physical, poured themselves into the mould of
poetry. He discovered conviction in the act of expression, as later he did in the pulpit. His creative
instinct achieved the synthesis of which his analytical
mind had despaired. Religion suddenly 'made her a
church,' and he could cry triumphantly:

> 'All will not serve; only who have enjoy'd
> The sight of Good in fullness can think it;
> For it is both the object and the wit.
> This is essential joy, where neither He
> Can suffer diminution, nor we.'

By the same stages therefore as he had refined his
passion for woman did Donne heighten his consciousness of life. He ceased to fear it as a force, so long as
he realized it as an idea. But although the poet was
now in creative moments convinced of the reality of
God, his faith in the negative and critical periods which
intervened, was less assured. And while doubt invited
a bleak detachment from human interests, mystical
certainty encouraged a self-absorbed indifference. In
neither was the realist satisfied. To satisfy him it was
necessary to merge imaginative faith in some practical
activity.

It remained to be seen whether Donne could relate
his personal conviction to the doctrine of any estab-
lished Church, and whether circumstances would
urge him to make the attempt.

§ 3

By the year 1612 Donne, in an atmosphere unfavour-
able to introspection, had escaped temporarily from

moody discontent. In the previous year he had penned his last purely casuistical pamphlet, his *Ignatius his Conclave*, which was more in the nature of an ebullient skit aimed at the arrogance of the Jesuits than a serious piece of dialectic. Indeed, he felt the necessity of apologizing for the flippancy of its tone. Even the sentiments and associations which attached to the faith in which he was reared did not here restrain him from ribald abuse of the Pope. In Sir Robert Drury's house the worldling, and not the mystic or the casuist, was in the ascendant, and the following year was to increase his self-esteem.

Life took on colour and incident. Donne was now within the ring of privilege and influence, and his blend of intellectual brilliance and vivacity of physical address, was exactly suited to fascinate a society young enough to appreciate the violence of Nature behind the graces of aristocracy.

His attachment to his new master made it particularly necessary that he should soothe the resentment of earlier patrons. For he was far too conscious of the precariousness of rich men's favour to wish to alienate any one of them, and his anxiety concerning the publication of 'An Anatomy of the World' was chiefly lest the 'Great Ladies' should (in the manner of later critics) interpret his panegyric too literally, and consider their charms and virtues slighted by the act. He even felt it necessary to apologize to the Countess of Bedford for having 'to others lent your stock,' and to testify in some flagrantly artificial verses his 'true devotion, free from flattery.'

The diversions of his new life, contrasted with the

'dull monastic sadness' of the old, more and more
delighted him. An 'even, moderate mirth of heart
and face' – he was to write in a manner far from pastoral
– was not to be had 'by a general charity and equanimity
to all mankind . . . nor from a singular friend . . .
but the various and abundant grace of it is good
company.'

In November of 1611, however, Sir Robert Drury
decided to go abroad, and wished Donne to accompany
him. The domestic complications which ensued from
this abrupt decision have been affectingly described
by Walton. He recounts how Sir Robert's resolution
'was suddenly made known to Anne Donne, who was
then with child (her eighth), and otherwise under so
dangerous a habit of body as to her health, that she
professed an unwillingness to allow her husband any
absence from her, saying, "Her divining soul boded
her some ill in his absence," and therefore desired him
not to leave her. This made Mr. Donne lay aside all
thoughts of the journey, and really to resolve against
it.' Agitated, however, by his sense of duty to his
patron, he at last prevailed upon his wife 'with an un-
willing willingness, to give a faint consent to the
journey, which was proposed to be but for two months,'
but actually extended to considerably more. It was
arranged for Anne to stay with friends or relatives in
the Isle of Wight, and, not without sore misgivings,
Donne accompanied his patron.

This incident and its sequel confirms all we have
said of Donne's deep attachment for his wife – an
emotion which needed only to embrace all life for his
religious education to be complete.

Parting from a mistress had in the past excited Donne to some of his bitterest satire and his most fantastic flights of metaphor. Very different in quality are the two poems which, if we are to believe Walton, the present occasion inspired. 'A Valediction Forbidding Mourning,' while it contains those loveliest of lines:

'So let us melt, and make no noise,
   No tear-floods, nor sigh-tempests move;
'Twere profanation of our joys
   To tell the laity our love,'

is also marked by such exquisite but complex ingenuity as:

'Our two souls therefore, which are one,
   Though I must go, endure not yet
A breach, but an expansion,
   Like gold to airy thinness beat,'

and ends with the oft-quoted geometrical simile, which compares the distant lovers to the two feet of a pair of compasses.

But the lines which Donne probably wrote after parting from his wife are truer in tone; they have that finely phrased simplicity, that delicate tenderness so different from delicate conceit, which we associate with the sincerest feeling. They are religious as Wordsworth is when he ceases to be didactic:

'Sweetest love, I do not go
   For weariness of thee,
Nor in hope the world can show
   A fitter love for me;

But since that I
At the last must part, 'tis best,
Thus to use myself in jest
By feigned deaths to die.

'Yesternight the sun went hence,
And yet is here to-day;
He hath no desire nor sense,
Nor half so short a way;
Then fear not me,
But believe that I shall make
Speedier journeys, since I take
More wings and spurs than he.

.   .   .   .

'When thou sigh'st, thou sigh'st not wind,
But sigh'st my soul away;
When thou weep'st, unkindly kind,
My life's blood doth decay.
It cannot be
That thou lovest me as thou say'st,
If in thine my life thou waste,
That art the best of me.

'Let not thy divining heart
Forethink me any ill;
Destiny may take thy part,
And may thy fears fulfil.
But think that we
Are but turn'd aside to sleep.
They who one another keep
Alive, ne'er parted be.'

In very truth 'out of the strong' was 'come forth sweetness,' and dramatic proof of the unity of spirit existing between Donne and his wife was shortly forthcoming.

The Drurys, with Donne in attendance, left London late in November, and after spending three months at Amiens, moved on to Paris. Donne suffered much anxiety, having heard as yet no news 'whether I am increased by the birth of a child, or diminished by the loss of a wife.' So active a fancy as his must have conjectured every kind of disaster. Sir Robert, returning unexpectedly one day, found Donne alone and clearly shaken by some startling experience. He begged him to explain what had happened, and, to quote Walton's words, 'after a long and perplexed pause,' he answered, 'I have seen a dreadful vision since I saw you; I have seen my dear wife pass twice by me through this room, with her hair hanging about her shoulders, and a dead child in her arms: this I have seen since I saw you.' Sir Robert was convinced that Donne had been dreaming, and advised him to be easy in his mind. But Donne persisted in his story, adding that on a second appearance his wife 'stopped and looked me in the face and vanished.'

Sleep did not alter his opinion, and after twelve days a messenger corroborated his vision by bringing news that he had 'found Mrs. Donne very sad and sick in her bed; and that, after a long and dangerous labour, she had been delivered of a dead child.' The day of the vision and of this sad event coincided. Walton's comment is as perfect in its poetry as its reticence: 'And though it is most certain that two lutes, being both strung and tuned to an equal pitch, and then one played upon, the other that is not touched being laid upon a table at a fit distance, will, like an echo to a trumpet, warble a faint audible harmony in answer to the same tune, yet many will not believe there is any such thing as a sympathy of souls; and I am well pleased that every reader do enjoy his own opinion.'

During the months which Sir Robert and Lady Drury spent abroad, Donne was a very assiduous correspondent with those exalted friends whose favour he wished to preserve against the time of his return. He was unwearied in messages of devotion to his Twickenham Countess, and his reiterated entreaties in prose and verse to various acquaintances to 'continue him' in somebody's 'good opinion,' or 'carry remembrance of his humblest services,' become a trifle craven. Doubtless every age has its epistolary euphuisms, and it is often very difficult to know when Donne is merely voicing the conventional courtesies of the day and when he is lowering himself to politic obsequiousness. But that he was often guilty of the latter there can be no doubt, and more and more we lose sight of that abrupt independence which at one time had been the fatal, but admirable, essence of the man.

Only too well had Donne now learnt the wisdom of worldly discretion. Having for the time rejected the Cloister and set his hopes on the Court, he was prepared, in pursuit of his purpose, as we shall see, even to descend to disreputable concerns. The truth was that panic was beginning to affect him. He was no longer young; he had a tantalizing host of influential friends, and great abilities, but he had no certain place in life. At any moment he and his ever-multiplying

family might once more be cast adrift on an open sea.
The security which middle age enthrones above all the
virtues had begun to allure even this doughty adventurer, and to its attainment he was to sacrifice with
growing desperation his dignity as a man, his gifts as
a poet, and at last the scruples of his conscience.

'I am now,' he wrote, 'in the afternoon of my life, and
then it is an unwholesome time to sleep. It is ill to
look back, or give over in a course; but worse never to
set out.'

The time, he felt, was drawing on when it would be
too late to set out. Every day tended to diminish his
chances of obtaining a remunerative appointment.
Already another hungry generation was treading upon
his heels, and his talents had reached their normal
meridian.

The taste too of 'high life,' which his position as a
rich man's attendant afforded him, served to whet his
appetite. He was strangely blended of the hermit and
the man who delighted in affairs, and now for the first
time since he was outlawed from York House the latter
received ample sustenance.

Consequently political gossip takes the place of the
'subtleties and spinosities' of theological argument, in
his letters. Kings, princes, and diplomats are of more
concern to him than the Deity. French theology, during his stay in Paris in 1612, was passing through a
most interesting reactionary phase, and more than one
eloquent Gallican divine had emerged to dispute the
claims of Protestantism. Two years previously we
should have expected Donne to be absorbed in the
controversy, to have listened to their oratory and filled

his letters with challenging comment; yet not a word on this topic survives amid the chatter of diplomacy, although the opinion expressed in Amiens that 'French papistry is but like French velvet – a pretty slack Religion, that would soon wear out,' must in Paris have received a startling refutation.

But theology at the time had ceased to offer any practical solution of his problems, while his personal religion had grown independent of it. He studied rather to better his legal status, taking up the threads which the improvident law-student of twenty had so carelessly thrown aside. He even wrote to his old theological patron Morton, consulting him as to 'whether the taking of the degree of a doctor of Law might be conducible and advantageous unto him to practise at home in the Arches, London.'

And as his thoughts waxed worldly, his spirits bounded up; no longer was life a graveyard riddled with worms. 'I learn,' he wrote, 'that there is truth and firmness and earnestness of doing good alive in the world; and therefore, since there is so good company in it, I have not so much desire to go out of it, as I had if my fortune would afford me any room in it. You know I have been no coward, nor unindustrious in attempting that; nor will I give it over yet.' The beneficial effect of the Baths at Aix confirmed his resolution.

Life, in short, in the comfortable company of Sir Robert Drury, was exhilarating; and in recounting the arrival of the Duke of Espernon's cavalcade in Paris, the various calls on the Queen's privy purse, or the darker traits of the King's character, there was considerably more 'relish of mirth' than

Mitcham even in its happiest moments had supplied.

In June the Drurys moved from Paris to Spa, intending to return home late in August, after passing through Antwerp and parts of Holland. But their plans for various reasons were changed. Sir Robert was now engaged on an informal embassy, connected with the contemplated marriage between the young Elector Palatine of Bohemia and that Princess Elizabeth whom Donne had probably known as a child, when Lord Harrington was her guardian, for whom he was to compose an 'Epithalamium,' and before whom, after she was wed to fatal fortunes, he was later to preach. In so far as this fostered the illusion of being engaged in distinguished diplomatic work, it made the idea of relapsing into unregarded privacy only the more intolerable.

The party returned to London in the early autumn, and Donne was unpleasantly aware that he had entered on his fortieth year. His free apartments at Drury House were agreeable enough, had they not seemed at times akin to stage scenery, which might be dismantled at a moment's notice, should the play cease to draw, or the producer meet with a fatal accident. Sir George More continued to pay his allowance, but a spendthrift and scarcely devoted father-in-law did not inspire confidence. And his wife was in no condition to face the rigours of another Mitcham life. She was the tired mother of a large family, still to be increased, and renewed poverty might well prove fatal to her fragility. Between Donne and such a disaster only two men stood, and both might fail him. He was still at the mercy of circumstance.

And so once again the contrast between the lively and prosperous society into which he plunged, and the loaned chambers at Drury House, crowded with children and presided over by a dispirited wife, made itself felt.

Despite the numbers of his family, he returned home as to some ominous solitude, and anxiety drove him to redouble his efforts to obtain a reliable appointment. The pending marriage of the popular Princess Elizabeth with the Elector Palatine offered him an opportunity of engaging the attention of the Court, and when the sudden death of her brother, the young Prince of Wales, delayed the marriage for some months, he embraced the sad theme with the same readiness as the glad. The results, however, were somewhat different in quality. His Elegy upon the 'Incomparable' Prince is a laboured piece of fustian.

He was in no mood to celebrate death, having so recently and sublimely exhausted his powers on the subject. His hopes and fears were now set on life. 'Heaven is expressed by singing,' he wrote, 'Hell by weeping,' and certainly in this Elegy there is not a single thrust of genius, not a single vivid image, to relieve the drab and eccentric obscurity.

How different is the Marriage Song dedicated in the following February to the radiant Princess! Here the compelling rhythm, the gleeful naturalism, immodest and yet innocent as in some of Goethe's 'Lieder,' fill with life alike the complicated structure, the recondite fancy, and the inevitable Platonism. The poem is both concentrated and garrulous, and no trace either of the Puritan or the Pagan discolours the buoyant stream.

This, we may fancy, was the Donne who in his happiest moments charmed with high, poetic spirits an appreciative society, forgetful of the cares of an overburdened family man. There is a tragic fitness too in the fact that the ill-starred Frederick and his adorable bride should have earned on their wedding-day so incomparable a pæan to the joy and innocence of life; and could we believe the theory that 'The Tempest' also was written to grace their nuptials, their subsequent ejection from Bohemia would seem but the inevitable Nemesis for so unexampled a distinction.

Donne's poem is so real, because the gentle, high-spirited Elizabeth, 'th' eclipse and glory of her kind,' awoke in him the same homage as he felt for the Countess of Bedford, and with it all the extravagant worship of youth and innocence natural to a perplexed middle age, still troubled with romantic cravings. To this devotion, reinforced later by a tender religious concern, he always remained faithful, and as he failed her in her happiness, so he was to comfort her in time of disaster.

His poetic loyalty, however, made no apparent impression upon the Court, and it seemed as if the King were still determined that Donne should do penance for his youthful indiscretions. Donne tried to still his anxieties by frequent journeying, now in the Isle of Wight, now at Bath, now at Windsor, and he turned to his old narcotics, Oriental and Spanish literature, and the Law.

Meanwhile he ventured a daring cast. Within two months of his return from abroad he had begun to reconsider the Church as a possible profession; instead, however, of confiding his idea to his old friend Morton or to some other clerical dignitary, he resorted to a man of worldly rather than religious pre-eminence. He aimed high, only to fall low.

For some years now a young adventurer, who had once under the name of Robert Ker belonged to the household of Donne's friend, Lord Hay, had been climbing to power in the Court. By 1611 he stood alone in the King's affections; he was made Viscount Rochester, and on the death of Salisbury in the spring of 1612, succeeded informally to the state, if not the office, of Lord Treasurer. With much capacity for intrigue, handsome and unscrupulous, this Favourite was at twenty-seven the key to the desired chamber of superlative patronage. To him in October, 1612, Donne addressed himself. Perhaps in thus combining a secular approach with a clerical objective, he strove to conceal from himself the full implications of his surrender, or even cherished a hope, well founded as events were to prove, that Rochester's patronage would take other than an ecclesiastical direction.

'Having obeyed,' he wrote, 'at last, after much debatement within me, the inspirations (as I hope) of the Spirit of God, and resolved to make my profession Divinity; I make account, that I do but tell your Lordship, what God hath told me, which is, that it is in this course, if in any, that my service may be of use to this Church and State. Since then your Lordship's virtues have made you so near the head in the one, and so religious a member of the other, I came to this courage, of thrusting myself thus into your Lordship's presence, both in respect that I was an independent and disobliged man, towards any other person in the State;

o

and delivered over now (in my resolution) to be a household servant of God.'

The 'inspiration of the Spirit of God,' we cannot but feel, had almost as little to do with the dictation of this letter as it had with the private and public character of Rochester. Donne's sudden 'resolution of a new course of life and new profession' was secular in its motive. To Lord Hay indeed he was more candid, writing that after bringing all his distractions together, he had concluded that in divinity 'a fortune may either be better made, or, at least, better missed, than in any other.'

Donne was neither the first nor the last to accept the Church as a profession and convert it later into a vocation, and the readiness with which he now allowed himself to be deflected from his course shows how material his aim was. Rochester, knowing by repute Donne's legal abilities, and needing at the time a secret but competent counsel, dissuaded him from entering the Church. He was in the midst of that infatuation for the Countess of Essex which was to work his ruin. She wished to obtain a divorce from her husband to enable her to marry Rochester; and knowing, as even her opponents could not then, the sinister evidence which might arise to prejudice a nullity suit, she found it desirable to enrol on her side, without undue publicity, the acutest legal intelligence. Donne's dialectical powers had been notably attested in his anti-recusant pamphlets, and Rochester soon discovered that, despite the revivalist tone of his first letter, a promise of later Court preferment was enough to persuade Donne to put his mind at the service of a woman whom he must

have guessed to be immoral, and who was eventually
proved to be criminal. He admitted, in fact, with entire
complacence that Rochester had 'bought' him, adding
that 'You may have many better bargains in your pur-
chases, but never a better title than to me, nor anything
which you may call yours more absolutely and entirely
than me.'

The bill is candidly drawn up by the expectant and
obsequious creditor, and Donne's humiliation is
scarcely lessened by the fact that for long Rochester
failed even partially to honour it.

Thus Donne's first approach to the Church brought
consequences in the last degree unclerical, and his
readiness to sell himself to Rochester cannot even be
condoned, as it might later have been, as the act of a
man rendered desperate by anxiety and sickness. The
incident is but another example of the deteriorating
effect of unemployment or parasitism on character.
A man who for years has been unable to adjust his
powers to any environment, who is conscious of his
forlorn status in the world, is willing to pay almost
any price for a ticket of entrance into its favoured
circle. The exile is inevitably kin to the outlaw. So it
was with Donne: he staked his integrity on a desperate
cast, and he lost.

Yet it is comforting to have evidence that the stain
was purely superficial. The heart of the man was un-
corrupted by any commercial enterprises, and his
religion was independent of Church or Court.

Riding on Good Friday of 1613 from his friend Goodyer at Polesworth to visit the Herberts at Montgomery
Castle, he doffed the sordid trivialities of intrigue in

which he was engaged – that 'pleasure or business' by which he lamented that men's souls were so pitifully 'hurried and whirl'd,' and 'being grown subject to foreign motion, lose their own' – and implored pardon for the debasement to which he had submitted.

'O Saviour, as Thou hang'st upon the tree,
I turn my back to Thee but to receive
Corrections till Thy mercies bid Thee leave.
O think me worth thine anger, punish me,
Burn off my rust, and my deformity;
Restore Thine image, so much, by Thy grace,
That Thou mayst know me, and I'll turn my face.'

Magdalen Herbert disposed him to devout resolution. She was not of the world as his Twickenham goddess was. Yet, capable as Donne was of rising at moments to the full height of his spiritual stature, he was too deeply involved in a worldly course to turn back. Montgomery Castle was but a fair retreat from the stress of intrigue, a retreat in which poetry blossomed as naturally as did obsequious letters in the world of fashion. On this occasion, taking the primrose as a symbol of beauty, innocence and intelligence, he associates it with the person of his hostess. Playful as are the poem's conceits, like those of St. Francis, they are flowers of perfect sincerity and devotion, delicately flushed and fragrant with emotion, frail and fluctuant as the air itself. It is a love-poem 'above all thought of sex,' a humble tribute to the inanimate spirit of womanhood.

But his happiness was the peace before the storm. He returned to London, not only to submit once more to the chains of Rochester, but also to succumb to serious sickness.

During his stay in France he had suffered an attack of fever, and so early as March, 1613, had reported his recovery from a short bout of illness in the old dismal dialect of Mitcham: 'I begin to be past hope of dying.' But in July the attack fell upon him which heralded the second dark period in his life, and urged him, protesting all the while, away from the secular world upon which he had set his hopes, into those regions of imaginative hope and realistic horror, where he was to end his days.

Perhaps severe sickness was a necessary initiation before so physical a personality would submit to a spiritual vocation. Poverty and neglect, alleviated as they had been, were not enough to force the issue. Drury House had in its turn to justify the title of 'my Hospital,' and that over an agonizing period, before the valiant egoist surrendered. From the midsummer of 1613 until the end of the following year, gastritis, rheumatism, ophthalmia, and the loss of three children, did their best and worst. It was a nightmare from which the worldly Donne, strive as he did until the last to avoid the inevitable, never really recovered. He was driven back into that 'reclusedness,' of which the 'disease and impotency' of his fortune were the dread preoccupation.

§ 4

At first, however, Donne lived on his hopes of Rochester. In June, largely through his subtle advocacy, the Commission granted the Countess of Essex her nullity

suit. Now surely Rochester would redeem his promises: and to strengthen his claims Donne completed
the 'Epithalamium,' part of which he had already composed before even the divorce was assured, presenting
it to the bride and bridegroom – somewhat euphemis-
tically entitled 'Blest pair of swans' – on the flaunting
celebration of their marriage in December, 1613. The
Marriage Song itself is little more than a composite
of flagrant flattery, ingenuous ornament and carnal
convention. But the pastoral introduction is of real
personal significance.

It is in the form of a dialogue between Idios and
Allophanes, the one upholding the virtue of a monastic
life, the other the charms of the Court. It is thus an
argument and apology conducted between the two
sides of Donne's nature, the religious soul and the
worldling, and the latter is the more convincing dis-
putant. Donne, in short, pays a politic tribute here to
the meretricious glitter of Court life, which he had so
often in earlier letters assessed at its true value. In the
hope of sharing at no distant time in the pageant of
Court functions, or in his desire to impress upon
Rochester how appreciative he would be of such a
privilege, he managed to extol even in the person of
his hermit Idios,

> 'those courts, whose princes animate
> Not only all their house but all their state,'

or in the words of Allophanes,

> 'from God religion springs,
> Wisdom and honour from the use of kings; . . .
> What hast thou lost, O ignorant man?'

He could not be more explicit, and yet his efforts bore
no fruit. The King disregarded his egregious compliments, and Rochester, now elevated to the title of
Somerset, preserved a discreet silence. 'I cannot tell
you,' wrote Donne to Sir Robert Drury, 'so much, as
you tell me, of anything from my Lord of Somerset
since the Epithalamium, for I have heard nothing.'

Throughout the dismal months of 1614 Donne
waited, ill, expectant, irritated. He hinted his claims
to Somerset in letter after letter, at first tactful and
deprecatory, but with a growing urgency which desperation at last clothed with candour.

Meanwhile he did not neglect his services elsewhere;
and in composing his 'Obsequies' in honour of Lord
Harrington, the Countess of Bedford's young brother,
personal affection, and the mystical fervour which
suffering had already awakened, enabled him to pro-
duce something more than ceremonial verse. Writing
at midnight, 'time's dead low water,' his thoughts
wavered between the sublunary conception that his
friend

'now dost bear
A part in God's great organ, this whole sphere,'

and the simpler sense of unseasonable loss:

'O soul, O circle, why so quickly be
Thy ends, thy birth and death, closed upon thee?'

In March an ambassadorship at Venice was likely to
fall vacant, and he begged Somerset to obtain it for him,
but the favourite's bounty did not extend beyond a small
gift of money to stay the importunity of creditors.

Soon after, in a letter to Sir Robert Drury, Donne described the plight of his household in almost identical
terms with those addressed to Sir Henry Goodyer, from
'my Hospital at Mitcham' five years before; indeed the
verbal similarity tempts us either to doubt the accuracy
of the lugubrious picture, or to suppose that Walton
in error attributed the passage quoted on page 149 to
an earlier occasion.

Yet things were bad enough. In May, to quote his
own words, he 'paid death one of my children for
ransom,' while his wife was prostrated by the birth of
another. The Epigram which he entitled 'Niobe' was
becoming applicable to himself:

> 'By children's births, and death, I am become
> So dry, that I am now mine own sad tomb.'

Like some reiterated dirge, now petulant, now resigned, letter followed letter from 'my poor hospital,'
telling of sickness without intermission, of beds that
are as well-named graves, of ten-day fasts and fevers,
and of imminent delirium.

With agitated servility Donne commended himself
to the memory of every Lord and Lady of his acquaintance, and at last, as the year advanced without any sign of a secular move on Somerset's part, he
reverted despairingly to his original plea. He begged
for religious preferment, if his lordly creditor were
'incapable of the favours . . . purposed to me.' He
added:

'I humbly beg . . . that after you shall have pleased
to admit into your memory that I am now a year older,
broken with some sickness . . . your Lordship will

afford me one commandment, and bid me either
hope for this business . . . or else pursue my first
purpose or abandon all.' He signed himself with
abject defiance: 'One who is by his own devotion
and your purchase your Lordship's most humble
and thankful servant.'

Somerset, however, seemed as loath to pay in the
clerical coin as in the secular.

Amid this depressing solicitation it is refreshing to
hear for a moment the tones of the true man. Poor,
distracted Anne Donne must have been less and less
of a companion to her husband during these months,
as the shadows deepened about her afflicted life; yet
his loyalty shows no signs of waning.

'When I begin to apprehend,' he wrote, 'that, even to
myself, who can relieve myself upon books, solitariness
was a little burdenous, I believe it would be much
more so to my wife, if she were left alone. So much
company, therefore, as I am, she shall not want; and
we had not one another at so cheap a rate, as that we
should ever be weary of one another.'

That he was disgusted, too, at the mendicant rôle he
was compelled to play is clear. He entitled himself
bitterly enough in one letter 'such an impertinency, as
I am.' Nevertheless, it was a sad blow to him when
even his Lady of Twickenham had to refuse financial
help. There were good reasons for her so doing, but
Donne was in no condition to view the matter im-
partially. If she could desert him, it was indeed useless
to put faith in any patron. The world, which he had
wooed so assiduously, to which he had prostituted his
manhood, even his honour, was surely rejecting its

hireling; yet still the glitter of the Court allured. 'No man,' he wrote, 'attends Court fortunes with more impatience than I do.' This impatience became almost hysterical as the year drew to its close; for two events occurred which promised to reduce his fortunes to a last extremity. Sir Robert Drury's health showed signs of failing, and rumour had it that Somerset was losing the King's favour. Upon the one he depended for sustenance, upon the other for preferment.

Panic drove him to adopt more truculent tactics. In November he wrote to Somerset reminding him that he himself had not 'hunted after' the business of the nullity suit, but that, having accepted it, he had carried it through with notable efficiency. He requested in polite terms that his debtor would speedily meet the bill.

It would be an exaggeration to call such a letter blackmail. Yet Donne must have known that Somerset was at this moment to some extent at his mercy: he too was approaching a crisis in his affairs, and he was most anxious not to add to his embarrassments. Donne might conceivably turn the knowledge which he possessed of his patron's past history to inconvenient uses. Whether this, or only weariness, or even a tardy compunction was the motive, it is impossible to say. But Somerset summoned Donne immediately to meet the King in Essex.

§ 5

When Donne presented himself in hot haste at Theobald's, where the King was in residence, Somerset met him in the garden with news that one of the Clerks of the Council had just died, and began to advise patience.

But Donne would accept no more prevarication, and Somerset yielded. He told Donne to wait in the garden until he had persuaded the King to appoint him to the vacant Clerkship; 'doubt not my doing this,' he added, 'for I know the King loves you, and know the King will not deny me.'

His confidence was, however, misplaced. The King's relations with his favourite had reached that point when as much pleasure was to be derived from refusing a request as previously had lain in gratifying one. He answered Somerset abruptly: 'I know Mr. Donne is a learned man, has the abilities of a learned divine, and will prove a successful preacher; and my desire is to prefer him in that way.'

For once James I showed real insight into character, and it proves how little Somerset had concerned himself, that, although he had been at least twice requested by Donne to interest the King in his clerical preferment, it was left to the King himself 'to descend to a persuasion, almost to a solicitation of him, to enter into sacred orders.'

Donne required little persuasion. Years later he could write: 'When I sit still and reckon all my old Master's royal favours to me, I return ever more to that – that he first inclined me to be a minister.'

Yet the King's part in this business was only the culmination of a process. He but cut the ribbons, and the ship which had been so many years a-building, released from its secular slips, gathered motion and launched itself. For appearance' sake Donne veiled his readiness to leap at the proposal and begged for some days to consider it and examine his qualifications; but in truth the die was cast. No other course was open to a desperate man. His secular hopes were in ruins: there only remained the profession against which he had so long rebelled as an idea, but to which now he must submit as a fact.

If circumstances were the deciding factor, the step was in a deeper sense miraculously opportune. The Ministry of the English Church achieved almost immediately a practical, and gradually a spiritual solution of his problems. It healed, as nearly as was possible with so violently dualistic a nature, the discord between the worldling and the mystic, the realist and the idealist, the casuist and the seer. 'The Divine Sonnets' which he was shortly to write, the 'Devotions' and the noble periods of his sermons are the ripe harvest of a life prodigally sown, the compositions in which the whole man, Dionysiac and Calvinistic, is at last completely and harmoniously expressive. He could not adapt himself to the change in a day. It needed in fact yet another agony of mind and of body to wean him wholly from the world, and death only could wean him from the flesh.

Walton therefore once again hastens on the time of his subject's holiness when he writes: 'Now, all his earthly affections were changed into divine love.'

None knew better than Donne that any conversion which pretends to a complete break with the past cannot but be fraudulent. Psychology refutes such a miracle.

'Thou art the same materials, as before,
Only the stamp is changed, but no more.'

Conversion may mean a sudden sublimation of a man's powers, but it cannot imply their contradiction; indeed too often it has only meant a translation of egoism into terms of despotic morality or prejudiced dogma. As Donne was to repeat constantly from the pulpit: 'Men do not change their passions, but only the objects of them. . . . God loves renovations, not innovations,' or, 'a covetous person converted will be spiritually covetous still. So will a voluptuous man, who is turned to God, find plenty and deliciousness in Him, to feed his soul, as with marrow and fatness.'

Donne did not then 'break out to an imaginary, and intempestive, and unseasonable Reformation'; he remained essentially 'a poison'd fountain' still, but the poison in his blood had an active vent; it no longer accumulated in self-consuming spleen. The King had prescribed better than he knew, and Donne was soon to acknowledge it.

'Joy,' he told a congregation, 'is peace for having done that which we ought to have done. . . . To have something to do, to do it, and then to Rejoice in having done it, to embrace a calling, to perform the Duties of that calling, to joy and rest in the peaceful testimony of having done so; this is Christianity done, Christ did it; Angelically done, Angels do it; Godly done, God does it.'

§ 6

Early in December he returned to London to prepare for ordination. He was anxious lest any rumour of his connection with Somerset should have reached the ears of ecclesiastical dignitaries, and particularly those of

the Archbishop of Canterbury, a man of somewhat
rigid piety. To quieten any suspicions which the
Archbishop might entertain, he hastened to compose
and dispatch to him a short set of 'Essays in Divinity,'
models of dull and learned propriety. He concluded
with four prayers, the first authentic utterance of that
devotion which he was to modulate through countless
keys. The 'music of a sinner, when he prays' he had
already preferred in verse to 'panegyric alleluias'; increasingly he found this 'shaking hands with God' a
necessary and consoling means of self-escape, and if his
Sermons are the Preludes and Fugues of his later life,
his Prayers may be fittingly called the Chorales.
Among these, one of his earliest is certainly not the
least beautiful:

'I beseech Thee that since, by Thy grace, I have long
meditated upon Thee, and spoken of Thee, I may now
speak to Thee. As Thou hast enlightened and enlarged
me to contemplate Thy greatness, so, O God, descend
Thou and stoop down to see my infirmities and the
Egypt in which I live, and, if Thy good pleasure be
such, hasten mine exodus and deliverance, for I desire
to be dissolved and be with Thee. . . . Hourly Thou
in Thy Spirit descendest into my heart to overthrow
these legions of spirits of disobedience and incredulity
and murmuring. . . . Thou hast given me a desire of
knowledge, and some means to it, and some possession
of it; and I have armed myself with Thy weapons
against Thee. . . . But let me, in despite of me, be
now of so much use to Thy glory, that by Thy mercy
to my sin, other sinners may see how much sin Thou
canst pardon.'

Plainly, although material considerations dictated the step, the Church had here a convert essentially sincere. Such words as these do but in fact take up in a religious dialect the burden of mystical vision which Donne had already borne so high in his 'Anatomy of the World.' There is the same deprecation of intellect, the same invocation of death, the same ecstatic consciousness of sin to be lived down. Donne's ordination implied no sudden elevation from mundane affairs. The argument which he had conducted with himself so long is continued, with this difference only, that it is related to an accepted idea of God, and that a purely private conflict became a public battle, witnessed by awestruck congregations.

Donne, the preacher, rolling forth his great periods on sin and death and God, analysing with an almost diabolic intricacy the refinements of lust and fear and ambition, is no less the historian of his own experience than was the poet of the early lyrics. It is as if another Rousseau declaimed his 'Confessions' in open assembly, announcing himself 'a volume of diseases bound up together.'

The conflict between hunger and recrimination, between the Pagan and the Puritan, was certainly less agonizing henceforth, because Donne, by surrendering himself to a God outside himself, to an embodied idea of life, tempered his self-consciousness. He could lean upon Him in his worst moments, and exult more confidently in his best, through having an accepted image in which to incorporate his distracted ideas. As when he so miraculously said:

'The contemplation of God, and heaven, is a kind of

burial, and Sepulchre, and rest of the soul; and in this death of rapture, and ecstasy, in this death of the contemplation of my interest in my Saviour, I shall find myself, and all my sins enterred, and entombed in his wounds, and like a Lily in Paradise, out of red earth, I shall see my soul rise out of his blade, in a candour, and in an innocence, contracted there, acceptable in the sight of his Father.'

But this confidence was never assured. 'Deceive not yourselves,' he said in another place, 'with that new charm and flattery of the soul, that if once you can say to yourselves you have faith, you need no more, or that you shall always keep that alive.'

He himself had to fight to the end against gnawing doubts and odious appetites, and, as we shall see, preaching became for him so triumphant a passion ·because it was only by aggressive and expressive action that he could purge his mind of terror; while it was because his congregations were always conscious of a man in very truth fighting for his life in the pulpit that they sat spellbound beneath his oratory.

But this was scarcely yet, although Donne was not long in preparing himself. He had written without delay to an old friend Dr. King, the Bishop of London, informing him of his determination, and on the 25th of January, 1615, being fittingly enough the Feast of the Conversion of St. Paul, he was ordained and attached as curate to the parish of Paddington.

§ 7

Donne, however, was far from concentrating all his thoughts at first on a spiritual vocation. A curacy was

not calculated to relieve him of his debts; the Countess
of Bedford had failed him, and Sir Robert Drury was
on the point of death. Lady Huntingdon now stepped
into the void and earned the inevitable complimentary
verses, and the assurance that he would 'reserve for her
delight not only all the verses, which I should make,
but all the thoughts of women's worthiness.'

But if Donne preserved some of the vices of the lay
mind, he also preserved its virtues. He donned no
professional prejudices with his surplice, nor did he
assume that the Church of his adoption was the sole
repository of truth. 'The channels of God's mercies,'
he still affirmed, 'run through both fields; and they are
sister teats of His graces . . .' He was too vital to be
either sanctimonious or sectarian.

Strangely enough he approached his task as a preacher
with great diffidence. The dialectician was at first
unnerved by the sound of his own voice in a public
silence, and the poet in him was not yet sufficiently
roused to sweep self-consciousness and even sophistry
away. On the 30th of April he preached before the
Queen at Greenwich, and it is hard to believe, although
it is an extreme example of his self-confession, that
when he gave out his text: 'Thus saith the Lord, Ye
have sold yourselves for naught; and ye shall be re-
deemed without money,' no fugitive thought of his
transactions with Somerset lurked in his mind. What
adds likelihood to such a conjecture is that during
these months, after his appointment as Court Chaplain, Donne must have been an eyewitness of the
favourite's decline from power and ultimate disgrace,
and his own, fortunately secret, connection with the

criminal scandal which accompanied it, must have caused him grave anxiety.

When therefore he was called to preach his first sermon before the King at Whitehall, he strained every effort to create a favourable impression. And clearly he succeeded beyond all expectation.

The figure who mounted the pulpit in these early days of his ministry was not the spectral divine, the emaciated, almost sardonic mystic, who was later to hypnotize his audience by the reverberations of his eloquence, the intensities of his imagination, and the sepulchral tones of his voice. He was a man, despite the ravages of ill-health, still in his prime, his beard indeed touched with grey, but in face and carriage retaining that air of buccaneering insolence, almost of dignified roguery, which we have remarked in the young man. Arrayed in vestments and uplifted by the sense of an august occasion, his appearance must have been singularly striking, suggesting indeed some challenging John the Baptist or one of Dürer's swarthy evangelists. At the same time he did not forget the courtier in the priest. There was a 'sacred flattery' in his address, which if it 'beguiled men to amend,' also gratified their vanity. His learning was beyond dispute, but the crabbed style of his correspondence, no less than the angular conceits of his poetry, could scarcely have prepared his friends for the miracle of eloquence which he was speedily to achieve, pungent, rhythmical, varied, and, even in its passages of scholastic argument, strangely sinuous and compelling.

The poet and the prose-writer came together in the pulpit, eliminating each other's faults and wedding the virtues. The abstract thought discovered its appropriate image under the stimulus of an emotion transcending anything that Donne had yet experienced. The 'naked, thinking heart' was at last sumptuously apparelled, the rough edges of his too masculine temper rounded by reverence and softened by faith.

The King was entranced by this preacher, in whom even the dead bones of theology clothed themselves with comeliness, and who made metaphysics and morality into an epic poem: while without any clerical unction he yet paid his service to God with something of the considered grace, the gesture and formality of the courtier.

From this moment Donne's career was made. The King insisted that each University should confer on his Chaplain its Doctorate of Divinity, and in the following year he presented him with two livings which, according to the convenient custom of pluralities, assured him a comfortable competence with the minimum of responsibility. In October, 1616, however, he was elected to a position which engaged his powers to the full for some years, proving an ideal, if exacting school for the great preacher: the Benchers of Lincoln's Inn appointed him their Divinity Reader. To preach two sermons on every Sunday during term and one on every other, and that before an invariably critical and learned audience, was no sinecure. Yet Donne was happy to accept the office, both because his mind was so well suited by training and aptitude to expound theology to lawyers, and for the devotion which he cherished for the haunt of his youth, a sentiment which the Society of the Inn cordially recipro-

cated. Moreover, the post was among the most lucrative in London, and, entailing as it did 'fair and newly
furnished lodgings with all necessaries,' supplied him
with just such a place of solitude as he needed, when he
wished to escape the bustle of domestic life.

How Donne housed his family after Sir Robert
Drury's death in 1616, we do not know. His wife
bore him another daughter and eleventh child in this
year, and in August, 1617, she died, a week after giving
birth to another still-born infant.

Thus Donne won to wealth and security too late for
his much-enduring wife to profit by it. Anne Donne
plays indeed a pitiable enough part in her husband's
stormy history. There is something infinitely pathetic
about her reticence. She never emerges from domestic
obscurity. From the day when she joined her lot so
recklessly with that of her impetuous lover, we know
of her sufferings only through his, and that but in
intermittent glimpses.

Yet if ever there was an appealing figure, it is hers,
quietly loyal to the life which, once it had seized her,
allowed her no respite until it had broken her. Always
behind the morbid fancies and self-accusations, the
frantic frivolities and ponderous sententiousness of her
husband's letters, we feel the eloquence of her silence.

It may be, as Walton wrote, that Donne's marriage
was 'the remarkable error of his life,' yet we can believe
that his wife suffered for it more than he. And now his
grief was barbed with bitter remorse. For her, always
delicate, and worn out by incessant child-bearing, rest,
even of death, cannot have been unwelcomed. But on
him, reviewing in forlorn retrospect the whole tale of

their passion, from its ebullient, disastrous preface, through drab years of domestic difficulty to this, its exhausted conclusion, there settled an overwhelming sorrow. He had succeeded too late to recompense her in anything save a loyal affection, save that communion of soul, of which he said:

> 'we were mutual elements to us,
> And made of one another.'

Doubtless it never occurred to Donne that a communion of soul which imposed maternity with such ruthless regularity on a delicate woman, in straitened circumstances, was somewhat lacking in mundane, yet human, consideration. But now the consequences of his insatiable egoism stared him in the face, and even he could scarcely avoid drawing damaging conclusions. He had dragged his wife away from ease, to plunge her into poverty, and from life he had hurried her unsparingly to death. Of a compensating hereafter too he had none of conventional piety's assurance. 'Here, in this world, we who stay, lack those who are gone out of it: we know they shall never come to us; and when we shall go to them, whether we shall know them or no, we dispute.'

Well might he take for the text of his funeral sermon at the Church of St. Clement Danes, where his wife was buried: 'I am the man that hath seen affliction by the rod of His wrath.'

But perhaps the words were even more desolatingly true of the woman whom he mourned.

¶ PART FOUR
THE PREACHER

Corporis hæc Animæ sit Syndon Syndon Jesu
Amen.

Martin ⒅ scup. And are to be sould by R R and Ben: ffisher

THE PREACHER

§ I

MANY years before, Donne had protested to his wife:

'O! if thou die before
My soul from other lands to thee shall soar.'

Certainly from this time he began to die to the world. Its values less and less intrigued him. Essentially henceforth, except for one brief period, he stood alone with his God, even though his god was still often himself. That process of education by suffering which we have traced was now far advanced; stricken, and once again morbid, he took religion to his arms. His surrender to some external and harmonizing idea, which had previously been momentary, gradually became habitual.

The fear and pain of solitude has probably driven more men and women into Churches than a zeal for social communion. Donne for long resisted. He tried to resolve the discords within himself without professional assistance. But circumstances, as we have seen, had compelled him to submit to a Church of which he was imaginatively independent, and now they challenged his egoism with a thrust that went deep into his heart. Suddenly his emotions were released. The sentiments which he had lavished on his wife for sixteen years were left objectless. But, as he admitted, they still in him 'abundant grew,' and to prevent them from 'smothering him,' he let them flow out in sympathy towards life and the God in whom he imaged life's principle. And so he could even write:

> 'This death, hath with my store
> My use increased.'

The gulf between his mind, that indifferent or caustic spectator, and his heart, which yearned for the serenity of self-surrender, was thus very considerably closed, while the Church and its doctrine served as an organ upon which the still vital individualist could sustain a noble music, previously but fitful.

It is difficult to define adequately a psychological condition at once so simple and so complex as 'a state of grace,' but certainly its reality has too often been clouded by exclusive association with formal creeds or conventional sanctity. Shakespeare, for example, experienced and expressed it in 'The Tempest,' and Wordsworth in 'The Prelude,' and Shelley in 'Prometheus Unbound'; and although the poet may generally only capture it in his high imaginative moments, while with the saint it is habitual, yet in both it would seem to be the reward of the individual who has subdued a personal discord by relating himself satisfactorily to the universe. For the subjective faculties cannot be truly harmonized without being reconciled with some governing idea, some intuition of external unity, which the individual rejoices to reflect.

Yet that sense of unassailable well-being which overflows us in our most entranced moments, as of being wonderfully clasped in the cool arms of life, our pulse in perfect accord with the heart that beats in stars and suns, winds and waters, in the elm-tree's tracery and the nodding daffodil – a rhythm which is at the same time beyond time and space, and the very principle of all creative form – is as often pantheistic as deistic. Such a condition the Romantics in their hazy way implied by 'a state of Nature,' and if Nature needs more careful definition than they could stop to give, many have discovered even in the spirit of the countryside the secret of a harmony which transcends all the trivial agitations of life.

The religion which Donne now embraced was, behind all the vocabulary of dogma, some such imaginative synthesis. In it, for ecstatic, precarious moments, he merged, without denying, his passion and his intellect. Unlike such later mystics as the son of his revered Magdalen Herbert, transfigured by their own innocence, he never forgot, to his own anguish, the facts of sin and death in the rapture of the idea. The flesh thrust itself between him and escape. No final and saintly serenity could descend on one doomed all his life to wrestle with rebellious devils. And so his faith implied, not some conclusive act of conformity, but just such a continual venture of the imagination as is entailed in the creative act of poetry, while the Church served exactly as the 'Sonnet's scanty plot' has for those 'who have felt the weight of too much liberty.' It canalized his energies, diminished their wasteful friction, and provided his distraught genius with a mould into which to pour itself. He too could have said:

> 'In truth the prison, unto which we doom
> Ourselves, no prison is.'

§ 2

It was through an agony of remorse that Donne strove
for this harmony of body and mind. Denying himself
even to his motherless children, he brooded alone. And,
to quote Walton's moving words: 'In this retiredness,
which was often from the sight of his dearest friends,
he became *crucified to the world*, and all those varieties,
those imaginary pleasures, that are daily acted on that
restless stage; and they were as perfectly crucified to
him . . . for now his very soul was elemented of nothing
but sadness; now grief took so full possession of his
heart as to leave no place for joy; if it did it was a joy to
be alone, where, like a *pelican in the wilderness*, he might
bemoan himself without witness or restraint, and pour
forth his passions like Job in the days of his affliction:
"O that I might have the desire of my heart! O that
God would grant the thing that I long for! For then,
as the grave is become her house, so would I hasten
to make it mine also: *that we two might there make our
beds together in the dark*." '

Donne was not yet quite so summarily crucified to the
world as Walton supposed, but certainly the Casuist
and the Courtier were not ashamed to go down on their
knees hereafter; while he had as something other than a
prudent profession, 'a new calling, new thoughts, and a
new employment for his wit and eloquence.' And if, as
Walton asserts, 'all the faculties of his soul were now
engaged in the conversion of others,' it was because in
so doing he continued to confirm his own conversion.

This he found to be necessary. He preached to others
to express and reassure himself, and when he spoke of

being 'within the pale of Thy Church and not in the wild
forest,' he referred to the ordered chaos of his own personality, rather than to any material institution. His
exhortation therefore was not the flower of any abstract
love of humanity, but of intense personal preoccupation,
and this, as we shall see, explains both the grandeur
and the limits of its expression.

Indeed had not Donne been so imperturbably, so
scornfully self-absorbed, it must have embarrassed him
at first to address in the Chapel of Lincoln's Inn a
congregation which numbered many well acquainted
with at least the rumour of his salad days. But the
practitioner of levity, returned as the apostle of sanctity, far from wishing to conceal his past, emphasized
it on every possible occasion.

'For mine iniquities,' he announced from the pulpit,
'are gone over my head, as a heavy Burden, they are
too heavy for me. . . . *We have wearied ourselves in the
ways of wickedness.* . . . Carnal pleasures are *dirty ways*,
and tire the licentious man; desires of gain are *thorny
ways*, and tire the covetous man; Emulations of higher
men are *dark* and *blind ways*, and tire the envious man.'
Doubtless such statements had a universal application,
but the reference was literally personal, and Donne
exulted in such public self-exposure.

Nevertheless, so long as he remained at Lincoln's Inn,
his pulpit style was necessarily curbed by a learned
environment and over-weighted with scholastic allu-
sions. The poet, seer, and proselytizer was less apparent
than the ecclesiastical attorney. Indeed it is when he
appeared as a preacher at St. Paul's Cross in the spring
of 1617 that we first hear, together with a reference

to Queen Elizabeth (in which he compares her worth and wisdom to 'Nestor's and Methusalem's and Adam's, if he had never fallen,' adding that 'in her death we were all under one common flood and depth of tears'!), a fine burst of that effusive music which strews the pages of his later discourse.

Meanwhile his emotions were finding another outlet. Poetry is a fair tranquillizer of pain that has passed its climax. And Donne, as the intensity of his grief over his dead wife declined, turned to the composition of sonnets.

It is significant that he had never employed this form in his youth, fashionable though it was. He was a poet in whom form and matter were, as they should be, intimately allied. He seldom practised forms for their own sake, or imposed one that was alien to its substance. This keen sense of artistic propriety is but another proof of his sincerity. He began to write sonnets when he had discovered for himself a synthesis, because the sonnet-form must, to be successful, image a unity of idea. The critical realist of the Songs and Satires had not yet subdued his nature to any ruling motive; but now the conflicting elements were at last partially reconciled, and consequently the 'Divine Sonnets' prelude the epic harmonies of the later Sermons.

§ 3

The 'Holy Sonnets,' composed by Donne during 1617 and 1618, were a tribute of regret and resolution to his dead wife. In gratefully recording his new conviction of 'grace,' he mourned its cause and occasion:

'Since she whom I loved hath paid her last debt
To Nature, and to hers and my good is dead,
And her soul early into heaven is vanished,
Wholly on heavenly things my mind is set.'

His religious faith was in fact the climax of his domestic, and in his approach to God he showed the same
remorse for past infidelity as he had to his wife. The
Platonist had known physical disenchantment, the
priest experienced a holy discontent.

The Sonnet therefore addressed to the Virgin, and so
for sectarian reasons omitted from the first published
version of 'Holy Sonnets,' beginning:

'Show me, dear Christ, Thy Spouse so bright and clear.
What? Is it She, who on the other shore
Goes richly painted?'

is more reasonably explained by the fact that Donne's
devotions, like Milton's, were still associated with
thoughts of his 'late espoused saint' than by any such
lingering fondness for Romish doctrine as has been
suggested. Indeed one of the analogies which he
employed most frequently and minutely was that
between his 'sacred' and 'profane love.'

The series of holy sonnets composed nine or ten
years earlier and entitled 'La Corona' are more
scriptural and less personal. They reveal in their
pattern a certain parallelism with the ingenious
'Metempsychosis' of his youth. But the milestones
of progress in 'La Corona' are the moments of crisis
in Christ's life: they are used to illustrate a
spiritual evolution as those of the earlier poem were
to denote a physical.

In all these sonnets, however, Donne was primarily
absorbed in asserting his emancipation from worldly

values, and, as an unfortunate consequence, lamenting past sin. The two conceptions met in the theme of Death, image alike of spiritual freedom and physical bondage, to which he constantly and, for all his assumption of faith, fearfully recurred. For as his sense of sin almost always tempered and even cast a lurid glare over his spiritual exaltation, so his fascinated horror of death embittered his boast of eternal life.

The theologian in 'La Corona' trespassed as considerably on the poet as the quibbler did once on the lover. Many passages are too much clogged by scriptural formalism to rise to the level of art. Yet pedantic as such terminology must be to many modern minds, it will trouble us less if we conceive of Donne as invoking, particularly when he addressed Christ in person, a harmonious idea of life, in which to forget his own perplexities, as when he wrote:

'Moist with one drop of Thy blood, my dry soul
Shall – though she now be in extreme degree
Too stony hard, and yet too fleshly – be
Freed by that drop, from being starved, hard or foul,
And life by this death abled shall control
Death, whom Thy death slew.'

In a later sonnet he used the dialect of the two professions with which he was now connected to contrast the letter and the spirit:

'but Thy all-healing grace and spirit
Revive and quicken what law and letter kill.
Thy law's abridgement, and Thy last command
Is all but love; O let that last Will stand!'

The poet, he knew, had been often in the past paralysed
by a too critical intelligence: the priest had to guard
against the same danger.

Certainly it is only in the conclusion of 'La Corona'
that he completely transformed doctrine into impassioned poetry, and scriptural metaphors become sym-
bolical rather than merely illustrative:

'O strong Ram, which hast batter'd heaven for me!
Mild Lamb which with Thy Blood hast mark'd the
        path!
Bright Torch, which shinest, that I the way may see!
O, with Thy own Blood quench Thy own just wrath;
And if Thy Holy Spirit my Muse did raise,
Deign at my hands this crown of prayer and praise.'

In the *Holy Sonnets*, written a decade later, this
personal veracity is become the rule rather than the
exception. Glancing backwards and forwards,
Donne submitted the flaws and fluctuations of his
nature to the criterion of his new ideal. His pleasures are 'like yesterday,' the brave glitter of the
world is faded. Conscious only of the subtleties of
sin, he stands terrified between 'Despair behind'
and 'Death before.' He thinks of his youth as of
God's picture marred, until it seems to him that
remorse, which was at first a punishment, is in its
turn a sin, because it perpetuates the discord which
he would resolve.

And yet he cannot escape remorse because he cannot
escape himself, cannot so absolutely purge himself of a
still latent relish for sin as to secure the serenity of
repentance. For, as he said six years later, laying bare
to a congregation the very roots of his own disharmony:

Q

'A Conscience is not clean, by having recollected all her sins in the *Memory*, for they may fester there, and *Gangreen* even to *Desperation.* . . . How many men sin over the sins of their youth again, in their age, by a sinful *Delight* in remembering those sins, and a sinful *Desire*, that their Bodies were not past them?'

And so once again he turns to Death as the liberator, and with a sudden blaze of imagination figures himself as about to endure the terror and triumph of dissolution:

'This is my play's last scene; here heavens appoint
My pilgrimage's last mile; and my race
Idly, yet quickly run, hath this last pace;
My span's last mile, my minute's latest point;
And gluttonous death will instantly unjoint
My body and soul, and I shall sleep a space;
Or presently (I know not) see that face,
Whose fear already shakes my every joint.
Then, as my soul to heaven her first seat takes flight,
And earth-born body in the earth shall dwell,
So fall my sins, that all may have their right,
To where they're bred and would press me to hell.
Impute me righteous, thus purg'd of evil,
For thus I leave the world, the flesh, the devil.'

It is significant that the diffident parenthesis 'I know not' was banished from the seventh line of this sonnet in other versions, where it runs: 'But my ever-waking part shall see that face.' Conventional piety doubtless demanded the emendation, but agnosticism was nearer the truth. Donne's naturalism and scepticism were not submerged in mystical faith; it was their persistence

which gave so terrible and sublime a reality to his
utterance, as of a man who did consciously, in his
assault on heaven, 'hell's wide mouth o'erstride,' and
knew that one moment's slackening of effort would
change victory into defeat. So here he repudiates sin
with the same violent subtlety with which he had
embraced it:

'I am a little world made cunningly
Of elements, and an angelic sprite;
But black sin hath betray'd to endless night
My world's both parts, and, O, both parts must die.
You which beyond that heaven which was most high
Have found new spheres, and of new land can write,
Pour new seas in my eyes, that so I might
Drown my world with my weeping earnestly,
Or wash it if it must be drown'd no more.
But O, it must be burnt; alas! the fire
Of lust and envy burnt it heretofore,
And made it fouler; let their flames retire,
And burn me, O God, with a fiery zeal
Of Thee and Thy house, which doth in eating heal.'

Donne clearly is more conscious as yet of sin than of
grace, and in one sonnet he asks graphically enough,
'What if this present were the world's last night?'
Could his soul rely on the forgiveness of Christ, should
that awful meeting be imminent, or would 'His countenance affright'? And then with a strange reference
to the days when he had assured his 'profane mistresses'
that Beauty was a sign of pity, he dwells consolingly
upon the beauty of 'the picture of Christ crucified.'
Bruised, agitated, and seeing in every attack of sickness

'death's herald and champion,' he casts himself upon the mercy of Christ, that in the fire of communion with Him he may forget a smouldering corruption.

But self-recrimination could never with such a nature descend to sentimental self-indulgence, and Donne, the analyst, is always examining his 'sin's black memory,' to discover in what lies his peculiar depravity. He imputes it to the fact that, while possessing to so remarkable a degree the divine faculty of Reason, it has only made him the more calculated and efficient a sinner. Reason, 'God's viceroy,' he complains, has proved alike the measure of his power and his impotence. It has made him both conscious of the brute in his nature, and able to exploit it. 'Why,' he cries,

'should intent or reason, born in me,
Make sins, else equal, in me more heinous?'

And the answer is that reason brings consciousness, but not necessarily virtue or harmony. It cannot quench lust, and may serve it only too capably. Reason in short enslaves, as instinct does; and freedom can only come when the two are related to some higher idea.

This idea Donne invokes as God, bidding Him, in a manner comparable to Francis Thompson's 'Hound of Heaven,' take his heart by force, 'like a usurp'd town,' 'break, blow, burn, and make me new.' The vehemence of this appeal is typical, and in its inspiration not only is the burden of sin for the moment lifted, but proud Death itself is dwarfed.

Donne now wooed his God with both the fervour and the self-disgust with which he had before addressed his mistresses; even the erotic imagery recurs. His religion was become a personal passion and a personal hazard, to which theology was no more than a prop. For the rest of his life he was to be in love with the spiritual and in dread of the material in this personal rather than priestly sense, to be torn between the forces of attraction and repulsion, to suffer all the torments of a frustrated lover to whom death only could bring alleviation, all a lover's agonized feeling of unworthiness, and all his yearning for that consummation, those ultimate bridals, which the flesh at best so tantalizingly, at worst so grossly denies.

§ 4

During 1617 and 1618 over-work and emotional tension threatened Donne with a breakdown. Even his congregations at Lincoln's Inn noticed that their preacher was lapsing into 'an infirm and valetudinarian state.' The old morbid symptoms returned. He himself was convinced that consumption was overtaking him, and even circulated copies of his 'Poems' and his 'Biathanatos' among intimate friends, to ensure their survival in case of his death.

Once again circumstances conspired to delay the inevitable collapse, and even to restore him for a short period to a more worldly state of mind. Political affairs in Bohemia, into which we need not enter, had assumed a serious complexion in 1618, and it was decided to send Viscount Doncaster (the Lord Hay of previous reference) on a mission of inquiry. The King, who had remarked the ill-health of his Chaplain, arranged that Donne should accompany Doncaster informally, hoping that change and relaxation would restore his strength and spirits. No happier scheme could have been devised. He received his appointment in March, 1619, and during the period of pleasant anticipation which intervened before his setting out in May, turned once more to poetry. His 'Hymn to Christ' is like a devout echo of those which he had addressed to his wife on parting eight years before; it is a beautiful and confiding address, absolutely innocent of conventional unction, of which the following is perhaps the finest stanza:

'I sacrifice this island unto Thee,
And all whom I love there, and who love me;
When I have put our seas 'twixt them and me,
Put Thou Thy seas betwixt my sins and Thee;
As the tree's sap doth seek the root below
In winter, in my winter now I go
Where none but the Eternal Root of true love I may know.'

To the benchers of Lincoln's Inn he also addressed himself in farewell terms, begging them 'in his long absence and far distance from hence' to remember his 'endeavours, at least his desire, to make sure their salvation,' as he for his part would remember their 'religious cheerfulness in hearing the word.' 'If I never meet you again,' he added, 'till we have all passed the gate of death, yet in the gates of heaven, I may meet you all.'

But even such a gentle melancholy as this ceased to affect him as, free of all responsibilities, he rode with the English ambassador through festive streets, or preached to some attentive Court circle, at once brilliant and devout. At Heidelberg it is worth noting that on two occasions he had the privilege of so addressing that 'devout, good, sweet Princess Elizabeth,' whose marriage his genius had adorned, and who was so soon, amid the ruins of her fortunes, to need all the consolation which religion could afford. We can imagine with what an affectionate fervour the poet, courtier and moralist in Donne bent to the task.

Doncaster's journey was prolonged far beyond its original intention. Brussels, Cologne, Frankfort, Vienna, the Tyrol, Nuremberg, The Hague – these were but some of its landmarks, and it was not till late in December that a renovated Donne resumed the guardianship of his family, and his duties at Lincoln's Inn.

§ 5

Donne's continental diversions again changed his outlook. So happy was he in body and mind on his return that, ceasing for a time from moral self-accusation, he began to view once more with an interested eye the world that a few months before he had so summarily dismissed. Indeed, had not 'every distemper of the body' been now increasingly 'complicated with the spleen' and its contingent 'heavy clouds of melancholy,' the enraptured seer and the fulminating moralist might even at this late hour have yielded place to the shrewd and worldly prelate.

It may be that the gathering 'vapours' of an organic disease were not 'so vehement a poison as those false ways in which we sought our comforts in our looser days,' but they were to prove even more effective in compelling an unworldly standpoint. Their force, however, was as yet far from decisive.

Donne still basked in the radiance of an Ambassadorial progress; the days of mortification were for the moment forgotten, and it was exactly this readiness to live extravagantly in the moment (as the natural man does) which prevented him, acute as his mind was, from ever completely evolving either a philosophy or a conviction such as circumstance was powerless to shake. Even his purest conceptions of the ideal had an element of hysteria in them, because they originated not in disinterested thought but in the fumes of physical fever.

Throughout 1620 and 1621, therefore, a temporary degeneration of character coincides with a temporary improvement in health. Donne renews his social intercourse and his keen interest in political small talk, and he grovels once again for preferment.

The Readership at Lincoln's Inn had doubtless proved a severe strain upon his powers, and it was natural that, when in August, 1621, the Deanery of Salisbury was likely to fall vacant, he should address himself to the King's new Favourite, the Marquess of Buckingham. But his exaggerated assertion that 'your Lordship knows how narrow and penurious a fortune I wrestle with in this world,' his wish that 'my Lord Keeper would have left a hole for so poor a worm as I am to have crept in at,' and his final protestation that 'I lie in a corner, as a clod of clay, attending what kind of vessel it shall please you to make of your Lordship's humblest and thankfullest and devotedest servant,' are unpleasantly reminiscent of his dealings with Rochester.

It was only after Donne had ensured the capture of an

illustrious post by every material means, that he could
piously advise others 'to leave all in God's hands, from
whose hands nothing can be wrung by whining but by
praying.' Certainly, however, his own efforts 'to knead
and mould' his destiny had not proved too successful,
and, as he later confessed, 'In the poor low way that I
have gone in which I have not made many nor wide
steps since my first leap which was my very entrance
into this calling, I have found that missing and failing
of some places have advanced my fortune.' This was
signally true of the present occasion; for while Salisbury
failed to materialize, only a month later Donne was
soliciting, in terms which protest a considerably greater
devotion for the person of the King's Favourite than for
the Deity himself, an even finer prize in the ecclesiastical lottery.

The Deanery of St. Paul's was both in dignity and
value pre-eminently suited to his requirements, and he
was not long kept in doubt. The King summoned
him to dinner, and employed a pleasant piece of imagery
to convey to his guest the news of his appointment,
saying before they had begun to eat: 'I will carve to
you of a dish which I know you love well; for, knowing
you love London, I do therefore make you Dean of St.
Paul's; and when I have dined, then do you take your
beloved dish home to your study, say grace there to
yourself, and much good may it do you.'

Unfortunately the dish was to remain for a short time
longer in the abstract region of metaphor, and Donne
had to content himself with repeating the grace. The
Archbishop of Canterbury had when hunting, to his
own extreme embarrassment, accidentally killed a keeper

with a barbed arrow, and had been compelled to refrain
from ecclesiastical duties until a Commission had decided
whether one guilty of even involuntary homicide
might continue to hold an arch-episcopal see; in two
months, however, Dr. Abbot was vindicated and on the
19th of November, Donne's dish was served.

It satisfied all his expectations. He became master of
a large and luxurious Deanery standing in its own
grounds, and of an ancient private chapel, to restore
which was one of his first cares. So affluent was he now
that at Christmas, 1621, he was even able to dispense
with the allowance which Sir George More had loyally
continued to tender. This was a cordial act, although
we can fancy, in spite of Walton's assurance that time
had made Sir George 'a lover and admirer of his son-
in-law,' that Donne was not sorry to be able to refuse
at last what had been originally a very grudging act of
charity.

Certainly it signified no saintly superiority to mam-
mon. He continued to hold a number of lucrative
pluralities, and even, with doubtful propriety, went to
law, when on his appointment to St. Paul's another
cleric had the temerity to apply for an incumbency
in the gift of the Benchers of Lincoln's Inn, which
Donne had probably received as part of the endowments
of his now relinquished Readership. Such an act is
ironically reminiscent of the clerical materialism which
the youthful moralist had denounced. And it seems
clear that the newly appointed Dean was very different
from the sinister evangelist, whose effigy stands to-day
in a side aisle of St. Paul's.

The office had attracted him quite as powerfully for

its earthly as for its heavenly eminence. Once again the
worldling tried to compromise with the mystic, the
aristocrat with the fevered fanatic. As Dean, he approxi-
mated to a Court dignitary, a position for which he had
always hungered, and to ingratiate himself with the
King or his advisers was probably more prominent at
this time in Donne's thoughts than to save his own soul
or another's. That burning sense of personal sin which
converted many of his later sermons into ecstatic self-
apologies, was by no means yet the obsession which it
became. He was pleasantly busied with his new duties,
with reorganizing the system of preachers, presiding
over the Chapter, and attending to his work as Preben-
dary of Chiswick; and while his labours as preacher were
light compared with those at Lincoln's Inn, the novel
routine ensured him against excessive introspection.

As a special pleader on those points of doctrine where
Theology and Politics touched, he served the King at
Paul's Cross as readily and efficiently as he had served
Morton in controversial pamphlets. It is interesting
also to find him, on the invitation of the Honourable
Company of the Virginian Plantation, extolling that
Commercialized Missionary Endeavour, which has
unintentionally done so much to prejudice Christianity
in foreign lands. Rumour indeed has it that Donne
himself was a shareholder in the enterprise which he
so feelingly consecrated from the pulpit; certainly no
alluring Company Prospectus could have rivalled his
sermon in its double appeal to men's conscience and
their pocket. The 'adventurers' and their imperialistic
successors, we have reason to know, did not take too
seriously to heart the duties with respect to the spiritual

welfare of the unregenerate heathen, which Donne urged romantically upon them, but the association of sanctity with a financial undertaking put the Company on a sounder basis by enrolling the devout as well as the hard-headed among its subscribers; and piety could scarcely resist such intercessions as these:

'Whom liberty draws to go, or present profit draws to adventure, are not yet in the right way. O, if you could once bring a Catechism to be as good ware amongst them as a Bugle, as a knife, as a hatchet: O, if you would be as ready to hearken at the return of a ship, how many Indians were converted to Christ Jesus, as what Trees or druggs, or Dyes that Ship had brought, then you were in your right way, and not till then.'

A year before, Donne had in similar terms commended the British Isles as having 'by reason of their situation, provision and trading . . . most means of conveying Christ Jesus over the world,' but impeccable as such sentiments were, their practical issue only proves how difficult it is to combine the moral and the financial. The sermon printed by the Virginian Company doubtless served as an admirable advertisement; and it is curious to learn that not only Donne, as preacher, but Nicholas Ferrar, the gentle mystic in later days of Little Gidding, as deputy-treasurer, were all unconsciously pioneers of that blend of Puritanism and Piracy, which has so often and successfully shouldered the white man's burden at the expense of the black man's back. Donne's Colonial interest is, of course, of personal interest only so far as it suggests that his thoughts were not quite so exclusively set on higher things as his earlier protestations would have led us to suppose.

Once again, and now with a final compulsion, sickness turned Donne's eyes from the open thoroughfares of the world to the sinuous bypaths of his own personality. The elixir of life which he had drunk in Germany, and which for nearly four years had saved him from himself, was at last to lose its virtue.

On the 23rd of October, 1623, the Serjeant's Feast, at which Donne was a guest, was held in the Temple, and the whole company walked in procession from Lincoln's Inn to St. Paul's, where the Dean was to address them. It was a wild night, and a dignified cavalcade, 'dabbling on foot and bare-headed,' was particularly exposed to the rain which drove across the streets. Donne was probably fatigued, and the exposure proved too much for him; he took a chill, which quickly developed into a gastric fever, more violent than any from which he had yet suffered.

Subject to successive attacks of extreme pain from internal inflammation, he also experienced that degree of heightened consciousness which fever so often induces. Material things under such conditions are apt to seem both luminous and insubstantial, while the individual is affected by an intense and obstinate self-awareness. So akin is such a state to mystical illumination that we are tempted to suppose the existence of some element of fever as necessary for the release of imagination from the clutch of the flesh. Generally, however, in sickness, imagination is distorted, because the mind of the patient shares the distress of his body, and at best can only imperfectly control or organize the intuitions, the finer vibrations which the nerves are laid bare to receive and record.

So in the delirium of the fever-patient, as in the vision of so many ecstatics, glimpses of pure reality are found coexisting with every kind of confused hallucination. But Donne's fever was remarkable in its combination of heightened consciousness and abnormal concentration. His retentive intellect never for a moment quailed, with the result that he interpreted his condition, with graphic and uncanny precision. The patient formulated his own diagnosis, and he extended it from the body to the hidden places of the soul. But if fever was impotent to shake the citadel of the mind, it shattered at a blow and for ever the defences of the complacent public dignitary. The resolute man of the world, the insolent, ingenious, Piratical Donne had suffered his last defeat; essentially he never recovered. Henceforth it is scarcely an exaggeration to say that he was to preach from a death-bed and in the grasp of fever; the fire thus kindled was to blaze and smoulder until it had burnt his body away.

The attack was as sudden as it was violent. Propped up in bed, where without intermission he was to register every phase of his condition, he described its onset thus:

'In the same instant that I feel the first attempt of the disease, I felt the victory; in the twinkling of an eye, I could scarcely see; instantly the taste was insipid and fatuous; instantly the appetite is dull and desireless; instantly the knees are sinking and strengthless; and in an instant, sleep, which is the picture, the copy of death, is taken away, that the original, death itself may succeed, and that so I might have death to the life. . . . I sweat again, and again, from the brow to the sole of

the foot, but I eat no bread, I taste no sustenance.'
'The original' did in fact nearly 'succeed.' For several
weeks Donne's life was in danger, and there were many
grave consultations, in which the King's own physician
took a part. Meanwhile the face grew drawn and
sunken on the pillows, and as the haggard hand inscribed
in tortured sentences a morbid medical chart, Donne
entered on the last stage of his pilgrimage, and that
which shares with the licentious era of his youth the
fascinated amazement of posterity.

The details of his distemper which the realist now so
minutely noted, the idealist was later to translate, during
convalescence, into spiritual terms, the heavenly Physician being then invoked in place of an earthly, to
prescribe other than pharmaceutical remedies; but the
reflections which Donne committed to paper during
the height of his fever surpass in vividness even the
'Devotions' which grew by analogy out of them. Doubtless this act of expression was, like so many of his
sermons, a vent to his acute anxiety: for despite all his
salutations of death it was his tenacious desire for life
which alone enabled him to prolong his mortification
over eight more years. 'My God, my God,' he wrote, 'I
find in thy book that fear is a stifling spirit, a spirit of
suffocation,' and he fought his way to the surface time
after time, like a drowning man.

And yet through all the symptoms of fear and pain,
the detachment of the man is astonishing. He studies
his body as he studied a theological pamphlet, recording the phenomena of his cosmos, its earthquakes and
thunders and rivers of blood, its sinews like mines, its
muscles like hills, its bones like quarries of stone – all

in the manner of some Geographer lecturing before the
Royal Society; while only the 'sad apprehension' which
he has to confess betrays the personal interest behind
the skilful exposition.

As the disease worsens, his agitation grows, and the
poetic faculty more and more supplements the scientific with all the force of biblical imagery. His fever,
instead of melting him like snow, 'pours me out like
lead, like iron, like brass melted in a furnace. It doth
not only melt me, but calcines me, reducing me to
atoms and to ashes, not to water, but to lime.'

Gradually the physical is consumed, as in all the
intensest moments of experience, and even pain becomes
an ecstasy. 'My stomach is not gone, but gone upward
to the Supper of the Lamb.' He is no longer mortal
and material, no longer 'clogged' by the body, but is his
'own Ghost,' hovering above his own sick-bed, comparing it, as so often before, with a score of *macabre* conceits to his grave, 'the common wardrobe,' 'the womb
of the earth.'

Day and night 'the moving finger writes, and, having
writ, moves on,' the eyes blaze beneath their shaggy
arches, the moist brow and the cadaverous temples pro-
trude in deathly transparency, at once fiendish and
sublime.

But as the climax of the fever passes, although the
danger still remains, the elemental voice assumes a more
human and incidentally more fractious tone. Sardonically he chides his friends for neglecting him through fear
of infection. They have only to bury him, he sneers, to
escape their dilemma. And now once again his body is
a matter of burning concern, and he divines its state by

reading sharply his doctors' faces, and drawing deductions from their treatment. 'I observe the physician, with the same diligence, as he the disease; I see he fears, and I fear with him; I overtake him, I overrun him in his fear, and I go the faster, because he makes his pace slow; I fear the more, because he disguises his fear, and I see it with the more sharpness, because he would not have me see it.' He consoles his pride by contending that 'I fear not the hastening of my death, and yet I do fear the increase of the disease,' but the distinction is plainly a quibble. The thought of death is agonizing; and every stage of his treatment is morbidly remarked.

The doctors prescribe, but without success; they use cordials to keep the malignity of the disease from the heart; they apply pigeons, to draw the vapours from the head; he develops a rash, and cannot sleep; the bells of an adjoining church remind him of funerals; they ring in his head, and all the bells which he has ever heard, or of which he has read, summoning, it may be, to vespers through twilit streets, or again to wintry funerals, herald his own burial. One tolling softly to another says: 'Thou must die'; it ceases, and in fancy he is dead. At last the doctors succeed in diagnozing correctly; they proceed to purge with happy results. Like Lazarus from the tomb, they raise him from his bed.

Not a Beaudelaire, a Marie Bashkirtseff, or a Barbellion can surpass Donne in the pathological exactitude, the poetical power or the awful intimacy of these sick-bed confessions. The inherent artist in him, as well as the terrified egoist and neurotic, dictated them. For these weeks of suffering were, like his agitated youth, the material out of which later he was to construct and

R

synthesize works of art, whether prayers, meditations, or sermons; and although no such conscious purpose can have been in the mind of the distracted fever-patient, the necessity of self-expression in such unexampled circumstances was as artistic as it was pathological.

It was the poet's direct response to violent experience, and 'The Devotions' in which he incorporated and expanded these realistic notes, during convalescence, reveal the second stage in the poetic process, that of 'emotion recollected in tranquillity,' of sensations enriched by leisured thought and aspiration at a time when the body, purified by pain, once again quivered to the touch of life. They are, in short, spiritual modulations on a physical theme.

He wrote them sitting by his bedside, where, 'as a prisoner discharged sits at the prison door to beg fees, so sit I here to gather crumbs.' It were better to say that he had already gathered the crumbs and here kneaded them into a lump. The sustained spiritual intensity of these 'Devotions' signify, as he claimed in his dedication to the Prince of Wales, that final conversion from the world which had been so long delayed — a 'præternatural,' as distinct from a natural, or merely clerical rebirth. The realist and the worldling are from this time absorbed in the mystic: they colour the mystic's language, they even trouble his peace, but they never climb again into the place of authority. Nothing is more striking in the 'Devotions' than the violence of Donne's abandonment of himself to God, the pathos with which he implores, as men have always implored their gods, for a revelation of joy, and light and expansion, in which to resolve his being, like some stagnant pool evaporated by the sun. He is frantic to escape the lusts and aches and corruption of his body, to breathe a purer air, to relax all effort, and submit to the healing hands of some subliminal harmony.

And yet he could not. A Puritan conscience still strove with a Pagan impulse. He never truly recovered either from his sense of sin or from his sickness, and so spiritual serenity was as unattainable as physical. The old warfare, which had now reached its culminating phase, was doomed to continue; the flesh was still too proud to submit absolutely, and peace was unobtainable on any qualified surrender. Thus the concluding paragraph of these 'Devotions' reveals the nervous sentry once more at his post, scanning the horizon for the lurking hosts of sin:

'Say to my soul, "*My son, thou hast sinned, do so no more*"; but say also, that though I do, thy spirit of remorse and compunction shall never depart from me. Thy holy apostle, St. Paul, was shipwrecked thrice, and yet still saved. Though the rocks and the sands, the heights and the shallows, the prosperity and the adversity of this world do diversely threaten me, though mine own leaks endanger me, yet, O God, let me never put myself aboard with Hymeneus, nor make shipwreck of faith and a good conscience, and then thy long-lived, thy everlasting mercy, will visit me, though that which I most earnestly pray against should fall upon me, a relapse into those sins which I have truly repented, and thou hast fully pardoned.'

The analogy between physical and moral disease has often been drawn, but seldom with such illuminating comment as in this 'sacred picture of spiritual ecstasies.'

But if we may see here 'the most secret thoughts that then possessed Donne's soul,' his 'Hymn to God the Father,' written in the spring of 1624, is the perfect epilogue to the tortured analysis of his sick-bed, and the meditations of his convalescence. It contains in its three stanzas the essence of his contrition, and in its conclusion reveals, for once without hysteria, the doubt which was to haunt his mind to the end.

A tree with a deep hold upon earth is not easily uprooted. Not even mortal sickness, save in its moment of climax, could dull Donne's taste for physical life, or fear of physical death. He sanctified death, because only so could he soften a repellent prospect or soothe an immanent terror, by promising himself an ultimate satisfaction.

Christ became a need to him as a consoling, if conjectural image of forgiveness and immortality. For Donne was at heart both pagan enough to accept death as dissolution, and mediæval enough to picture a hell in which sin received a very physical requital. For a moment, however, in this spring of renewed and rarefied vitality, he was able to confide his fear to God without groans and crepitations:

'I have a sin of fear, that when I've spun
    My last thread, I shall perish on the shore;
But swear by Thyself, that at my death Thy Son
    Shall shine as He shines now, and heretofore;
And having done that, Thou hast done,
    I fear no more.'

Unfortunately the Deity is not given to swearing oaths even for the reassurance of agitated Deans. But Donne

had the words of his 'Hymn' set to a most grave and
solemn tune, which was often sung by the St. Paul's
choristers. And we can picture well with what an ineffable contentment, a delicious sense of the solution of all
discord, the boys' voices stole upon the Dean's ears, as
he sat huddled and haggard in his stall in the dim light
of an evening service; sanctifying his hopes, and silenc-
ing for a time the demon of egoistic doubt that in cold
daylight still mocked his loftiest aspirations. 'O the
power of Church Music!' he wrote, 'that harmony,
added to this hymn, has raised the affections of my
heart, and quickened my graces of zeal and gratitude;
and I observe that I always return from paying this
public duty of prayer and praise to God with an unex-
pressible tranquillity of mind, and a willingness to leave
the world.'

One who was privileged to contribute daily to such
music under the 'branching roof' of King's College
Chapel is not likely to undervalue its assuaging power;
nevertheless even the exquisite purity of boys' voices
is in the nature of a narcotic, and no narcotic could long
anæsthetize the body and mind of Donne. Belief, so
substantial in the tinted twilight, is apt to prove but a
wraith in the candid stare of morning.

For Donne fear remained, sinister and persistent, a
ghost which could at best be only temporarily laid by
the dying fall of music, or the aggressive act of preaching, or by veiling its stark features in elaborate ceremonial. Throughout his remaining years Donne
wrestled in public and in private with the thought of
death, under whose sentence he knew himself to stand,
and only after eternalizing his own corpse, so far as

stone can eternalize, did he surrender himself with
embittered solemnity to the 'necessary defect of
dying.'

§ 6

Donne returned from what he called at one time 'a
parenthesis,' at another, 'the gates of heaven,' both a
new man and an old. 'So the Spirit of God,' he said
five years later, looking back upon this time, 'moves
upon the face of these waters, the Spirit of Life upon
the danger of death. Consider the love, more than love,
the study, more than study, the diligence of God, he
devises means, that his banished, those whom sins, or
death had banished, be not expelled from him. I sinned
upon the strength of my youth, and God devised a
means to reclaim me, an enfeebling sickness. I relapsed
after my recovery, and God devised a means, an irre-
coverable, a helpless consumption to reclaim me; That
affliction grew heavy upon me, and weighed me down
even to a diffidence in God's mercy, and God devised a
means, The comfort of the Angel of his Church, his
Minister, The comfort of the Angel of the Great
Counsell, the body and blood of his Son Christ Jesus,
at my transmigration.'

His 'transmigration' was now so far advanced, his
clay already so 'sublimed,' that, when he mounted
the pulpit, he no longer impressed his congregation as
primarily a confident and learned divine, magisterial in
his utterance, as who should say: 'I know my worth
and enjoy the dignity of this occasion'; rather the
emaciated face, the mouth drained of its fullness and
frivolity, save for a hint of sardonic mirth, the dusky

hollows in the cheeks, the painfully protruding cheek-
bones, the nose stark purged of all its grossness, the
eyes incandescent between puckered lids, the brow a
battlefield of twisted furrows, the lean arm and fingers
that like talons stressed a point or grasped greedily
the hour-glass — all fascinated as something more or less
than human. Was it death or life that was eating this
face away? Did it portend a soul in anguish or in
ecstasy? It was sometimes difficult to say.

Nor did the preacher make it easier, when with a kind
of demented glee he announced himself in such terms as
these: 'I am a reciprocall plague; passively and actively
contagious; I breathe corruption, and breathe it upon
myself; and I am the Babylon that I must go out of, or
I perish.'

But in the full tide of preaching all the elements of
cynicism, disillusionment, hunger and fear, that lurked
in those features with such sinister intent, were submerged. There was a fervid benignity, a compelling
exaltation, a ghostly grandeur about his address. He
preached as one to whom everything had assumed
symbolic significance, to whom the flesh had become
the temple or the tomb of life, and Kings' Courts some
celestial antechamber; as one uplifted to a middle region
between earth and heaven, there, like an astronomer
'spying a new-found star,' to spy out God and report
of him, 'as Angels out of clouds,' to men.

The pulpit, therefore, was now in Donne's eyes not
only a place of public self-confession, but a supernatural
platform. To what a pinnacle he raised it we may
judge from many references in his sermons, from his
own necromantic style, and from such lines as these,

addressed to a 'Mr. Tilman after he had taken Orders':

'What function is so noble, as to be
Ambassador to God, and destiny?

. . . .

How brave are those, who with their engine can
Bring man to heaven, and heaven again to man !'

At another time he indued it with the terror of some
cosmic process: 'His Ordinance of preaching batters
the soul, and by that breach, the Spirit enters; His
Ministers are an Earthquake, and shake an earthly
soul; They are the sons of thunder, and scatter a cloudy
conscience; They are as the fall of waters, and carry
with them whole Congregations; 3,000 at a Sermon,
5,000 at a sermon, a whole City, such a City as Nineveh
at a Sermon; and they are as the roaring of a Lion,
where the Lion of the tribe of Juda, cries down the
Lion that seeks whom he may devour.'

On yet another occasion he compared the Preacher
to an Eagle, who, after making 'a holy noise in the
conscience of the Congregation, and when he hath
awakened them, by stirring the nest, he casts some claps
of thunder, some intimidations, in denouncing the judg-
ments of God, and he flings open the gates of Heaven,
that they may hear, and look up, and see a man sent by
God, with power to infuse his fear upon them.' For only
after infusing 'the fear of God into his Auditory' is the
Minister, in Donne's opinion, justified in 'spreading his
wings over his people, as to defend them from all
inordinate fear, from all suspicion and jealousy, from
all diffidence and distrust in the mercy of God.' That
a terrified people were not likely to confide themselves

to God save in a craven spirit entered as little into
Donne's mediæval mind as into that of his like in all
the ages.

Preaching, however, to one who could clothe it with
such ferocious and world-shaking epithets, was no
merely pious, academic or edifying activity. It was epic,
lyrical and dramatic art, and in it, as we shall see,
Donne satisfied by sublimating not only his fear and
remorse, but also his desire for social distraction, for
courtly distinction, for poetry and spiritual reassurance.
His energies, no longer diffused, now concentrated
upon the pulpit, and all his hope of heaven at war with
his lust for earth, poured down from this eminence like
some fugue of Bach's, rolling in complicated currents
along a shrouded roof.

Nevertheless, he was not destined to pursue his path
of ecstatic self-expression without at least two experiences of that clericalism which had alienated the younger
man from every Church. 'Our times,' he was bitterly
to confess once more, 'abound with men that are busy
and litigious about trifles and church ceremonies.'
Unsectarian himself, and appreciating the truth latent
in the dead matter of every creed, he failed to satisfy
the petty prejudice of some material-minded prelate,
who therefore sought to harm him by whispering
malicious slanders in the ears of the King.

Donne's secret scepticism preserved him from faith's
worst flaw – intolerance; but he knew enough of the
whims of exalted patrons, and had crept with such
difficulty into a favoured preserve, that he did not
neglect to accommodate himself to his royal master's
particular brand of doctrine, or to embellish most

eloquently from the pulpit on suitable occasions the Royal Character, the Royal Stock, and the Royal Environment.

Had he not said of James I, with all a courtier's grace, that 'it would have troubled any king but *him*, to have come in succession, and in comparison with such a *Queen*'? and had he not on more than one occasion drawn a gratifying analogy between the Royalties of Earth and Heaven?

But in that age so quibbling was the regal and ecclesiastical view of Christianity, that though a man preached from his heart on death, sin, God and immortality, he could not be certain that he had not, quite unconsciously, transgressed some negligible dogma, or roused suspicions of Romish or Puritan leanings in the niggard mind of some pretentious priest. Twice indeed did this happen, to Donne's intense alarm; for his fear of death was only greater in degree than his dread of being cast out once more into the social wilderness. Fortunately on each occasion he was able to satisfy the king in question that 'their Doctor was an honest man.' Honesty of such a kind was certainly the best policy, but it was little more.

Very different was the homely ideal of the parish priest which Donne sketched in the first sermon that he preached in the church of St. Dunstan's in the West, a living of which the reversion had been given him some years before, but to which he did not succeed until March, 1624. He compared it to a marriage between the minister and his congregation, in which mutual love would soften reproof and intensify communion. And forgetting himself for a moment in the upturned faces of his listeners, he cried with something of a dreadful forethought: 'What sea could furnish mine eyes with tears enough, to pour out, if I should think, that of all this Congregation, which looks me in the face now, I should not meet one, at the Resurrection, at the right hand of God.'

In the Donne of these last years we detect not only the solitary ascetic, craving a direct and undistracted communion with God, but one who felt often the need of the affectionate, we might almost say the domestic regard of simple men and women.

And if the pulpit of St. Paul's invited him to become some elemental power, striding the gulf between heaven and hell, a voice of cosmic revelation, a haunted soul lost in lonely monologue amid the immensities of space and the obscenities of matter, that of St. Dunstan's tempted him to descend somewhat nearer the plane of unassuming humanity, as near at least as was possible to one who resolutely refused to indulge in 'uncircumcised lips or an extemporal or irreverent or over-homely and vulgar language,' and to whom the pulpit could never be anything more sedate than 'my exultation.'

These gentler sentiments were now to be reinforced by public instead of personal sickness. The plague descended upon London, and throughout May and June, 1625, there was a general dispersion. Donne scattered his family, and retired himself to Sir John Danvers' house in the village of Chelsea – an ideal haven indeed, since there his hostess was none other than Magdalen Herbert, who had in 1608 married Sir John, a gifted and wealthy man, much her junior. Thither the plague quickly followed him, and compelled

so absolute a retreat that he described himself as being
confined in a 'secular monastery.' His imprisonment,
however, was in no sense a burden to him, and, being
happy himself, even the abnormal loss which his parish
of St. Dunstan's suffered in that awful visitation did
not unduly depress him.

'I make it another argument,' he wrote, 'that our good
God hath a holy and precious purpose to enwrap us in
the same everlasting communion of joy, that enwraps
us now in the same communion of calamity.' It is only
when the devout suffer acutely themselves that they
begin to question the beneficent purpose of God! The
wails of a stricken world penetrated the household at
Chelsea like whispers from another sphere.

Enveloped in that love of hospitality to which Donne
was to pay a melancholy tribute in a later funeral sermon, 'shutting up the day, at night, with a general,
with a cheerful singing of Psalms . . . the last Act of that
family, united in itself and with God,' one who was
peculiarly sensitive to his environment, who scintillated
in secular society, aspired in devout, and moulted in
solitude, came perhaps during the next six months
nearer the knowledge of tranquillity, nearer a solution
of all discord in himself than ever in his tempestuous
life.

Besides the 'good angel' for whom he cherished so
deep a devotion, and whose presence had always harmonized and exalted his faculties, he enjoyed the com-
panionship of George Herbert, now in his thirty-second
year, and passing, during these very months, in his
gentler way through a crisis identical with that which
Donne had prolonged over so many years. Herbert

was one in whom the spirit of the Renaissance burned purely, discoloured by no mediæval smoke. And so when he turned to piety, it was with all the graces of culture. As Charles Cotton wrote of him: he had 'a soul composed of harmonies,' and although we are told in the same poem that his

'education,
Manners, and parts, by high applauses blown,
Was deeply tainted with ambition,'

the taint in so melodious a nature must have been very superficial. For while Donne lusted after experience in his uncouth egoism, Herbert wooed it with the exquisite sensibility which he inherited from his saintly mother. None was more responsive to life than he, more tremulously appreciative even of its allurements:

'I know the ways of pleasure, the sweet strains,
The lullings and the relishes of it;
The propositions of hot blood and brains;
What mirth and music mean; what Love and wit
Have done these twenty hundred years and more.'

But he was essentially a cultivated, a fastidious spirit, alike in his worldliness and his mysticism, and thus incapable of the barbarism to which Donne descended in search of reality, or of the obscene and violent depths over which he hung. In Herbert the artist predominated, in Donne the scientist; in the one the saint, in the other the seer. One was native to the forces of light, the other to those of darkness. Sensibility predominates in the one, self-assertion in the other. Herbert's soul is like a cool glade, Donne's a sultry marsh.

The two had known each other for many years, but it was a remarkable coincidence that they should have been thrown into the closest intimacy, prolonged over several months, at the moment when Herbert, saddened by the events of the time, 'had many conflicts with himself, whether he should return to the painted pleasures of a Court life, or betake himself to a study of divinity, and enter into sacred orders, to which his mother had often persuaded him.'

Donne was speaking of himself when he said that 'these were such conflicts as they only can know that have endured them; for ambitious desires, and the outward glory of this world, are not easily laid aside,' and we can believe that as a sympathetic confidant of a dilemma parallel to his own, he was, second to George Herbert's mother, the most influential agent by which 'at last God inclined' the hesitating courtier 'to put on a resolution to serve at his altar.' It is curious to think that even two years previously his influence might well have weighed in the other scale.

In earnest and affectionate argument with a congenial spirit Donne was able to exercise the priestly functions of which circumstances had temporarily deprived him; and the long summer days passed blissfully enough in revising and transcribing his sermons.

But nothing reveals more luminously the wistful contentment of these months, upon which neither fear nor passion could encroach, than the poem which Donne addressed to his hostess as the autumn drew on. The Elegy that he wrote in celebration of her beauty emerges

with a strange rarity of tone from amongst those others
in which, in years gone by, he had ranged the whole
scale of amorous agony and delight, had spun out his
ingenious wit or prolonged a crude indulgence.

Those days of passion burning to possess are gone.
Even the humanized passion of marriage is surpassed.
Love, Donne averred, which 'as wine in June, enrages
blood' 'comes seasonablest, when our taste and appetite to other things is past.' It was this 'seasonable'
emotion that he now expressed.

'The Autumnal,' as he named this poem of homage
to Magdalen Herbert, embodies the Platonism of the
soul as distinct from that of the mind. Donne had, as
we have seen, been well able to appreciate the Platonic
idea of love as an abstraction, but it is doubtful whether
he had ever succeeded in completely incorporating it in
his realistic passion. Now at last, in the waning of his
desire, it lost all its detachment and became, so to say,
indigenous; it was truly grafted on to his instinct, and
achieved a natural flowering. He was arrived at last at
that moment when human life halts before definitely
falling into decay, when it realizes beauty, not in the
flushed and wasteful efflorescence of the spring, in the
multiplication of the physical, but rather, like art itself,
in the abstract image, the trembling impression of a
creative tide after it has ceased to flow, like some calm
echo of stormy music in the mind, or an afterglow
that lingers precariously when all the day's daring is
done.

At this psychological moment he was privileged to live
in intimate communion with her who for twenty years
had imaged his ideal of spiritual womanhood. Provi-

dence, after so ruthlessly pitching him upon the high
seas, brought him thus at last into a quiet harbour as the
late sunlight lengthened, granting him this short inter-
lude before he had to face the ordeal of his last voyage
into the unknown. The tribute is nearer that ultimate
wisdom of love, in which there is neither expectancy
nor regret, that idea at the heart of life which the poet
must ever pursue and never attain, than anything that
Donne wrote. Even his prosody is smoothed by the
prevailing calm.

> 'No spring nor summer beauty hath such grace,
> As I have seen in one autumnal face;
> Young beauties force our love, and that's a rape;
> This doth but counsel, yet you cannot 'scape.
> If 'twere a shame to love, here 'twere no shame;
> Affections here take reverence's name.
> Were her first years the Golden Age? that's true,
> But now they're gold oft tried, and ever new.
>
> .   .   .   .
>
> . . . who asks more heat than comes from hence,
> He in a fever wishes pestilence. . . .
>
> .   .   .   .
>
> Here, where still evening is, not noon, nor night;
> Where no voluptuousness, yet all delight.
> In all her words, unto all hearers fit,
> You may at revels, you at council, sit.
>
> .   .   .   .
>
> If we love things long sought, age is a thing
> Which we are fifty years in compassing;
> If transitory things, which soon decay,
> Age must be loveliest at the latest day.
>
> .   .   .   .

I hate extremes; yet I had rather stay
With tombs than cradles, to wear out a day.
Since such love's motion natural is, may still
My love descend, and journey down the hill,
Not panting after growing beauties; so
I shall ebb out with them who homeward go.'

The unsparing realist, we must admit, is not absent
even from this poem, as when he contrasts with the
grace of her whom he celebrates the ugliness of an
unlovely old age,

'Whose every tooth to a several place is gone,
To vex their souls at resurrection.'

But essentially there breathes through the whole a
quiet, tender as the evening sky, before it has begun to
pale with the premonition of night.

§ 7

But the night was at hand. For the next five years
Donne was seldom to forget it. He had already proclaimed and protested against death's dominion over his
dead wife, and the corpse of a king. 'How poor,' he
had pleaded, with a blend of fear and flattery, 'how
faint, how pale, how momentary, how transitory, how
empty, how frivolous, how Dead things, must you
necessarily think *Titles*, and *Possessions*, and *Favours*,
and all, when you see that Hand, which was *the hand
of Destiny, of Christian Destiny*, of the *Almighty God*, lie
dead? It was not so hard a hand when we touched it
last, nor so *cold* a hand when we kissed it last.' He had
even described death as a place of execution in the

tender hearing of the Princess Elizabe that Heidelberg, and thrust its inevitability with dreadful insistence and a mass of naturalistic analogy upon his Twickenham Countess, now sobered by the sorrows of the world. And now the first text which he delivered from the pulpit on his return early in 1626, when the plague had abated, was fittingly enough 'For there was not a house where there was not one dead.'

'All must die' – this was the bell that tolled through his latter years: he was to repeat it month by month as occasion invited. For it was comforting to forget, if only for a moment, the individual horror in its universal application, or to close his eyes to the ghastly incidents of the death-bed which would rise up so graphically before him – the sun setting for ever, the cloud of faintness, the awful strangulation, the livid feast of the worm – in such philosophic parallelisms as 'Doth not man die even in his birth?'

Sometimes he could bury himself in metaphorical rapture, in an ecstatic sepulchre, in that divine contemplation of which Saint Gregory spoke, when the body was consumed without a pang as by some instantaneous combustion, and the soul rode free upon the wings of vision. Then for a moment he would vindicate his soul 'against the dying life and living death of the body,' pouring his scorn on the physical and its pretensions either to pain or pleasure, comparing it to a caterpillar or a mildew, with the same frenzy of exultation as he hailed the spiritual triumphant, in virtue of its own largesse of joy, 'perfected, sealed with an everlastingness.' Or in the climax of some peroration he would, as in his 'Hymn to God the Father,' invoke the

face of God to discountenance the face of death, 'when
he lays hold on me . . . so in the agonies of death, in
the anguish of that dissolution, in the sorrows of that
valediction, in the inversibleness of that transmigration,
I shall have a joy, which shall no more evaporate, than
my soul shall evaporate, a joy, that shall pass up, and
put on a more glorious garment above, and be joy super-
invested in glory'; or again of 'The Last Day':
'The grave itself shall be open again; and . . . the
heavens shall be open, and I shall see the Son of man,
the Son of God, and not see him at that distance, that
Stephen saw him there, but see him, and sit down with
him. I shall rise from the dead, from the dark station,
from the prostration, from the prosternation of death,
and never miss the sun, which shall then be put out,
for I shall see the Son of God, the Sun of Glory, and
Shine myself, as that Sun shines.'

These were great moments, moments when the fugitive
outdistanced his pursuer, and thrilled with the conviction of eventual escape. But they were brief as they
were ecstatic. Still with 'unperturbéd pace' the dread
feet followed, and they were those not of the 'Hound
of Heaven,' but of Hell.

Seldom did 'the passing bell and the Angel's trump
sound all but one note.' Far more often he conceived
a prolonged and ghastly hiatus between the two; and
to rid himself of this nightmare he was driven to
enumerate every detail of it, to pass his burden on to
his congregation each time his fancy accumulated it
anew, and to spare them nothing.

'Corruption upon our skin (our outward beauty); corruption upon our *body* (our whole strength, and constitu-

tion). And, this corruption, not a green paleness, not a
yellow jaundice, not a blue lividness, not a black mor-
pheu upon our skin, not a bony leanness, not a sweating
faintness, not an ungracious decrepitness upon our
body, but a destruction, a destruction to both. *After my
skin my body shall be destroyed.* Though not destroyed
by being resolved to ashes in the fire (perchance I shall
not be burnt), not destroyed by being washed to slime,
in the sea (perchance I shall not be drowned), but destroyed contemptibly, by those whom I breed, and feed,
by worms.'

We cannot help regretting that cremation was not in
fashion in Donne's day. It would surely have saved his
imagination its worst moments. It would at least have
delivered him from the necessity of arguing inconclusively with the worm, which was to devour him, or of
questioning it, 'Will you change places with me?' – only
to conceive the ungenerous reply: 'No; for you are like
to live eternally in torment; for my part, I can live no
longer than the putrid moisture of your body will give
me leave, and therefore I will not change; nay, would
the *Devil* himself change with a damned soul? I cannot
tell.' If truth be told, Donne himself could not tell.
For although doubtless all that was devout and desperate in him believed what he so often reiterated, that
'Thou shalt be recompensed at the resurrection of the
just,' his own life had not been of the kind to encourage
an implicit confidence that he would be ranged with
the just, while the same physical relish for life that had
made him, at least for a time, an undeniable and even
deplorable sinner, compelled him now to visualize
death in all its most loathly detail.

So powerful indeed was this physical faculty still, that
often the assurance of religion, its texts and its sanctified
formulas, even the image of the resurrected Christ
Himself, proved the frailest of barriers against a blood-
shot realism. Body and mind together would argue that
Death was a final, a hideous dissolution, against which
no argument could be advanced and no excuse pleaded;
that it was as hopeless to elude the inevitable by visionary rapture or pious ejaculation, as it was to reconcile
the contradictions of human nature; that man was in
truth despicable, a mere battlefield of forces, trampled
at last into the loam from which he sprang.

And then a premonition of the grave would literally
make his flesh creep; for what he figured was no abstract region of blank nothingness, of dark silence,
without star or sunrise, but a puddle of human flesh,
formless, squirming, obscene. Against such imaginings
even the heroic 'O Death, where is thy sting?' rang
hollow. It was a specious boast. For death did sting;
it lacerated him almost daily. And just because of the
passivity of this opponent, this lurking expectant fact,
the position was intolerable.

There was nothing objective to attack, but only monstrous images, vile, abominable creeping things that
dragged their putrid length about his mind. And then
it was that he turned to the pulpit as a purgative. 'I
have been always,' he wrote, 'more sorry when I could
not preach, than any could be that they could not hear
me. It hath been my desire (and God may be pleased
to grant it me) that I might die in the pulpit.'

Because God did not grant this desire, Donne was
driven, as we shall see, to substitute another piece of

ceremonial, in which to drape himself from the naked realism of the death-bed. Since he might not die publicly in his surplice, he would die publicly in his shroud.

Incapable of that self-immolation by which alone he might have won serenity, Donne chose henceforth the pulpit as the public altar on which to burn the ever-replenished fuel of his tormented senses; and by this expressive sacrifice of his desires and fears he not only gained relief, but even a tortured pleasure. The sensuousness of his imagery is proof enough of that, while if his congregations witnessed in the process the slow bodily consumption of their preacher, they saw him also rise to the zenith of his spiritual power. For, as in the illness from which his 'Devotions' had flowered, and from which he had never in fact recovered, Donne's preaching shows all the symptoms of fever. It combines to an unrivalled degree an intoxicating sense of the infinite with an almost clenched grasp of the finite; but, unlike Pascal, it was the finite which terrified him.

Whether in the homelier atmosphere of St. Dunstan's or in the royal arena of St. Paul's, it was now as a man 'possessed' that he mounted the pulpit, as an evangelist that he expounded the mysteries of God, or peered awfully into the abyss of mortality, as a rhetorician of the old school that he piled up his inexorable periods, and above all as a poet that he delivered himself of his message, swaying to every tide and eddy of emotion, his voice now rolling onward in some stately period, now stressing some word or phrase again and again, like the thud of recurrent waves on the shore, now crooning softly in persuasive suggestion, now winding

skilfully through the mazes of argument and analogy,
now strident in denunciation, now mellifluous in bene-
diction, haling on his audience to transports of felicity,
or melting and moulding them into 'a companionable
sadness.'

The very term 'Rhetoric' has become debased and
suspect, since it passed from the preacher to the politi-
cian. We think of it as a device to capture the facile
attention of the mob, as at best the medium of half-
truths, at worst the trumpet of lies. Not so was the
rhetoric of Milton and Bacon, of Jeremy Taylor and
Shakespeare and Donne. Here was no shallow bombastic eloquence, no attempt to drown sense in sound or
deck inanity in vulgar ornament. To quote De Quincey's words: 'It laid the principal stress upon the
management of the thoughts, and only a secondary one
upon the ornaments of style.' Moreover, Rhetoric to
men of the seventeenth century, as to the Greek masters
in whom it originated, was an elaborate art like poetry;
its system was indeed more complicated than any system of prosody, and he who had to master so intricate an
instrument was in no danger of enjoying that surplus
energy which explains so much of the empty inflation
of modern oratory.

Donne, as we have seen, had studied much in dialectical writing and its system of controlling and developing a train of thought. It was, to our modern taste, a
somewhat cramped and creaking instrument, and one
which, on the evidence of Donne's letters and pamphlets, we should scarcely have expected to interpret
adequately the thunders and lightnings of apostolic
frenzy. Yet when Donne in the enraged agony of his

later years resorted to its time-honoured stops, how magnificently it responded! The convulsed chaos of the natural man was subdued to marvellous significance by the machinery of the casuist.

To quote De Quincey again: 'He combined what no other man has ever done – the last sublimation of dialectical subtlety and address with the most impassioned majesty.' The flesh, so to say, of his speech was strictly conditioned by the anatomy of his thought, and his description of the style of the Holy Ghost is, typically enough, a true account of his own: 'The Holy Ghost is an eloquent Author, a vehement, and an abundant Author, but yet not luxuriant; he is far from a penurious, but as far from a superfluous style too.'

When Donne erred it was not in being too sumptuous, but in being too bare. Often the bones and framework of the preacher's dialectic protruded in just as deathly a fashion as did the bones of his face, and the habit of expounding a text word by word, of returning upon a phrase in laboured fugal development, is apt to prove both cumbrous and monotonous. But it was never a mere artifice. Donne's sincerity in the pulpit was so concentrated that he modulated even a mannerism into a higher key. As a result of this fusion of his faculties in an act of expression, his prose is more consistently poetical than his verse. Both have the same flaws, such as the pursuit of forced and fantastic analogies; both can be harsh and crabbed, but seldom in his poetry were emotion and thought so perfectly wedded as to generate either the pure image or the pure idea. The poet was now too sensational, and so too realistic in expression, now too logical or abstract, and so in style

too quibbling or fantastic. But the preacher far more
often resolved such self-consciousness in the unity of
an overmastering impulse, achieving an equilibrium,
doubtful though it was, between body and mind, concrete experience and abstract meditation, thus becoming creative in that full sense where no friction lurks.

Many records testify to the impression which Donne
made as a preacher on his contemporaries. Jasper
Mayne, for example, praised the grace of his delivery
in the lines:

'I have seen thee in the pulpit stand,
Where we might take notes from thy look and hand,
And from thy speaking action bear away
More sermon than some teachers used to say.'

But artist as Donne was, and therefore studious of the
technicalities of his craft, and even of the 'elegant
phrases' of the Fathers, these were more and more
submerged in the volcanic urge of passion. He was a
fashionable preacher, not because he lowered himself
to attract audiences by any theatrical artifice, but
because he was inevitably acting in a personal drama
of absorbing interest.

His face, we are told, flushed and paled with the
violence of his feelings; he preached the word, to quote
Walton's famous if rather too romantic description,
'so as showed his own heart was possessed with those
very thoughts and joys that he laboured to distil into
others: a preacher in earnest; weeping sometimes for
his auditory, sometimes with them; always preaching
to himself, like an angel from a cloud, but in none;
carrying some, as St. Paul was, to heaven in holy

raptures, and enticing others by a sacred art and courtship to amend their lives; here picturing a vice so as to
make it ugly to those that practised it, and a virtue so
as to make it beloved even by those that lived it not;
and all this with a most particular grace and an inexpressible addition of comeliness.'

Yet his clerical brethren were less appreciative of his
eloquence than the laity. It may be that they disliked
being compared to earthquakes, thunders, lions, and
falls of water; while the starched theologian or earnest
moralist is seldom sympathetic towards the poet.
Doubtless there was justice behind their complaint as
well as jealousy. An 'angel in a cloud,' an elemental
force, is scarcely the ideal pastor for simple men. The
congregations that flocked to hear Donne preach were
not athirst for pure edification. They appreciated in
Donne the great actor or musician as much as the
great preacher, and Donne himself fostered the idea
by frequently comparing his function to that of 'a
watchman on a tower sounding a trumpet,' to the beating of a drum, or the tolling of a warning bell.

Often enough his 'sacred flattery' was moral only in
the ultimate sense in which any profound æsthetic
experience purges by pity and terror. And since an
hour, the usual length of his discourse, added to its
complicated substance, put a severe strain upon attention, many of his 'great and curious auditories' must
have quietly slept through the carefully penned
doctrinal parts of the sermon, thus reserving themselves for those periods of cadaverous rhapsody or
divine inebriation, which they greeted with such
'periodical murmurings' as actually drew from Donne a

rebuke, on the ground that their 'impertinent inter-
jections' swallowed up one quarter of his hour.

In fact Donne, like all 'possessed' people, held his
audience by a hypnotic power, by a capacity to speak
from outside the circle of ordinary consciousness and
to shock the normal vision by monstrous images of
darkness or almost unbearable shafts of light. But as a
moralist he was too subtle and learned for the humble,
and too menacing. He could terrify like some frenzied
natural force, but he could not persuade. Indeed, he
seldom makes any attempt to appeal to men's reason
or virtue. He denounces or adjures, he drags his congregation by force to the Day of Judgment, strips
them metaphorically naked, reveals them 'foul and
sinful and unclean,' and promises them 'terrible
things.' What he said of God could really be applied
to himself – that the word of His Preaching 'may be
the savour of death unto death.' The odour of corruption was indeed often in Donne's breath.

And all this was the consequence of his egoism: he
was preaching to himself, and not to his hearers. It
was the same of his public Prayers, which he described
as having the nature of violence: 'We threaten God in
prayer . . . we besiege God . . . we take God prisoner,
and bring God to our conditions.' The measure of his
own sin and morbid self-flagellation he passed on without qualification to his audience. It did not matter that
their difficulties may have been other than his own,
their flesh less rampant, or their minds less twisted by
fear. He forced his own ordeal upon them, convinced
that the essence of religion was in it. Fundamentally
he was right, but he sacrificed in the process that

intimacy of contact with his fellows which is always denied to dominating egoism.

It is only the man who has risen above the battle who can touch the secret places of the heart, who can convince without denunciation, and warn without a threat. Donne might write of his sermons in a quiet moment: 'I chose to build in this poor fashion some spittles and hospitals, where the poor and impotent sinner may find some relief, or at least understanding of his infirmity'; but no description could be less justifiable. He may indeed have humbled complacent minds, but the poor sinner (in whom vice is something far less theatrical than the snarling monster of Donne's imagination) scarcely entered his purview. And if he touched him at all, it was only to terrify and amaze.

To-day, however, we are not primarily interested either in the theological or moral value of Donne's sermons. We approach them as works of art and as the biographical data of his last years. Their style, as with everything Donne wrote, is an exact index of the man. Unlike the gentle fluidity of Jeremy Taylor's sermons, those clear pools that mirror a 'great and lovely mind,' those honeycombs of 'delicacy and sweetness,' Donne's discourse is both congealed and voluble, hard and expansive, cramped and compulsive. It is like a smouldering river of lava, now molten, now livid, here coiling liquefaction, here contorted granite. But invariably the spirit animating the style is one of intense self-consciousness; and it is this self-absorption which gives them their permanent value. The substance of practical edification or theological argument is ephemeral enough: the voice of personal confession, the artistic expression of profound emotion, survives the ages. As Donne drew onwards towards death, his ecstasy became less and less qualified by temporal considerations. We hear only the voice of crooning supplication, of cumulative rapture, of stuttering, horrified self-exploration, and above all 'the storms and thunders and earthquakes of his own despair.'

§ 8

In the sermons then of these latter years, the Donne whose personality we have explored puts a trumpet to his lips. There is no miraculous transformation. The difference is only in degree. He has, maybe, 'put a new, and a spiritual tincture and form and habit in all his thoughts,' but the thoughts, the impulses and dilemmas, are basically the same. He is still 'pregnant with th' old twins, Hope and Fear'; his hope of heavenly delight, of that eternal glory, which 'makes all worldly prosperity as dung,' and 'all worldly adversity as feathers,' is spiced with memories of earthly gratification: and his fear of hell is the exact complement of disgusted satiety.

He cites all the loathsome details of corruption with the same avidity with which he mapped out the body of woman; he wooes God's favour with the same self-debasement as he had that of exalted patrons, and even compares the Holy Ghost to a good courtier; he loves God with the same baffled sensuality, though he call it a 'holy amorousness,' with which he had loved his mistresses, and he directs the same suffering analysis to the task of unravelling the flaws in his devotion.

And when for a time the discord is resolved in the

'serenity and sweet air of a good conscience,' when the 'howling' that is the 'noise of hell' is quenched in 'singing, the voice of heaven,' when his whole being goes out suddenly in joy, 'in a continual dilatation of the heart, to receive augmentation of that which is infinite' (such joy as the realist typically describes elsewhere as likely to work 'a liquefaction, a melting of my bowels'), we recognize once again the worried husband, who, amidst a brilliant society, drowned his care in a flood of genial expansiveness. Many also of the pictures which he draws for the purposes of illustration and edification are directly autobiographical. Thus when he says: 'It is well with us, if we can ride out a storm at anchor; that is lie still and expect, and surrender ourselves to God, and anchor in that confidence, till the storm blow over,' his memory is surely reverting to that storm which the Azores expedition failed to ride out. When he quotes beggarly poverty as responsible, even more than excessive riches, for sin, and urges his audience to 'labour earnestly in the ways of some lawful calling,' he is criticizing his own life.

When he speaks of 'the sociableness of God, the communicableness of God; he loves holy meetings, he loves the Communion of saints, the household of the faithful,' he is sanctifying in his mind the society of Twickenham Park and Montgomery Castle. When he describes the best and the clearest time as being in the sunshine, when God 'appears to us in the warm and cheerful splendour of temporal blessings upon us . . . when thou hast a good estate, and good children to let it descend upon . . . good health, and a good profession to exercise thy strength, and thy labours in

. . . when the dishes upon thy table are doubled, and thy cup overflows,' he is picturing all that he longed for and lacked in Mitcham days. When he refers to 'a perpetual revolution and transmigration of souls through bodies, which hath been the giddiness of some Philosophers to think,' he is chiding the poet of 'Metempsychosis.'

But it is in his savage and yet gloating onslaught on sin that Donne owes most to his past. 'As long as we are in the valley of tentations,' he wrote, 'there is nothing, no not in spiritual things, not in faith itself perfect,' and though he conceived himself as having been delivered 'out of the womb and depth of darkness,' he was always in terror of returning to it, always fearful 'that God should let my soul fall out of his hand into a bottomless pit and roll an unremoveable stone upon it . . . that of that providence of God, that studies the life of every weed, and worm and ant and spider and toad and viper, there should never, never, any beam flow out upon me.'

His morbid consciousness of sin was like his horror of death, the rebellious stab of the physical within him that would not submit to a spiritual dispensation; and to purge himself of the discord, of licentious memories which at once allured and outraged him, he was driven to express them in words, as when, recording doubtless an experience of his own youth, he speaks of 'the adulterer, whose eye waits for the twilight, going forth, and casting his eyes upon forbidden houses.'

The purpose is, of course, always moral, but the voluptuous, the relished imagery is proof enough of the power which the flesh still exercised over him. Even

when he describes his ultimate communion with God,
the physical savour is almost overpowering:

'It was the flesh of every wanton object here, that
would allure it in the petulancy of mine eye. . . . But,
in heaven, it is Caro mea, *My flesh*, my soul's flesh, my
Saviour's flesh. As my heart is assimilated to my flesh,
and made one flesh with it; as my soul is assimilated
to my God . . . so there my flesh shall be assimilated
to the flesh of my Saviour.'

That he is still subservient to the physical he pathetically admits on many occasions in weighty illustration of the doctrine of Original Sin, as when he
says:

'With what a holy alacrity, with what a heavenly joy,
with what a cheerful peace, should I come to the
participation of those means and seals of my reconciliation, and pardon of all my sins, if I knew myself
to be delivered from Original Sin, from that snake in
my bosom, from that poison in my blood, from that
leaven and tartar in all my actions, that casts me into
Relapses of those sins which I have repented? And
what a cloud upon the best serenity of my conscience,
what an interruption, what a discontinuance from the
sincerity and integrity of that joy, which belongs to a
man truly reconciled to God, in the pardon of his
former sins, must it needs be still to know, and to
know by lamentable experiences, that though I wash
myself with Soap, and Nitre, and Snow-water, mine
own cloathes will defile me again, though I have
washed myself in the tears of Repentance, and in the
blood of my Saviour, though I have no guiltiness of
any former sin upon me at that present, yet I have a

sense of a root of sin that is not grub'd up, of *Originall sin*, that will cast me back again.'

Such confessions as these (and there are many by far more precise) are not vague pulpit oratory. They leave no doubt that Donne had still an intense craving for physical indulgence which he could not harmonize with any doctrine of 'grace' or exorcize by religious formulas. And the subtlety with which he diagnoses every variety and every degree of sin is only equalled by the terror, as of one trembling on the edge of some seething crater, with which he summons up before his audience 'what passes between God and those men, upon whom the curse of God lieth, in their dark *horrors at midnight.*'

Sometimes in his multiplication of the horrors of hell we are inclined to class him with those writers of whom Lamb said, 'they terrify babes with painted devils: but they know not how a soul is capable of being moved; their terrors want dignity, their affrightments are without decorum.' And yet Donne is so stammeringly sincere, so elemental in his terrified foreboding, that his accumulations of horror almost rival in their effect a Websterian concentration.

'What extraction of wormwood,' he cries, 'can be so bitter, what exaltation of fire can be so raging, what multiplying of talents can be so heavy, what stiffness of destiny can be so inevitable, what confection of gnawing worms, of gnashing teeth, of howling cries, of scalding brimstone, of palpable darkness, can be so, so insupportable, so inexpressible, so unimaginable, as the curse and malediction of God?'

Only one who had himself known the horrors and

T

squalor of a personal hell, of being suffocated in the vile embracements of the flesh, could impute such devilry to the Deity, to the spirit of life with which he longed to reconcile himself, pleading deliriously: 'What torment is not a marriage-bed to this damnation, to be secluded eternally, eternally, eternally from the sight of God?'

But to Donne the punishment of sin was never merely negative, a withdrawal from the light of life, just as death was other than nescience. Both figured in his mind as states of seething and polluted activity, and he firmly believed 'that every sin casts another shovel of Brimstone' upon unfortunate malefactors squirming in hell. In this stirring of hell-broth, as in his dynastic conception of the Deity, he was completely mediæval, being equally incapable of disentangling the idea of death from the fact of corruption, and the idea of God from the force of life. Any such thought as 'the marriage of Heaven and Hell' was alien to his dualistic being. His God was not only a beneficent creative spirit, all radiance and joy, but also His antithesis, violent darkness and pain; he was not only a sublime idea, but, if rebuffed, a malevolent force. In fact Donne, like Milton, imputed to God both the physical and spiritual attributes which he himself reflected.

After the sins of the body came the sins of the mind. For logic denied him harmony, as well as lust. It was a subtle rather than a ferocious opponent; and he had measured its limits, as will be remembered, in 'An Anatomy of the World,' and in much of his earlier correspondence. Nevertheless his was too bold and inquiring a mind ever to allow him to anchor in faith;

his difficulty therefore was to preserve on the open
sea the balance between superstition and scepticism.
In reality he plunged frequently into either the one or
the other, upon alternate waves of panic and honesty.

'We may search so far,' he said, 'and reason so long of
faith and *grace*, as that we may lose not only *them*, but
even our reason too, and sooner become *mad* than *good*.
Not that we are bound to believe anything *against
reason*, that is, to believe, we know not why.' Or again:
'*Knowledge* cannot save us, but we cannot be saved
without knowledge; Faith is not on this side knowledge, but beyond it.'

These are excellent truths, but Donne was unfortunately compelled by his ordination oath to believe
and preach a number of doctrines which ran directly
counter to reason, in the true rather than the casuistical
sense. And although he could plead a lawyer's case
for them, the conflict between dogma and that natural
intelligence, once so scornful of compromise, is often
apparent, and there is even something pitiable in the
spectacle of the intellectual rover of other days seriously
discussing as fact the domestic economy of Angels and
Devils, arguing whether the Serpent walked upright
before the Fall, and deprecating metaphysical inquiry
as 'forc'd dishes of hot brains, and not sound meat.'

But if Donne's hands were tied as far as doctrine was
concerned, he was able to bring the same detached and
minute observance to bear upon his own spiritual
lapses as before upon his physical excesses.

'I throw myself down in my chamber, and I call in
and invite God and His angels thither; and when they
are there, I neglect God and His angels for the noise

of a fly, for the rattling of a coach, for the whining of a door; I talk on, in the same posture of prayer; eyes lifted up, knees bowed down, as though I prayed to God; and if God should ask me when I thought last of God in that prayer I cannot tell: sometimes I find that I forgot what I was about, but when I began to forget it, I cannot tell. A memory of yesterday's pleasures, a fear of to-morrow's dangers, a straw under my knee, a noise in my ear, a chimera in my brain, troubles me in my prayer.' How vivid and how subtle in self-analysis it is! And what a phenomenon is this of so modern and self-conscious a mind moving in a world of mediæval thought!

But if Donne in his worst moments of twisted naturalism was apt to 'tear open the jaws of Earth, and Hell, and cast himself actually and really into it, out of a mis-imagination, that God had cast him into it before,' there were other times, when his senses drank life as voluptuously as death, when his soul, 'as a flower at sun-rising, conceived a sense of God, in every beam of his, and spread and dilated itself towards him in a thankfulness,' in every small blessing that he shed upon her.'

Nevertheless we must admit that the materialist is as apparent in his descriptions of heaven as the mediævalist in those of hell, as when he says of it: 'A new earth, where all their waters are milk, and all their milk honey; where all their grass is corn, and all their corn manna; where all their glebe, and all their clods of earth, are gold; and all their gold of innumerable carats'; a vision to whet the appetite alike of the Board of Agriculture and of Wall Street!

Even such material blisses as these were few in his
latter years. Death was in the air and dimmed the
sun. His body, as it wasted away, seemed to transform
itself into a sickly miasma that at once stifled and morbidly aggravated his desire for liberated consciousness.
The cheerful, reasonable, courtly cleric drifted more
and more into a mediæval twilight, preoccupied with
the intricacies of temptation and the niceties of lust,
warning his congregations against 'the sinful remembrance of former sins, which is a dangerous rumination,
and unwholesome chewing of the cud,' and yet as
constantly returning to it himself.

For there was no conception of life upon which this
man, at once materialist and mystic, could rest serene,
as in some clear and steadfast illumination. That
which fed the physical in him tortured the spiritual,
while the spiritual itself piled up the fuel of remorse.
And before him loomed death, that moment of con-
vulsive grappling between the two, so long delayed
and compromised, but which at last no ingenuity, no
elaborate appeals to the Fall of Man or the Redemption, could either defer or really relieve of its tragic
awfulness. Nevertheless Donne set himself not only
to rehearse the part which he dreaded to play but to
discover also some kind of decorative ritual, which
might mitigate the horror, and even rob the physical
of something of its material triumph, by compelling it
to serve a ghostly symbolism.

§ 9

Death attacked Donne from without as well as from
within. Early in 1627 he lost one of his daughters,

and in May and June, within a few weeks of each other, the two patronesses who had inspired respectively his secular ambitions and his religious aspirations. It was sad as it was difficult to think of one who had ruled a court of poets with such grace and distinction, of one so brilliant and vivacious as the Countess of Bedford, dying slowly and painfully in reduced circumstances and with 'spirits far spent.' But Donne had never gone to her for spiritual sustenance, and for material he had long ceased to depend on her. It was otherwise with Magdalen Herbert. With her crumbled a living prop upon which he had leant long, and since he could never again invoke her living presence to exorcize the dæmons of his blood and brain, he comforted himself with picturing the beauty of her death-bed, and the disarming smile with which she greeted that 'fearfullest *Messenger*, Death.' 'She shew'd no fear of his face, in any change of her own; but died without any change of *countenance*, or *posture*; without any *struggling*, any *disorder*; but her *Death-bed* was as quiet as her *Grave*.' The thought of it almost cleansèd his mind of putrefaction.

The next year brought the deaths of his faithful friend Sir Henry Goodyer and of the comrade of his elopement, Christopher Brooke. But if the roots of his life were being torn up, there was still sap enough in his branches, both to put forth foliage and attract new friends to its shade. He found a new circle of intimates, chief among whom was a Mrs. Cokain, a lady introduced to him by Goodyer before his death. She had been deserted by her husband, and lived with a family of seven young children at Ashbourne. To her

Donne confided himself in many letters, as 'a friend, a brother, and a priest of God,' and if the professional priest rather wearisomely preponderates, there seems no doubt that he had a real affection for this 'dearest, noblest and lovingest sister,' to whom he could write that 'nothing returns oftener with more comfort to my memory than you.'

Among other new acquaintances was Isaak Walton, who, as a parishioner of St. Dunstan's, was drawn on by curiosity and by admiration for the extraordinary eloquence of the preacher to study the nature and history of the man. As an eye-witness of these last years and days, Walton is invaluable, although his piety even here is apt to blunt the edge of his psychology.

The significance of Donne's life passes now altogether from the stage of external event into that of inward conflict – 'that solitariness and arraignment of myself,' which issued in his sermons. The need of preaching became imperative. The great festivals of Christmas, Easter and Whitsunday he still reserved, to speak colloquially, for his star-performances; but, if we are to believe Walton, it was his habit now to preach once a week, if not oftener, and 'after his sermon he never gave his eyes rest, till he had chosen out a new text, and that night cast his sermon into form, and his text into divisions.'

From such incessant study, as from some vault where he wrestled with slippery shades and confluxes of darkness, he emerged on Saturdays, to renew himself for the struggle by contact with humanity. And then it was that Walton and other friends gathered round him, and the challenge of death was forgotten for a few hours in the cheerful interchanges of conversation and reminiscence.

In August, 1628, Donne's daughter Margaret took the smallpox, and compelled him to withdraw from the Deanery to Peckham, and thence into Bedfordshire. Soon after his arrival there he suffered so serious a return of his old fever that he was driven to return to London to consult his physician, Dr. Foxe. On the journey he also developed tonsillitis, but after being blooded and starving for ten days he 'returned to a convenient temper, and pulse, and appetite.'

Nevertheless, as he cannot but have suspected, this was the first of death's final assaults. He found his clerical work 'more than my present state will bear,' and on Dr. Foxe's advice retired for some months into the country. But he was incapable of that vegetation which alone might have restored his strength, and it was plain that his vitality could not indefinitely sustain the incessant strain imposed upon it. The fire was eating into the fuel too speedily for it to be replaced.

He returned, however, to London in time to occupy the pulpit of St. Paul's on Christmas Day, and to continue in regular attendance there and at Whitehall until May, 1629. His health then broke down again, and compelled another complete retirement for six months.

He was come now, in his own grim words, 'to pay a fever every half-year as a rent for my life,' and at every new demand he felt less confident of his exchequer being able to meet the bill.

What agonies of doubt, what writhings of conscience, accompanied the 'damps and flushings' that pervaded his system, during these months, we cannot say. For the first time in his life, he suffered in silence. Certainly his vital forces were failing, and despite the last flare of his egoism, which was yet to come, it may be that he began to view his end with something of resignation, that the idea of release from the unending friction of body and mind was, in jaded moments, not unwelcome. Nothing else can explain the sudden cessation of all self-expression, even of correspondence, unless it was that he had now no friend intimate enough to entrust with the unconquerable terror, which he despised: while 'it was not,' he wrote, 'for my gravity to write of feathers and straws.'

In November he preached at St. Paul's Cross, but for the first time was unequal to his Christmas Day sermon in the Cathedral. Through the early months of 1630 he was able, by nursing his strength, to continue his duties, but he preached for the last time in St. Paul's late in March, on Easter Day.

The summer brought no new lease of life, and in August, when he went down to visit his eldest daughter at Aldborough Hatch, in Epping Forest, his fever returned never to leave him. There he lingered as autumn darkened into winter, the fever smouldering in his blood, incapable at times of moving, occasionally 'breaking prison and walking into the garden.'

He was troubled by some malicious rumours that 'he was not so ill, as he pretended,' but had withdrawn 'to live at ease, discharged of preaching'; and sardonically entertained by others that he was dead. 'I have never good temper,' he wrote, 'nor good pulse, nor good appetite, nor good sleep,' and confessed that he was 'more affected with coughs in vehemence, more with deafness, more with toothache, more with the uvula, than heretofore.' 'I humbly thank God,' he wrote at another time, 'I am only not worse; for I should as soon look for roses at this time of the year as look for increase of strength.'

That lifelong process by which the physical in Donne was slowly transformed into the spiritual was in truth reaching its last stages, and he himself was perfectly conscious of it. 'All this,' he was happy to note, 'mellows me for heaven, and so ferments me in this world as I shall need no long concoction in the grave, but hasten to the resurrection.' It was satisfactory to think that the more thoroughly the fever did its work, the less would there be for the worm.

More than two years before he had announced in St. Paul's: 'Thou pursuest the works of the flesh, and hast none, for thy flesh is but dust held together by plaisters: Dissolution and putrefaction is gone over thee alive; Thou hast overliv'd thine own death, and art become thine own ghost, and thine own hell.' It was indeed increasingly true of himself, and to so doughty a lover of life, death itself began to wear a more favourable aspect, as it promised a dramatic end to so neutral a state.

'My noble sister,' he wrote to Mrs. Cokain, 'I am afraid that death will play with me so long, as he will forget to kill me, and suffer me to live in a languishing and useless age, a life, that is rather a forgetting that I am dead, than of living.'

Such was his condition in the lethargic periods which intervened between the actual attacks of fever, when he was affected rather, as in the past, with an abnormal self-consciousness, an ecstasy, which he described as being 'at the gates of heaven.'

Late in December he drew up his will, in which he gave 'God an entire sacrifice of body and soul'; and now fully conscious that his days were numbered he determined, say rather he was compelled, to enter the pulpit for a last time, in the hope it may be of realizing his oft-expressed wish to die there, or at least to engage publicly in one final bout with his adversary death, and thus by purging himself of the torments which had been fermenting within him all these months, prepare himself for his death-bed.

It had always been his custom to preach at Whitehall on the first Friday in Lent, and, weak as he was, he returned to London in January to consult with Dr. Foxe how best he might strengthen himself for the ordeal. Dr. Foxe prescribed cordials and the drinking of milk for twenty days, and extreme as was Donne's distaste for milk, he agreed to follow this advice for ten days, at the end of which time he told his doctor that 'he would not drink it ten days longer, upon the best moral assurance of having twenty years added to his life; for he loved it not; and was so far from fearing death, which to others is the King of Terrors, that he longed for the day of dissolution.'

That he longed for the day may well have been true, but that its approach was void of terror the astounding sermon that he was now to deliver sufficiently refutes.

His friends, seeing his extreme emaciation, were anxious to dissuade him from undertaking a task beyond his powers. But he passionately insisted. 'And when, to the amazement of some of the beholders, he appeared in the pulpit, many of them thought he presented himself not to preach mortification by a living voice, but mortality by a decayed body and a dying face' – a conjecture which subsequent events might have confirmed. 'And doubtless many did secretly ask that question in Ezekiel, "Do these bones live?" or, can that soul organize that tongue, to speak so long time as the sand in that glass will move towards its centre, and measure out an hour of this dying man's unspent life? Doubtless it cannot.' And yet, after some faint pauses in his zealous prayer, his strong desires enabled his weak body to discharge his memory of his preconceived meditations, which were of dying: the text being 'To God the Lord belong the issues from Death.'

'What kind of issue,' announced that seamed and shrunken visage, 'we shall have out of this world, whether prepared or sudden, whether violent or natural, whether in our perfect senses, or shak'd and disordered by sickness . . . the issue of death is a deliverance in death . . . for our very birth and en-trance into this life is an issue from death . . . and a delivering over to another death, the manifold deaths of the world. . . . We have a winding-sheet in our mother's womb . . . and we come into the world wound up in that winding-sheet; for we come to seek a grave. . . . We celebrate our own funeral with cries, even at our birth.'

And then the strained voice proceeded to recount with cumulative intensity all the deaths that are in life from its beginning to its end:

'This whole world is but an universall churchyard, but our common grave. . . . That which we call life . . . is but a dying seven times over, and there is an end. Our birth dies in infancy, and our infancy dies in youth, and youth and the rest die in age, and age also dies and determines all. . . . Our youth is worse than our infancy, and our age worse than our youth. Our youth is hungry and thirsty, after those sins, which our infancy knew not; And our age is sorry and angry, that it cannot pursue those sins which our youth did.' And beyond 'every day's death and every hour's death' lay 'the final dissolution of body and soul, the end of all.'

'But then,' he cried, as the tears crept down his haggard cheeks, 'is that the end of all? is that dissolution of body and soul, the last death that the body shall suffer? (for of spiritual death we speak not now;) it is not . . . though it be an issue from the manifold deaths of this world, yet it is an entrance into the death of corruption, and putrefaction, and vermiculation, and incineration, and dispersion, in, and from the grave, in which every dead man dies over again. It was a prerogative peculiar to Christ, not to die this death, not to see corruption.' For Christ, he argued, was 'embalm'd with eternity' . . . with divine nature 'even in his body as well as in his soul,' and by this 'hypostatical union,' this so perfect marriage of the human and the divine, there was no flaw by which friction and so dissolution might creep in.

The thought emboldened him to conceive of the extension of such a state to man at Christ's second coming, until the tired voice swelled in power and rich-

ness as it proclaimed: 'Behold I show you a mystery.
. . . In an instant we shall have a dissolution, and in
the same instant a redintegration . . . and that shall
be truly a death, and truly a resurrection, but no sleeping, no corruption . . .'

Meanwhile, however (and the voice assumed once
again its sepulchral tones), 'for us, who die now, and
sleep in the state of the dead, we must all pass this
posthume death, this death after death, nay this death
after burial, this dissolution after dissolution, this death
of corruption and putrefaction. . . .'

'Miserable riddle,' he exclaimed, his voice, we fancy,
suddenly becoming shrill, 'when the same worm must
be my mother, and my sister, and myself. Miserable
incest, when I must be married to mine own mother
and sister, beget and bear that worm, which is all that
miserable penury, when my mouth shall be filled with
dust, and the worm shall feed and feed secretly upon
me. . . . One dieth at his full strength, being wholly
at ease, and in quiet, and another dies in the bitterness
of his soul, and never eats with pleasure; but they lie
down alike in the dust, and the worms cover them. . . .
That all that Monarch, who spread over so many
nations alive, must in his dust lie in a corner of that
sheet of lead, and there, but so long as that lead will
last, and that private and retir'd man, that thought
himself his own for ever, and never came forth, must
in his dust of the grave be published, and (such are the
revolutions of the graves) be mingled with the dust of
every highway, and of every dunghill, and swallowed
in every puddle and pond; This is the most inglorious
and contemptible vilification, the most deadly and

peremptory nullification of man, that we can consider
. . . If we say can this dust live? perchance it cannot.
It may be the mere dust of the earth which never did
live, nor ever shall; it may be the dust of that man's
worms which do live, but shall no more; it may be the
dust of another man that concerns not him of whom it
is asked.'

Such conjectures were too awfully, too insidiously
attractive to dwell upon longer: the preacher tore himself away from them. He turned from the visualiza-
tion of his own death to an assessment of his own
life.

'Our Critical day is not the very day of our death, but
the whole course of our life'; better were it to consider
this than to 'nourish a vain imagination of immortality
and immutability.' And yet the consideration of the
past brought no relief, but only added terrors to the
future. What waste, what wantonness, what blasphemy
there had been! Surely the wages of sin must be paid?
How then might death be made tolerable? In the
Christian religion only, with its claim to hold 'the keys
of death,' might he escape from the paroxysm of himself. 'There was nothing more free, more voluntary,
more spontaneous than the death of Christ.' The
thought was like a cool breeze fanning his fever. If
Christ could die so wonderfully, with such cleanli-
ness and heroism, could not he too? And the worm
was forgotten, the turmoil of the grave was hushed
for awhile, as he lived again through the incidents
of Christ's passion, from Herod to Pilate and the
Cross.

'There now hangs that sacred body upon the cross,

rebaptiz'd in his own tears and sweat, and embalm'd in
his own blood alive. There are those bowels of compassion, which are so conspicuous, so manifested, as
that you may see them through his wounds. There
those glorious eyes grow faint in their light, so as the
Sun asham'd to survive them, departed with his light
too. . . . There we leave you, in that blessed depend-
ency, to hang upon him, that hangs upon the Cross.
There bathe in his tears, there suck at his wounds, and
lie down in peace in his grave, till he vouchsafe you
a Resurrection, and an ascension into the kingdom
which he hath purchas'd for you with the inestimable
price of his incorruptible blood.'

The 'faint and hollow' voice ceased, the features so
writhen and demented before, seemed bathed now in
some sublunary ecstasy. The idealist had wrestled
with the realist for the last time in open assembly, and
he had gained his usual momentary victory, by invoking the scriptural story to oppose the combined forces
of his body and his mind. In the exultation of it Donne
forgot his exhaustion, forgot everything but the sense
of relief, of immeasurable satisfaction, which stole over
his senses. He even 'hastened' back to his house, 'out
of which he never moved, till, like St. Stephen, "he was
carried by devout men to his grave." '

§ 10

In the five weeks which intervened before Donne
finally took to his bed, he continued to prepare himself
against the event. He could no longer relieve the
tension by acting in the pulpit, by converting a private
problem into a public parable, and so was driven to

discover some other sort of symbolism, of picturesque
ceremonial in which to drape the obscenity of fact.

He belonged to an age which could well appreciate
this craving for gesture and ritual; for man was grown
rational enough to realize the indignity of his servitude
to nature, but not to assert his superiority. He therefore played the actor to hide his humiliation from himself, as one who is secretly ashamed of a humble birth
and upbringing will over-emphasize etiquette when
he enters privileged society. To those doubtful of the
spirit, form is an invaluable refuge. Thus it was with
Donne.

His end was so extremely mannered because its
material aspect terrified him. He had always exploited
his material as an artist to escape it; and now he
honoured death with both a private and a public
performance.

His family crest was, perhaps fittingly, a sheaf of
snakes; it was an unpleasant, a squirming emblem,
and he determined to rid himself of it and incidentally
bid a symbolic farewell to his closest friends, by having
a new seal made, representing the body of Christ
crucified upon an anchor – the emblem of hope. This
he dispatched to them, engraven very small in helio-
tropium stones, and set in gold.

Chief among the recipients was George Herbert, and
Donne accompanied his gift with some lines in which
he displayed himself once more as a poet, and explained
the personal application of the symbolism:

> 'Adopted in God's family, and so
> My old coat lost, into new Arms I go.

U

The cross, my seal in Baptism, spread below,
Does by that form into an anchor grow.

.　　　.　　　.　　　.　　　.　　　.

But he that makes our crosses Anchors thus,
Is Christ, who there is crucified for us.
Yet with this I may my first Serpents hold; —
God gives new blessings, and yet leaves the old —
The Serpent, may, as wise, my pattern be;
My poison, as he feeds on dust, that's me.
And, as he rounds the earth to murder, sure
He is my death; but on the Cross, my cure.
Crucify nature then; and then implore
All grace from him, crucified there before.'

The whole problem of Donne's personality is incorporated in this little poem. He does not dismiss the
serpent with the vague obloquy of the pious: it is not
only 'my poison' but 'my pattern' — poisonous as the
emblem of corruption, inspiring as the symbol of human
intelligence. And Christ, as the ideal intelligence, is
the serpent transformed, purged of all grossness, completed in all wisdom. Thus once again Donne, faithful
as ever to the earth he loved and dreaded, attested the
evolutionary nature of things and refused his credence
to any supernatural miracle. Even Christ was the ultimate fruition of the worm, born of the crucifixion of
nature, and not of her denial.

Death itself, Donne argued, was a like crucifixion, and
that Christ should have endured and survived it was
indeed full of consolation and hope, if only he himself
could have silenced the lurking incredulity of his mind
and the gross awareness of his senses.

Fortunately in February an incident occurred which served to divert his thoughts in the direction of a theatrical tableau. His doctor, who saw that his patient's vitality was rapidly failing, begged him to arrange without delay to have a monument made of him, to stand in the Cathedral. Donne seized upon the idea with avidity, his mind grimly playing with a score of fantastic notions. Thus would he conquer death, thus should marble mock the tickling of the worm: thus could his egoism trick the teeth of time. Posterity should never owe to him a pompous platitude in stone, but he would awe it, as he had awed his contemporaries from the pulpit; so long as marble survived and men could see, he would remain a parable of life in the arms of death. For, on his own admission, 'As our pride begins in our cradle, it continues in our Graves and Monuments.'

First he 'sent for a carver to make for him in wood the figure of an urn, giving him directions for the compass and height of it; and to bring with it a board, of the just height of his body. These being got, then without delay a choice painter was got to be in readiness to draw his picture. . . . Several charcoal fires being first made in his large study, he brought with him into that place his winding-sheet in his hand and having put off all his clothes, had this sheet put upon him, and so tied with knots at his head and feet, and his hands so placed as dead bodies are usually fitted, to be shrouded and put into their coffin, or grave. Upon this urn he thus stood, with his eyes shut, and with so much of the sheet turned aside as might show his lean, pale, and death-like face, which was purposely turned towards the east, from whence he expected the second coming of his and our Saviour Jesus.'

It seems probable that Donne's strength failed before the painter had completed his task, and that he lay down while the drapery was studied. The fall of the folds, at least in the statue modelled later, presumably on this picture, by Nicholas Stone, betrays a recumbent position.

The picture afforded Donne extreme delight. What shudders it would cause posterity! Perhaps his only regret was, as expressed ten years before in a sermon, that 'Painters have presented to us with some horror, the skeleton, the frame of the bones of a man's body; but the state of a body, in the dissolution of the grave, no pencil can present to us.'

He gloated over this, the most expressive of all his acts, as an artist over a masterpiece achieved after years of barren toil. He could not tear himself away from it, but 'caused it to be set by his bed-side, where it continued and became his hourly object till his death.'

His earnest endeavour now was to make the fact worthy of its pictorial representation. Here was a model, so to say, to die up to. 'Upon Monday, after the drawing this picture, he took his last leave of his beloved study; and, being sensible of his hourly decay, retired himself to his bed-chamber.' He spent the week in taking 'a solemn and deliberate farewell' of friends, and after completing any outstanding business let it be known that henceforth 'he would not mix in thoughts with anything that concerned this world; . . . but as Job, so he waited for the appointed day of his dissolution.'

'And now he was so happy as to have nothing to do but to die, to do which he stood in need of no longer time; for he had studied it long, and to so happy a perfection.' Yet Donne was not one to be idle even on his death-bed, or to succumb graciously to that air of sanctity with which Walton has so feelingly invested him. The restless mind still chafed, the eyes blazed, the emaciated hand began to scribble. Eight days before his death the poet bade farewell to life with the same concentrated uniqueness, the same chemistry of fancy and analogy, of geography and devotion, as he had brought to the celebration of his mistresses in the hey-day of his youth. He called his poem 'A Hymn to God, my God, in my Sickness,' and it ran thus:

'Since I am coming to that Holy room,
　　Where, with Thy choir of saints for evermore
I shall be made Thy music; as I come
　　I tune the instrument here at the door,
　　And what I must do then, think here before;

'Whilst my physicians by their love are grown
　　Cosmographers, and I their map, who lie
Flat on this bed, that by them may be shown
　　That this is my south-west discovery,
　　Per fretum febris, by these straits to die;

'I joy, that in these straits I see my west;
　　For, though those currents yield return to none,
What shall my west hurt me? As west and east
　　In all flat maps – and I am one – are one,
　　So death doth touch the resurrection.

'Is the Pacific sea my home? Or are
   The eastern riches? Is Jerusalem?
Anyan, and Magellan, and Gibraltar?
   All straits, and none but straits, are ways to
      them,
   Whether where Japhet dwelt, or Cham, or Shem.

'We think that Paradise and Calvary,
   Christ's cross and Adam's tree, stood in one place;
Look, Lord, and find both Adams met in me;
   As the first Adam's sweat surrounds my face,
   May the last Adam's blood my soul embrace.

'So, in His purple wrapp'd, receive me, Lord;
   By these His thorns, give me His other crown;
And as to others' souls I preach'd Thy word,
   Be this my text, my sermon to mine own,
   "Therefore that He may raise, the Lord throws
      down." '

   How wonderfully the taut mind controls the quailing
nerves! To the end Donne's brain preserved its grip
upon his body.
   'He lay fifteen days earnestly expecting his hourly
change; and in the last hour of his last day, as his body
melted away, and vapoured into spirit . . . he said: "I
were miserable if I might not die." ' It was his first
and last complete surrender.
   'His speech, which had long been his ready and faithful servant, left him not till the last minute of his life
. . . as his last breath departed from him, he closed
his own eyes, and then disposed his hands and body

into such a posture as required not the least alteration
by those that came to shroud him.'

The artist had played the part for which his whole
career had been a painful rehearsal, to perfection. There
was a precision, a formality about Donne's death in
fitting contrast to the turbulence of his life. And who
that knew that picture of him 'drawn by a curious hand,
at his age of eighteen, with his sword, and what other
adornments might then suit with the present fashions
of youth and the giddy gaieties of that age,' would have
recognized the same being in the haggard face that lay
– was it in agony or peace or derision? – beneath the
jaunty rosette of the winding-sheet?

> 'How much shall I be changed,
> Before I am changed!'

had been Donne's motto, and it was literally true. The
dead face was the ruin, almost the caricature, of the
young one. The flesh had been burnt away and what
remained of it puckered in the flames of life: the bold
eyes were sealed within their bulging lids, the once full
and insolent lips were stretched tight and thin, the upper
one curling backward beneath the cropped moustache
with a faint but undeniable suggestion of malice and
mockery; the gross nose was wasted, and where it met
the brow formed a delta of contorted wrinkles; the
swarthy beard, once so luxuriant and yet trim, was
withered, the skin on the cheeks and temples was so
shrunk, so scorched and lined, that it seemed like a
wasted parchment stretched precariously over the bare
bone.

It was a face at once grotesque and sublime, sinister

and sanctified, fiendish and devout, seared and purified, cynically ecstatic. The craftiness and arrogance of his youth were sobered into a hungry, a cadaverous simper, while his mysticism seemed to glimmer through the shadowy hollows with a phosphorescent light.

In this enigmatical face was concentrated a complete biography, the history of a mind and a body for ever at warfare, of senses tormented by greed and weariness, and a soul strangled with self-disgust, of one for ever defeated and for ever unconquerable.

Many years before he had written:

> 'But soul we find too earthly to ascend,
> Till slow access hath made it wholly pure,
> Able immortal clearness to endure.'

And now that at last he had wholly 'left his nature to converse with fire,' did that vexed spirit rejoice in a harmony achieved, or did it drown only in the cool deeps of nescience? Surely so vital a force, so tense a consciousness, spurned the thought of blank annihilation? And yet the sardonic lips gave no encouragement to pleasant conjecture. It was enough that the fire had so effectively burnt itself out as to leave little more than a pile of pallid ashes.

'Thus variable, thus virtuous was the life,' wrote Walton; and virtuous it was, although in another sense than Walton's. Donne's life had the cardinal virtue of honesty. 'For more than forty years through the wilderness of the many temptations and various turnings of a dangerous life,' he preserved a native integrity and a native discord. He failed to harmonize, but he refused to compromise. And so his life is at once the crudest of conflicts and the fiercest of fevers, a conflict that could never end in peace and a fever that could only burn itself out.

How greatly circumstances aggravated his dilemma, the facts of his life have sufficiently shown. Yet even if, avoiding the fatal indiscretion of his marriage, he had shone like a star in the social firmament, or grown into a prosperous diplomat, it is difficult to believe that the internal conflict could have been indefinitely delayed, that he could have escaped in the activities of a profession the agonies of a personality.

'Poor intricated soul!' he once said of 'The Atheist,' 'Riddling, perplexed, labyrinthicall soul!' and essentially it was of himself that he spoke. His theology, his doctrine may have been unexceptionable on grounds of orthodoxy, but his Christianity was no more than the veneer of the savage. He did not so much evolve a religion as represent a complex, and because that complex is typical of Puritanism in its origin, and, as such, of a stage in the spiritual development of man, repeated from generation to generation in the individual, his life has more than a personal significance.

It should make a particular appeal to an age such as ours, which is even more puzzled how to bring the head into harmony with life than the heart. We, in a very different way, are in danger of losing touch with any unifying idea external to ourselves, of being prisoned within the relativity of our own conceptions, and so of becoming dwarfed and mechanical for want of that apprehension of creative purpose in the universe which invites to self-forgetfulness, and which it is art's and religion's aim to supply.

To the Puritan of the seventeenth century a gulf suddenly yawned between nature and man. The old joy of the senses, the old care-free innocence of instinct was tarnished, because man had begun to be self-conscious and to exploit the material of life to his own hurt and to the disturbing of Nature's economy. He had discovered how consciously to abuse and criticize the physical impulses which before he had almost unthinkingly accepted.

And from such criticism sprang self-disgust and cynicism – or, as religion names it, a sense of sin – the first symptoms of man's superiority to the flesh, of his human and rational prerogative.

But if intellectual man was born out of natural man, he was still the slave to the physical which he criticized. It was that which made his criticism so agonized. He was drowning, even while he cursed the ocean that engulfed him.

At the same time he had frayed the organic thread which connected him with nature, and through which the primitive man absorbs rude strength and health as indifferently as the tree or the flower draws moisture from the atmosphere. He enjoyed neither a physical nor a spiritual harmony, but was torn in the strife between his intelligence and his impulses. Thus the Christian ideal acted as a poison on the natural man in the process of proving a purge, and self-consciousness was the only discipline by which his egoism might learn the wisdom of selflessness. It was the discipline of war, since before the physical and the rational could be reconciled in a spiritual, a completely human, ideal, a dreadful battle had necessarily to be fought – has likewise, though generally in a modified form, to be fought to-day.

It was Donne's great and tragic destiny to experience the worst agonies of that inconclusive battle, and to bequeath to literature the tale of it. With a kindred fierceness he loved life and hated it, accepted and denied it. He was as sensual in his later asceticism as in his earlier indulgence, at once too Pagan to be a Christian and too Christian to be a Pagan. The corollary of his lust for life was his dread of death; for death meant surely an end to sensation, against which his goaded instinct rose in horrified rebellion which no philosophy might quell.

The battle still persists, the reconcilement is still grievously hard, the redemption always uncertain. But it is less intense perhaps for us, because evolution has made us less Pagan and more rational. Few of us lust after life with Donne's ferocity, and the horizons of our mind are wider. We are less hopeful of heaven or fearful of hell, and we are inclined to temper the problem of evil with tolerance, even to regard the dilemmas of a conjectural hereafter with a certain quiet indifference.

Similarly we approach life with less assurance and less arrogance. Whether out of weakness or strength, we are less afflicted by a sense of sin, and so less given to moral denunciation. Impressed by the relativity of things, we are perhaps too content to be merely tentative and experimental, and to deprecate any absolute conclusions. We have ceased to accept the large and material generalities once denoted by such terms as God and Satan; we wish to examine and discriminate; and, being content to admit that if our knowledge of this life is small, our knowledge of the next is nil, our thoughts are more set on making this life tolerable than on imaging some incorporeal ecstasy, or agonizing over a corporeal corruption.

But the primitive Puritan, being physically and mentally crude, is ruthless in his lust, his logic, and his condemnation. His anxiety inhibits his pity. By contrast, the Puritanism of our day is first cousin to Science. It seeks to exclude egoistic prejudice from its understanding, and its motive is Compassion. In this way only, it seems to us, can the chasm between the natural and the spiritual be bridged, and man's conscious intelligence and nature's blind disinterestedness unite in a morality which accords alike with the forces of life and the principles of humanity.

Such a morality, such a self-sufficiency of soul and emancipation of mind as is plain to read not only in a modern like Tchehov, but in the purest utterance of almost every great artist in the past, was beyond the scope of Donne's discordant personality. And so his style, whether as poet or preacher, never achieved either the fresh, effusive gaiety or the assured serenity of Absolute Beauty.

He could not create beauty out of life, he could not

even see the beauty in which the limbs of life were veiled, which flowed through and over the bleak anatomy of fact, consecrating the perishable dust and redeeming it of squalor and grossness – because he lacked harmony in himself; and for the same reason he could only aggravate the horrors of death by endowing it with his own animality.

Too mature for that Classic Grace which even in its wantonness preserved an innocence of body and of mind, a divine naturalness, he was yet too primitive for Romantic vision. He represents as it were only the tangled roots of the Gothic, that turbulent obscurity out of which were born, in purer souls than his, not only grinning gargoyles but a miracle of tapering spires.

But as the violence of the sunset sky is wrought out of the dust-laden air, the particles of matter through which the pure light passes, so the soul of man glows with the most lurid colour in proportion to the degree of the physical which it has to penetrate and subdue.

It is the rich physical nature of Donne that makes him so passionately expressive, even in his defeat; and in his rare moments of imaginative victory, of conflict culminating in unity only to relapse again into discord, 'through the ragged apparel of the afflictions of this life; through the scars and wounds and paleness, and morphews of sin, and corruption, we can look upon the soul itself.'

And this soul is worthy of all honour; for though defeated, it never accepted a fraudulent peace. Haunted by funeral phantoms, swooning beneath the horrors of a self-conceived hell, it continued to fight on.

In the stress of such a nature the problem of human life is starkly presented. Like some distracted microcosm, Donne reflects and condenses the long labour of the man to outgrow the beast and approach the divine. And he shows that religion for an honest man is something other than an escape: that it is an adventure which demands in the region of the ideal as much moral courage and tenacity, and reveals the same flaws of character, as do the yards in a pelting gale for the sailor rounding the Horn.